THE AUDUBON BOOK OF TRUE NATURE STORIES

THE AUDUBON BOOK O

True Nature Stories

Selected and Edited by *JOHN K. TERRES*
Former Editor, AUDUBON MAGAZINE

Illustrated by *WALTER W. FERGUSON*

Thomas Y. Crowell Company, NEW YORK
Established 1834

BY THE AUTHOR

Songbirds in Your Garden
The Audubon Book of True Nature Stories
The Wonders I See
Discovery: Great Moments in the Lives of Outstanding Naturalists
The Audubon Nature Encyclopedia (Editor-in-Chief)
Flashing Wings: The Drama of Bird Flight

All the stories in this book originally appeared in Audubon Magazine, *copyright 1942–1944 and 1948–1958 and published by the National Audubon Society. They are reprinted by kind permission of the authors. In addition, "Smoky, the Catbird" appears in* Discovering Nature *by Charlotte Orr Gantz, copyright 1949 by Charlotte Orr Gantz, published by Charles Scribner's Sons.*

DESIGNED BY JOSEPH F. WEILER
LIBRARY OF CONGRESS CATALOG CARD NO. 58-9716
MANUFACTURED IN THE UNITED STATES OF AMERICA
SECOND PRINTING

TO MOTHER—*who always knew what the*

animals in these stories

have meant to me

I should like, personally, to invite every reader of this book to become a member of the National Audubon Society, 1130 Fifth Avenue, New York, New York 10028. As a part of your annual membership fee you will receive *Audubon Magazine*, from which the stories in this book were taken. The remaining part of your fee will help to support the splendid work of this organization in helping to conserve the wildlife of America. THE EDITOR

Introduction

EVERY ONE OF THESE STORIES IS TRUE. IN THEM YOU WILL find not only much about the personalities of each animal but much about some of the people who knew them. In a way most writing is autobiographical, especially when we write about a subject that is close to our hearts.

Ever since Ernest Thompson Seton's collection of stories, *Wild Animals I Have Known,* was first published in the 1890's, the "wild animal story" has been popular with American readers. Its appeal is just as strong now as ever. Possessed of a different kind of intelligence than our own, wild animals survive in a natural world where death or injury stalks them constantly. In some of these stories you will read about birds and other animals playing, courting, mating, building homes, and raising families—all struggling to live, and all living lives that are in many ways much like our own. Beautiful, graceful, gentle and fierce, comic and tragic, these are wild children, sometimes near to being human, but never quite, and never meant to be. Our sympathy for them is deepest when the odds against them are greatest. In their very "childishness," in their inability to reason, we may find them helpless when they face dangers that are not of their animal world—dangers they are not fitted, by nature, to deal with successfully.

Some time ago, in the Sunday book review section of one of our greatest newspapers, I saw a drawing of a man reclining in a woods. His back was against a log, and he was contentedly reading a book of poetry. A large black bear, a deer, and two pheasants were leaning over his shoulders. They, too, appeared to be absorbed in the book, but their eyes, rolled sidewise, were watching two hunters who stood near, their guns partly lifted, a look of anger and frustration on their faces. The cartoon had no caption, nor did it need one. The wild animals had sought the protection of the gentle spirit who lay reading his book, and it symbolized more clearly than anything we can say that wild things recognize tolerance and sympathy and fly to it as quickly as they dash away in terror from human violence and persecution.

In reading the true animal stories in this book, you will be impressed, as I have always been, by the sensitivity of wild animals to kindness. As a boy I hunted and, to this day, I hold it against no one who wishes to hunt. But I, personally, can no longer inflict pain and death on creatures who have shown me that they, too, enjoy being alive. Once you have truly *known* a wild animal and have been charmed by it, I doubt that you will ever be so keen to hunt one again. Perhaps these stories will show you that, as someone has so wisely said, "a man might kill a rabbit, but he could never kill *Peter Rabbit.*"

J. Frank Dobie once wrote: "Sympathy for wild animals, sympathy that is intellectual as much as emotional, has not been a strong element in the traditional American way of life."

If some of these stories—of Alta, the eagle; of the baby mountain lion, Quito; and many, many others—will make readers feel a little closer to some of our native wild things, then this book will have done its greatest service.

JOHN K. TERRES, *Former Editor*
Audubon Magazine
New York, New York

Contents

THE AUDUBON BOOK OF

TRUE NATURE STORIES

Quito

FREEMAN TILDEN

THE LITTLE KITTEN WAS LYING ALONGSIDE THE ROAD when the car full of tourists came along. There was deep forest on both sides of the road, for it was in Olympic National Park, Washington, the great preserve of primeval rain-forest on the peninsula that faces upon Puget Sound and the Pacific Ocean. The driver saw the kitten and stopped. One of the occupants of the car got out, picked up the little mewing thing, and they drove along.

Perhaps the tourists thought the spotted tabby was a lost domestic kitten; maybe they had merely acted on a generous impulse, without thinking at all. Whichever way it was, the fact remained: they had kidnapped a baby mountain lion, otherwise known as a cougar. It was probably fortunate for the kidnapper that the mother cougar was at the moment some distance away. A cougar is rarely dangerous to human beings except under some provocation. This might have been one of those challenges that the wild—large or small—meets with instinctive, quick action.

Very few Americans have ever seen a cougar. People have lived their lives in the Rocky Mountains and in the Pacific west-coast country without glimpsing one, though they are not uncommon enough to please the owners of livestock or the deer hunters who believe that man alone has the right to be a predatory animal. I have seen their tracks but have never seen the live animal itself outside a cage.

When the tourists who had picked up the baby mountain lion reached the park superintendent's house, they stopped and left the young animal with him. It was too late to return it to the wild because they couldn't remember the place where they had found it. There were now three things that could be done with the cougar kitten: it could be turned loose, and would likely die a lingering death of starvation; it could be put out of the way painlessly with chloroform; or someone could try to feed it and care for it until it was able to fend for itself.

Major Tomlinson, the park superintendent, asked Al Rose, his ranger what he thought about it. Al said, "I'll see what I can do." And thus began one of the strangest and most delightful friendships —with a man and woman on one side, and a wild animal on the other. The story makes one wonder just how wild is a wild animal? How wild would they be if they were not hunted? Even cougars!

A full-grown cougar may weigh 150 pounds and more. It may slink away from man, going noiselessly on its big feet to avoid meeting him, but it can be a thing of concentrated muscle, determination, and fury when it finds itself put on the spot. This tiny cougar kitten, weak and with eyes only half open, had the same qualities in miniature, as Al was soon to experience.

Albert Rose and his wife Margaret love animals. They love all animals, whether they are called "predatory" animals or not. They are just as fond of bears, coyotes, and mountain lions as they are of deer, skunks, or squirrels. Albert Rose is now chief ranger of Mount Rainier National Park, and his experience with Quito the cougar happened some years ago.

"If our house had been the least bit dull before we took over that bit of snarling, scratching, biting bunch of fur, it didn't take it long to develop activity," Al Rose told me. "We fed her from a baby bottle, and each feeding was a skirmish. The only way she would drink was lying on her back in our laps, and wildly clutching the bottle with all four feet. If the milk didn't come fast enough she would chew up the nipple and fly into a rage. The claws flew, and so did the milk. For this regular performance we had to put on long leather gloves and pad ourselves with thick towels. We bought rubber nipples by the dozen and iodine by the pint."

After the first few days of this exciting nursing, the cougar kitten fell sick. The Roses diagnosed it as constipation; a shrewd and accurate guess. The animal needed an enema. The ensuing treatment with the syringe was something the Roses would long remember. "It was like fighting a buzz-saw and threading a needle at the same time," says Al. "After the battle we turned her loose outside and followed her with a flashlight for a couple of hours, so she would not get lost. Then we took her in, put her in her box, and dressed our wounds."

They named her Quito. In a very short time, Quito must have concluded that human beings were not so bad, after all. Her manners at mealtime were rough, but apparently well-intended. She learned to eat and drink from a small pan, but the Roses had to nail the pan to a board; otherwise the food flew in all directions, and Quito would seize the pan and would walk around with it, growling defiance. She ate canned pet food, eggs, and vegetables. Whatever human children might think about it, Quito doted on boiled spinach. Canned salmon was—well—scrumptious! The Roses added a little cod-liver oil, suggested in the care and feeding of infants. Born with spotted fur, Quito soon had her sleek, tawny coat of an adult cougar, and was lovely to see.

Quito was a stickler for the conventions. She was not merely housebroken; she was housebroken in reverse. She got the basic idea perfectly, but she had her own interpretation of it. If she happened to be playing out in the woods, and felt a call of nature, she would rush into the house and go modestly to her sandbox. This fulfilled the expected proprieties.

The growing cougar was allowed the freedom of the surrounding forest, but she did not wander far, and came back at a whistle, bounding happily to her friends. She loved Margaret Rose, and had a good-natured tolerance of other women. Men she did not trust, especially strange men. The milkman was a special object of toothy snarling, and his German-accented cry of "Come take dat tam lion away!" was a regular occurrence at the Rose's house where he made his daily delivery. Quito never tired of romping with children. The more they mauled her, the better she liked it. The greatest fun was hide-and-seek and when the children were all hidden Quito would hunt for them. When she found them, she capered with delight; and when it was Quito's turn to hide, she was overjoyed to be "found."

At night the Roses let Quito sleep at the foot of their bed. But she found that this was not quite chummy enough. Soon after she was allowed that liberty, she improved on it. Waiting till the Roses were asleep the little cougar would crawl up to the head of the bed and insert herself between Al and Margaret, with just her nose out of the bedclothes. With her head resting on Al's shoulder she signified her happiness with a purr that was like that of a domestic cat, only several times louder. "Why she chose my shoulder instead of Margaret's," says Al, "I don't know, except that she probably thought I could better withstand the vibration."

There was one game Quito invented that was not quite so pacific, and it used to make bystanders gasp a little. Quito would have called the game "snatch." She would suddenly seize a hat, a glove, or a galosh from someone, take it to the center of the floor, and defy the world to take it away from her. To meet this challenge required speed and nerve. Al Rose learned how to do it—without losing a hand. He picked up a small rug and threw it over Quito, then pushed it back until some part of the trophy came into view. With a quick grab he got hold of the object to which Quito's teeth were fastened, and then started spinning the cougar. As she wouldn't let go, and because the spinning was rapid, Quito became as dizzy as any young child who turns around and around. At last she would let go, stagger helplessly for a while, and finally come over sheepishly to Al to be fondled. This was the sole game played with Quito that Al was afraid might sometime get out of hand. There was something of a savage reversion to the wild in it.

When the Roses went away for the day, they took Quito in their coupe. She loved to lie on the shelf at the rear window of the car and watch the world go by. If the Roses parked, they locked the car; and often came back to find people around the car, waiting in confidence that the car-owners would be surprised and possibly frightened to discover a mountain lion in their vehicle. The crowd was always astonished when Al opened the car door and Quito greeted him with affectionate violence. On other visits about the country, Quito walked sedately on a leash beside Al and Margaret.

The charming association of Quito and her friends was approaching its end. In late autumn of that year, when Quito weighed a little more than twenty pounds, the Roses had to move to another station in the national park. It was adjacent to the park boundary, and the Roses knew that Quito, who considered all forest land to be her domain, would probably wander away on private land, and meet a quick death at the hands of someone anxious to collect the bounty on cougars. All animal life, whether predatory or not, is safe in the park sanctuary—or we like to think so. We had better say "theoretically" safe. At least, it is the intent of Congress that they should be. It was foolish to think of turning Quito loose within the park. A housebroken cougar, carefully nourished on boiled spinach and canned salmon, could not meet the competition in the wilderness. There was nothing to do but try to find Quito a suitable home. Who wants a nice housebroken cougar, sound, and kind to children? There was only one candidate—the Woodland Zoo in Seattle, who said they would take her.

"That was a sad day for Margaret and me," Al said. "We arrived in Seattle with Quito perched behind the seat, at her window. We didn't go directly to the zoo. We just drove around, weakly postponing the evil moment. Finally it had to come. I left Margaret crying in the car while I led Quito into the wild animal area. Instantly all hell broke loose! Either seeing Quito, or smelling her, every animal that could roar, bark, or scream cut loose. The din was terrifying. With a frantic leap Quito ran up my legs and jumped on my shoulders. She was trembling. I staggered with her to the quarantine cage, her claws embedded in my back, and managed to get her inside. Then my wife and I drove our dismal hundred miles home. We didn't talk. We just went."

Three weeks later Al and Margaret went to the zoo to see how Quito was doing. She was still in her quarantine cage. When they were still two hundred feet away Margaret called to Quito. There was a noisy crowd all around, but Quito heard the familiar voice and went "mildly insane," as Al put it. An attendant let the Roses into the enclosure and stood shuddering while Al walked up to the cage and put his fist in Quito's mouth—an exchange of affection which had always pleased the cougar.

"Good gosh!" said the attendant, watching the endearment. "And we can't even get near the cage: we have to push the food in from back here."

That was the last Al and Margaret saw of Quito. The news came a few months later, that Quito had died. No reason for her death was given. It might have been the change of food. It might have been that Quito could not adjust herself to the cries and odors of so many animals so strange to her. Who knows? Perhaps it may not be unforgivably sentimental to think that Quito— pacing her cage and recalling the nights when she slept so happily with her head on a man's shoulder, and of the gay times at hide-and-seek with shouting children, and the wonderful game of "snatch," and all the other happy hours with Al and Margaret—it might not, I say, be too absurd to believe that Quito just lost her will to live.

A Whooping Crane Named Bill

S. W. OLIVER

For many years, there have been less than fifty whooping cranes in the world. The author of this article, now deceased, wrote of an era, late in the last century, when cranes were far more numerous than they are now, and were not protected by law. Today, were he alive, neither Mr. Oliver nor others of his family and friends would think of shooting at a crane. Most people along the migration route of this bird, from Canada southward through the Dakotas, Nebraska, Kansas, Oklahoma, and Texas, know of the rarity of the big whooping crane, and try to protect it during its migrations. The notes at the end of this book tell of efforts to save the whooping crane from extinction. —*The Editor.*

WHEN I WAS A YOUNG BOY MY PARENTS SETTLED NEAR the central part of what was then Dakota Territory. It was in the early 1880's and, though the big game had all disappeared, there were plenty of wild fowl. We seemed to be on the main line of travel of all the migratory birds. It was easy to shoot most of them, but difficult to get near enough to a crane, even the little sandhill crane being very wary and always having sentinels posted to warn of danger. It was next to impossible to get a shot at the big white whooping crane. However my chance came at last.

The white crane starts south early, and one evening in September my father reported that three white cranes had just alighted at the farther end of the cornfield, a little over a half mile from the house. Taking the gun and Prince, our big shepherd dog that I had trained to hunt with me, I started up through the cornfield.

It was Indian corn, short, and did not furnish a complete cover while I was walking upright, so I soon had to get down on my hands and knees, and as I got closer, down on my stomach, with Prince doing the same as I. We finally got close enough and, rising up on my knees, I shot, killing one old bird and wounding the smaller and younger bird. It ran off, using its wings and legs, and I could not have caught it excepting that Prince ran under the crane and tipped it over on its back where it lay fighting until I overcame it and tied the legs together. Then I picked up the dead one, and took both home.

The old daddy bird was a beautiful specimen, snow white and would have stood five feet high. The other parent bird remained in the vicinity for three days, never alighting in the cornfield again, but flying back and forth and calling for her mate and young one.

Upon examining the younger bird, which was a nice bronze color, we found that the only injury was where a large shot had lodged in the last joint of the left wing. We decided not to kill and roast him with his daddy, but to put him in the hen house until the wing healed.

We decided to let the bird make his own choice as to whether or not he wished to take his freedom or stay with us. One morning we brought him out in the yard and let him go. Stretching himself and shaking his wings he walked about looking things over, then began picking up bits to eat, as much as to say, "This suits me fine, I will stay." And stay he did for about three years.

The cranes had not all gone south yet and flocks of both gray sandhill and white whooping cranes were still migrating. Our crane would watch and call to them. He kept the birds circling above our place for over an hour, trying to call them down but he never offered to go with them.

As the winters in Dakota are very severe, we wondered whether he would survive. He did not seem to suffer from the cold as he spent most of his time in the warm hen house. He had not yet attained full growth or the dignity that comes to a crane with age and experience, but he was awkward and gangling. We named him "Bill" after a neighbor boy of about the same gangly build. In a short while he learned to recognize his name and would come when called, even if he was out of sight. I would let him get a quarter of a mile on his way up the creek bottom to feed and would then call "Bill!" He would stop, answer me, and come back.

We soon found that we could not fool or tease him. My older brother offered him a piece of bread; and as Bill stretched his long neck to reach for the bread, my brother jerked it back, which no doubt gave Bill's neck quite a jar. Immediately his eyes showed his anger. His feathers rose and, spreading his wings, he leaped upon my brother's shoulders, beating him with his wings, striking at him with his long, strong bill, and making a loud, throaty noise. The rest of us had to come to the rescue and pull him off my brother. We never tried anything like that with him again.

In a few months Bill became known throughout the countryside. We never marked or clipped his wings. He was free to go any time and anywhere he wanted.

When the first spring returned after his capture and the wild cranes began passing over on their way north, he would keep them in the vicinity for a long time, where they called to each other with their loud trumpeting. The white, or whooping cranes, are high flyers and although you can faintly hear their trumpetlike call coming from the sky, they are difficult to locate until they get between the sun and you. Bill, with his sharp eyes and ears, would see and hear them and, turning his eyes skyward, would answer their calls and direct our eyes to them.

We lived on Swan Creek which drained quite a large territory. In the spring there was plenty of water in the creek but the rest of the year it dried up, leaving small ponds and sloughs which were good feeding places for the water fowl. Bill would go to these sloughs and ponds to feed, leaving early in the morning and returning home at sunset. He seldom used his wings, as he seemed to enjoy this daily walk. Often Bill would stay at the feeding places overnight and return home early in the morning. He would come up to the house, making a guttural kind of noise which we called talking. We boys always believed he understood a good part of what was said to him.

He tolerated the farm fowls but made no friendships with them. One fall we captured a wild goose and the crane and goose became pals at once and were together most of the time. The following spring they were out in the yard when a flock of geese came honking over. Our goose answered the call, spread her wings and flew away with them, leaving Bill standing there, looking after her.

Bill seemed to think the most of our father. He liked to go walking with him and was always ready to go. During the early part of the grain season after the evening meal, which was about six o'clock, my father liked to take a walk around a field of wheat of about eighty acres near the house. Bill was usually waiting at the door for him. If he was not there Father would call, "Billie, come on, let's go," and Bill would come on the run and they would go walking up the road together. Bill would keep up a continual drone of throaty noises to show how happy he was. He enjoyed those walks with father and showed it.

At various times when we were in the fields, we had seen large flocks of sandhill cranes having what we called a "crane hop." They would spread their wings, bow or curve their necks, and hop and skip around and sometimes jump over each other. My father would say, "Well, Billie, let's dance" and he would spread his arms out and wave them. Bill would spread his wings, put two or three curves in his long neck, and go hopping and skipping around Father and sometimes jump clear over him.

One day our cowpuncher captured a sandhill crane, which he brought home. We boys thought that Bill would now have a pal, a relative of his. I put the stranger in the hen house and closed the door, intending to let Bill in when he came home.

Later, after I had finished the evening chores and was on my way to the house, I heard a great commotion in the hen house. Chickens were coming right through the windows, breaking the glass, and out of a small opening at the bottom of the big door. I ran to the hen house and opened the door to see what was the matter. The place was so full of dust and feathers I could scarcely see. I discovered that Bill, somehow, had gained entrance and had the other crane down on its back and with wing, beak, and foot was proceeding to finish him off then and there. I rescued the stranger, and took him out in the yard and set him free. He left in a great hurry.

One night in June Bill did not come home. We did not worry for he had stayed away over night before. After several days, and still he had not come home, we began to worry for fear that something might have happened to him. We searched all the ponds and sloughs for miles around, but could not find him. One morning after he had been gone for two weeks, I heard a faint trumpet call way off to the southwest. I strained my ears to get the next call and sure enough it was nearer, and soon I saw a speck away off in the distance. It was Bill, flying higher than usual, showing he had come from a great distance. When within a half mile of the house he began to drop down and how he whooped, one whoop after another, as fast as he could, seeming to want to let us know that he was coming and his joy at being home again. Soon he swooped into the yard a little below where we were all standing and came up to us as fast as he could walk, talking loud and fast and showing his pleasure at seeing all of us again.

Now comes the most remarkable incident in Bill's career; an incident which shows how he, a creature of the wild, was completely captivated and so in love with his new life and human friends that, instead of going back to his own kind, when he had the chance, he would try and bring them into his changed environment.

The next fall there was another night when Bill did not come home. I was around home keeping an eye turned in the direction from which I expected him to come. It was about ten o'clock in the morning when he came in sight over the hill about a half mile from the house. Walking with him were three big, beautiful white cranes like himself. When they saw the buildings and heard the dogs bark they stopped. Bill stopped with them and we knew he was talking, assuring them that all was well.

Finally he drew off a little from them and stopped and began picking at the grass and walking around and talking until he got them up to him. Then waiting for some time, he again drew off a little way and did the same thing until they came to him. He repeated these tactics time and time again, walking back and forth and talking. When he got so far, he would wait a little while before repeating. The nearer he drew the birds to the house the harder he worked. He began to walk farther and faster, back and forth, and he began to talk louder.

You could see he was excited. He worked on the wild cranes this way from ten in the morning until four in the afternoon, bringing them within about two hundred yards of the house, but try as hard as he would, he could not bring them nearer. Once or twice he came into the yard and then walked back to them, showing them that no harm would come to them. He came into the yard in front of the house, while the other cranes stayed where they were for another hour, but they and Bill called back and forth to each other. Finally they flew away. Bill stood in the yard and watched them go.

Well, all earthly things come to an end and so did Bill come to his.

He was some four or five miles up the creek feeding in a little pond when a youth came along bringing some oxen to put on our pasture. He saw Bill there and, not knowing anything about our crane, began throwing stones at him. Bill did not try to get away, but just took his time moving away. A rock finally hit Bill on the side of the head, knocking him out completely. The boy thought he had killed the bird so he tied the legs together, thrust his ox goad between them and slung the burden over his shoulder.

When he got to our camp our cowboy told him that that was our pet crane. He discovered that Bill was not dead but only unconscious so he brought him home to us. Bill could now stand, but what a head! You could not see one eye at all. His feelings were hurt the worst, since he had received a shock he had not expected. He would not let any of us come near him so we shut him up in the hen house, intending to keep him there until his head healed. This was in the evening.

The next morning when I went to the hen house to look at him he was gone. No one had let him out. It was the same as when I found him trying to kill the sandhill crane; no one had let him in. We boys believed he had learned to pull the string which would open the door. He had seen us open the door so often to let him in that he had learned how.

We searched for days, everywhere, but found no trace of him. It was two years before we learned of his fate. Some weeks after Bill's accident, a young boy from the East was hunting along the creek about eight miles from our place. He came to a small pond and a big white crane came walking up the bank toward him making a lot of noise.

The boy had never seen a crane before and did not know what it was. Without stopping to think that a wild fowl would not come up to him like that, he shot and killed it. It was Bill, who had evidently recovered from his injury, and, although he did not readily make up to a stranger, was ready to renew friendship and no doubt would soon have come home again.

The White-Tailed Deer of Pimisi Bay

LOUISE DE KIRILINE

IT WAS A BRILLIANT MORNING IN MARCH. THE SUN BLAZED down upon Pimisi Bay and on the Mattawa River of southern Ontario. The high vertical cliffs on either side of the river reflected the sunlight and its glorious warmth. Below Talon Chute the water lay open and smoking. But on the lake the ice was hard and granulated from the effects of deep-freezing nights and daytime sun-thaw, and it gave off translucent heat waves visible only against the distance.

All of a sudden, a deer leaped out in front of me from behind the point. Bouncing high as if made of nothing but air and rubber, it

bounded over the ice, flag aloft, showing the long silky hairs underneath flounced into a magnificent white rosette. A smart crunchy tattoo with a hollow undertone resounded from the ice under the deer's hoofs.

The deer stopped, all four legs spread disorderly in the pose of the last interrupted motion. With irrepressible curiosity, it looked around at me who had disturbed its lazy browsing in the sunshine. Then, up went its head in a movement of playful defiance, and it set off in a parade trot, the like of which was never equaled in the highest equestrian school.

Hoofs scarcely touching the ice in the high-stepping gait, the deer flung wide its forelegs in elaborate semicircles and swung its graceful head from side to side in a high mood of extravagance and show, born, surely, of the life-giving brilliance of the sun. Never has any choreographer designed a *pas seul,* nor a Nijinsky executed a measure, of more plastic perfection than the dance over the sparkling ice of this wild and free fawn. There was no negative element in this show of motion, no fright in the speed, nor desire to be gone out of sight. Here was all the pithy reality of pure exuberance, of pure beauty, set against a backdrop of ice and sky and wooded shoreline, a natural performance such as no stage has ever witnessed. For minutes I stood watching in spellbound delight, until the hoofbeats died away and the deer vanished behind wreaths of rising vapors at the First Rapids.

A winter and a half passed from the time the deer first arrived in our territory until we saw them. In all this time, we read the fresh evidence of their presence nearly every day in the marks left by their dainty hoofs as they stopped along our paths, or made four-footed take-offs into the soft snow, or stamped around amid the white cedar brush on the terrace below the Loghouse where we lived, overlooking Pimisi Bay. So close they had been under our windows, yet never seen. Elusive they were, like mirages, forever vanishing, discrediting even the signs of their own passing.

Then, on the second day of the New Year, it happened. Well-nigh a hundred times I had come outside stealthily, trusting to luck that someday I would surprise these shy animals. But this day I forgot. Scared by my sudden appearance, a deer bounded away with a startling snort into the dawn twilight. And all I knew was that it had been there, that I had seen it at long last.

The spot where the deer had been browsing was about fifty feet from the house. Hardly any cedar leaves remained within their reach in the small grove after their frequent visits in the past. So we put a block of salt on a rock and tied fresh bushy branches of cedar to a trunk. The next morning we knew that our efforts had been appreciated.

This gave us the idea of enticing the deer yet closer to our windows by means of a gradual advance of the cedar boughs to a place in front of the house where we planted a small forest of branches in the snow. We moved the salt, too, and cleared a place for it beside the path. Very soon the deer caught on and they began coming to this feeding bower regularly, without displaying any surprise at the everlasting resources of their favorite winter food. And it was here that we eventually learned something of the ways and plays of the northern white-tailed deer, *Odocoileus virginianus borealis.*

There were two of them, a buck and a doe. The buck was small, young probably, and grayer than the doe. With only tiny knobs replacing the three-pointed antlers he shed back of the Loghouse last fall, he looked like the doe's baby. His large liquid eyes were fringed with long curved lashes and gazed upon the world with trusting naïveté. He stepped daintily as if on limber stilts, and the spread of his cloven hoofprint revealed his mood and the speed of his advance. Nearly always he took the lead ahead of the doe in an apologetic way, as if begging forbearance with this bravado of his, due solely to her safe conduct. Even when she was out of sight, his constant and acute consciousness of her whereabouts was never in doubt. He kept throwing back his head over his shoulder, his munching jaws still and his eyes fixed in the direction from whence, sure enough, she eventually emerged to pose like a figure carved on the brow of the hill.

In shape and temperament the essence of fleetness, the deer in moments of danger, as I was to learn in time, were past masters of slow motion. The doe took exactly twenty minutes to descend from the brow of the hill to the feeding place at the window, a distance of a scant 150 feet. Her large ears twitching nervously, she came down with extreme cautiousness, stepping as if on pine.

She withdrew and set down her hoofs, one at a time, precisely in the buck's tracks and without disturbing a speck of snow or leaving an additional light mark of her own slender shins. She took advantage of every bit of cover provided by naked bushes that stuck out of the snow or by the lower branches of the evergreens, behind which the outline of this large and deliberate animal became so confused as to render her all but invisible. On bright, moonlit nights, when the interplay of silvery light and blue-black shadows created fantastic patterns upon the snow-covered forest floor, I saw her retire into an obscure patch and become totally engulfed by it in all her ruminant amplitude, as if she were no longer there.

I knew the doe from the buck anywhere because she was curiously unlike him. She was of a lighter fawn color, and her head was more elongated than his. An odd kind of dignity and maturity characterized her poses and movements; her girth was ample and her flanks spacious; and she lacked only the fawn at her side to complete the maternal mammalian picture. Oftentimes she merely stood, interminably, wearing a vastly bored expression and chewing the cud thoroughly and endlessly.

After she got his "all-safe" signal she took no further notice of the buck. Only on occasion, when the two met at close range, she displayed recognition that they belonged together. She would throw up her head and snap at him, and sometimes she reared against him with pawing forefeet and ears flipped back flat as if annoyed at his proximity. But how could I guess her feelings with accuracy?

Their approach to the feeding place was a matter of grave importance since it involved the security of an existence perhaps more vulnerable and precarious than that of any other sylvan inhabitant. They used two main avenues: down the steep incline from the brow of the hill or along the path from the spring. Both these approaches had the advantage of enabling them to survey the feeding place and its surroundings spread out below without themselves being seen before they emerged from behind a curtain of evergreen branches. Often they stood there for half an hour or more, as if to outwait any chance disturbance, before they decided to come down at last. But when, during a number of visits, the place proved to be devoid of upsetting elements, the deer rapidly became accustomed to the peacefulness of the situation and began moving about with greater confidence.

Yet, even as they stood munching the cedar boughs below our window, every muscle and nerve of their bodies were constantly aquiver. A leaf rustled, a chickadee twittered, and the deer's ears flicked, always on the *qui vive.* When the wind in the pine above dumped a pad of snow on the roof with a thud, the little buck sank to his knees in a spontaneous motion of avoidance. But the conditioning of the deer to the cars, trucks, and buses that rumbled, roared, and backfired, racing up and down the hill on the highway only a few hundred feet away, was of long standing. Provided none stopped, provided no other sound was mixed with their noise, such as the clatter of a horse's hoofs or the crunching of a man's soles against the pavement, and that no unfamiliar movement could be detected except that of the speeding vehicles, the deer treated them as air. Not even did the animals shy away from them during a playful canter in the moonlight; instead the prancing deer often danced alongside these roaring monsters with their glaring eyes as if they belonged to the play.

Our faces in the window were a source of apprehension to the doe especially. Were they there before she arrived, she appeared oblivious of them until a movement gave them away. Then she bounded off. But she soon returned, trying out various new approaches, watching the window intently, until she was apparently reassured that either the faces did not see her or she could no longer see them. At other times she stood her ground and gazed upon the odd apparitions, raising and lowering her head to make sure her eyes did not deceive her. But in due time, the faces in the window, like the cars on the road, were accepted as harmless and inescapable accessories to this particular environment. For the deer's own safety, this was as far as we wished to pursue their taming.

At that time the Loghouse harbored a cat which, quite naturally, considered the surroundings as his territory and the deer as illegitimate trespassers. He made this known by racing up a tree trunk, tail fluffed and claws noisily scratching the bark; or he jumped on the roof and galloped around, finally pretending to spring upon the heads of the jittery deer but saving himself by a hair's breadth. The deer fled. But soon they gained courage, since this toy panther apparently lacked both the size and attributes that to them meant danger. One night, as the cat commenced his intimidation routines, the buck faced him in front of the doe. With tails lifted and the long white hairs of their flags spread and stiffened, the deer met threat with threat; the buck gave an explosive snort, and with a motion almost too pretty to convey belligerency he stamped the ground three times with his dainty front hoofs. The effect of these moves upon the cat was spectacular, and all further demonstrations on his part were inhibited.

This was what we saw of the deer at the feeding place. They came there at all times, at dawn and at dusk, in the dark of the night and in the bright light of midday; but most often they came in the afternoon. Often they came in snowy weather with their backs, shoulders, and long eyelashes powdered white. Only on cold days, when the thermometer dipped below zero, they stayed away, sometimes for several days. Those days they took shelter back in the woods under the spruces and balsam firs, whose lower branches were caught in the deep snows and formed snug circular tents around the trunks. There, underneath, the snow was tramped hard by the deers' hoofs. It was here, too, that I sometimes surprised them bedded down in the snow, once the two together just beyond the brow of the hill, but more often a little apart, and always on a small elevation with a view commanding the surrounding country. Almost before I saw them, they were gone, arisen on knees and hind legs in one motion, to cast themselves off and away in a giant first leap. And only the steaming hollow where they had lain, scooped out by their body heat, remained to tell that they had really been there.

One day, blood-curdling yelpings cut sharply and grimly through the dawn silence. The next instant a deer in a wild panic crashed through branches and bushes down the slope in front of the Loghouse. Another raced across the spring and took the highway like a broad ditch almost without the touch of a hoof. I got my snowshoes on fast and ran back into the woods to see what was happening. And there in the snow and in the gathering light I pieced together the story of that dawn.

That morning the timber wolves whose 5½-inch tracks I had measured on the lake only a short while ago had their day among the deer back of the Loghouse. I saw where one wolf had come upon the standing deer and sent them racing for their lives in all directions. I saw the evidence of tight pursuit between cloven hoofs and padded feet. I followed it, and some time later I came upon the end far out on High Point.

It was all over, all finished. Death feeds upon life and life upon death, and this is the law. Only two deer were down: one, then a little farther on another, hamstrung, then stumbling and falling in their tracks. For many a day a few wolves and at least one fox fed undisturbed and well upon these two and sought no other prey. When they had finished, there was nothing left save tufts of hairs scattered about for the birds to use in their nests, come springtime. There was no carnage. If left to herself nature does clean work and seldom exacts the penalty of prolonged suffering.

The snow was gone and the sun beat down upon the warming fragrant earth. On a sunny slope I saw two deer. One of them threw up his head and looked at me as if recognizing something it was used to seeing, then continued his browsing. I could not mistake that doe nor the little gray buck escorting her. And, inconsequent as our affections make us, I could not suppress my relief knowing that just these two were the ones which escaped that fateful dawn.

The following winter only the doe returned to the feeding place she remembered, but she was not alone. Two small bucks accompanied her. They had lost their spots but by looks and behavior clearly marked themselves as none other than the doe's twin fawns born early last spring. For there is no loss, no end, only a change, and all shall profit thereby.

Crip, Come Home!

RUTH THOMAS

ON OCTOBER SIXTH, CRIP, OUR OLD BROWN THRASHER with a stiff wing had started south.

Thinking of him all that day, I had watched him moving through woods, slipping from thicket to thicket, watching, always watching. Crip could fly less than a hundred yards; I had seen him force his wings till his strength was spent and he fluttered to the ground. There would be open spaces to cross in the woodland and, night or day, there would be enemies quick to pounce on a weary, crippled old thrasher. The owl sees in the dark, the Cooper's hawk watches from the noon-bright sky, and cats forever prowl on silent feet. Dangers enough in a bird's home garden, I thought but many, many more to beset Crip's miles of travel through strange country in his journey south.

When Crip first came to our hill in Arkansas and claimed the east yard as his nesting territory, he was like other brown thrashers, having two good wings and no name. I knew him only by the aluminum band, 308978, that I had placed on his left leg. Three summers he and a faithful mate built their nests in a great tangle of climbing Van Fleet and Silver Moon roses that flung their canes far and high, and each year he waited there for the time to fly south.

The spring that Crip was four years old, he lost his territory in the roses to a pair of strange thrashers. His old mate had failed to return; he was a long time at winning a new mate, and he finally settled in my north flower garden. On June 9 of that year, he fluttered across our lawn, his right wing dragging, plainly broken. We never knew how the hurt had befallen him or whether he had a family at the time.

For the rest of the summer, he lived alone in my garden. Still and fluffed, every morning he waited in the old lilac bush by the gate for the grain and nutmeats that I scattered on the ground. He grew very gentle, and even as I stood close by, watching, he would begin to eat. At noon, and again in the evening, I went out with food, and always something eased in my heart when I found the thrasher safe. And yet, I thought, what hope for a bird that cannot fly? Tomorrow, or the next day, Crip would surely die.

The summer ran out, no enemy struck, and the wing healed in a crooked way. It drooped from the shoulder and the wrist would always be stiff. With his molt finished, Crip became more active, went in long leaps across the lawn, and often got into trees by springing to the lowest branches.

In the middle of September, the wonder of it! he could fly! I had several times seen him glide down from a tree, landing with a topple to the right, but now he made short level flights from tree to tree, and then came the proud day that he lifted himself from the ground. It was awkward and labored flying. Whether the sound wing's strokes were shortened to match the injured one's jerky beats, or the compensation was in the line and tilt of the body, I did not know, but I never saw Crip fly without feeling in myself a sympathetic straining.

That first autumn following the injury, Crip knew his weakness. When it was time to migrate, he moved only from the north garden to the roses, and the thorny canes that had sheltered his nests became his winter castle and stronghold. During that winter, many times a day I took him food, and on winter evenings I listened for the muttered notes, *"kunnh, kunnh,"* that told me he had made his way to the cedar tree to sleep.

Winter and then summer passed, and another autumn came. Again Crip stayed on his hill. Through October's sunny days he had perched in the roses. Wrapped in a moody silence, he heard the geese going over and watched the migrating warblers in the oaks. There must have been conflict in his being; on the one hand, the fear that grew in him all the weeks he hid with his hurt; on the other the old, old restive fever, like a command, "Go South!" By the next autumn he had grown so used to the stiff wing, so confident in his use of it, that on that October day he had joined the bird travelers moving southward. On October twelfth he had gone, and with a sigh I resigned myself to a winter of hopeful waiting.

Winter in Arkansas is short. By March first the jonquils were in golden bloom; cardinals were whistling, blue birds warbled and fluttered at their nest boxes, and the mockingbird sang and shouted and mimicked his bird neighbors. The warm days, the songs, and the greening of the earth gave me a small hope. Crip was wise and cautious; he might have escaped his enemies in October and on the beat of his homeward journey.

On March fourteenth a brown thrasher sang from the north garden, and I hurried out with my binoculars. The bird high in the white oak had two bands on the right leg—one, my own red celluloid identification band; the other, the metal government band. Red, Crip's neighbor, had come home. Last summer, Red had owned as his territory the north lawn and garden, while Crip's land of the roses was to the east of our house. The two thrashers had established a dividing line, and seldom did either one trespass on the other's property.

It must have been next morning that the thrasher that had been Crip's mate for the last two seasons returned. That afternoon I found her in a banding trap in my garden, knowing her not only by the number of her metal band but by the green celluloid band above it. Greta, I had called her, because she was GR, "green on right," in my file.

Red moved uneasily in the branches above us. As soon as I released Greta, he flew to her side. They moved on down my border of shrubs, tossing the old brown leaves of winter, digging into the soft earth; and Red, in the way of a thrasher newly mated, whispered a song. Faithless Greta, not grieving over Crip nor waiting for the old thrasher, had accepted his neighbor as her new mate.

If only these thrashers could talk to me! "Red, did you see Crip as you hurried home? Greta, did you pass the thrasher with a lame wing, resting, perhaps in a tangle of catbrier?"

Then it was March eighteenth. All day I watched. "Crip, come home! The roses are in leaf, a bower for your nest. Come claim your own, take back your wife. Are you even now hurrying with the hard beats of your wings?"

My hope grew faint; perhaps it was the time for grieving.

Seven more days went by. "Crip, are you coming? Too late to have your wife. Red and Greta are building a nest on Red's land, in the big honeysuckle of my flower garden. But they also claim the territory of the roses. They eat at your table and loiter in your thicket of thorns. Hurry, Crip!"

On the morning of March twenty-sixth, Crip came home.

At six o'clock I went to the kitchen and put on the teakettle; then I ran up the window shade. At the edge of the roses I saw a small whirlwind of old leaves flying around and around. I rubbed the sleep from my eyes and looked again. Two brown thrashers were in a furious fight; and even as they leaped at one another and tumbled in the leaves, I could see that one had a stiff right wing. *Crip!*

In my excitement I was foolish and panicky, thought Red was killing the old thrasher, and ran out. Our two Scotties rushed after me, and at such a commotion the thrashers separated, Red flying up and away, Crip streaking to the roses. So Crip *would* have back his territory—for, with birds, he who runs is loser; he who stays is the victor.

That was a wonderful morning, and I think I was happier than the old thrasher that had come to the end of his migratory journey. Only half believing what my own eyes saw, I hurried to tell my husband, "Crip's home!" and then out again with a handful of chopped nuts. From the window I watched the thrasher patter out of the roses and across the lawn to the table; and I saw that he looked old (he would be eight that spring), that his color was faded and his tail and right wing were frayed at the edges. But never mind, the winter and the journey were finished; now he would rest and know happier days.

Then to the barn to tend my milk goats. It was thirty minutes later, returning with the pails of milk, that I saw Crip and Greta and Red on the lawn and realized that Crip had come home to grief and trouble. Up to then, I had not thought of his reaction to Greta's desertion. Now he and his old mate, Greta, were only two feet apart, pretending to forage, while Red was a few yards to the north. Crip's feathers were puffed; he was on truculent guard and kept eyeing Red. Red, I thought, was uneasy and afraid. He was the first to fly up to a tree; Greta followed; and then old Crip, lifting himself in his hard way, flew up to the perch between them. Immediately Red and Greta flew to their garden, leaving Crip huddled in dejection.

Through the afternoon, Crip rested in the roses; and at twilight, going to the top of the nearest oak, he began to sing in earnest phrases. Next morning Greta was at his table for the first serving of nutmeats. What could Crip think but that he had called her home?

That was the thrasher pattern of courtship—songs to summon a mate. As he hurried to her side, she gulped the last mouthful and flew off.

Crip might have quickly accepted the loss of his former mate if she had stayed in Red's territory. But Greta had no regard for the males' territorial lines. Crip's home had been her home, and she continued her visits, thus keeping him in a state of alternate hope and bafflement. He offered himself, whispered songs, carried twigs and leaves as symbols of his eagerness to be at nesting. Greta's nest in the garden was finished, Red was the mate that had helped her build the nest, and the new bond was stronger than the memory of the two summers with Crip. Rebuffed, the old thrasher turned in fury on Red, who usually followed Greta to wait in a nearby shrub. Perhaps Red remembered the fight by the roses and knew that he was trespassing, for he retreated to his own territory.

Scene followed scene, the details varying little. I wrote in my notebook: "At ten o'clock, Greta eats at the table; Crip leaps up beside her and she threatens with her beak. And still he hopes! Jumping down, he picks up bits of leaves. . . . One o'clock, Greta is again at the table, and after eating, goes to the ground to forage. Crip is encouraged and, seizing a leaf, runs to the roses; but Greta flies away. . . . Two o'clock, Crip and Red and Greta are on the lawn near the old line between the territories. Red plainly wants to avoid a fight with Crip and flies up to a tree on his side of the boundary. Crip moves to Greta and both toss leaves, but she gives no sign that she sees him and presently flies to her nest in the honeysuckle; there Red joins her. Crip, still and forlorn, watches them."

On the third day, Crip seemed weary and confused; his occasional songs were thin and perfunctory, his manner toward Greta changed to timid doubt, and the rushes at Red took more and more of his strength. Now Red was the confident thrasher. He had learned that Crip was slow and clumsy, especially at rising from the ground, and he grew bolder at trespassing into Crip's territory.

On the fourth and last day of this strange situation, Crip was visibly drooping, worn, I think, by the frustration as well as the frequent clashes with Red. At two in the afternoon, both Red and Greta ate at the table, and then, defiantly, both flew to the roses. Crip, huddled in the old leaves at the edge of the tangle, had ignored the two at the table, but no thrasher's pride could endure a neighbor male in the home sanctuary. He roused, ran a few steps, then faltered as though one leg was hurt and spread his wings for crutches. With an obvious effort he pulled himself up, leaped into the roses and chased Red a few yards toward the north garden. And then Crip fluttered to the ground and slumped against a tree. His eyes closed, wings sagged, all his feathers were curiously loosened. Was my thrasher dying! Red, knowing his advantage, slipped back to the roses. And old Crip, fierce and pitiful, started up. It was time to interfere, and I went out and drove Red and Greta away.

Crip rested then, and his feathers smoothed down, but for a long time he held his right foot against his breast. At six-thirty I saw him in a furtive running to the cedar. My poor thrasher! That was the way he had traveled the long miles to reach this unhappy home.

On the fifth day, Crip's luck changed. For one thing, I piled extravagant heaps of nutmeats on a shelf in the north garden, so that Red and Greta would have little reason for going into Crip's territory. Of far greater importance, a single female thrasher arrived. It was March thirtieth, very late in the season, and I had not dared to hope that a prospective mate for Crip would arrive.

Crip forgot Greta, and all the forenoon he sang the bold and beautiful songs of courtship from an oak on the south hillside. Somewhere below him was the thrasher that he was asking to be his mate. By afternoon, he had called her to the roses where I saw her sprawled, sleepy and basking, at the sunny edge of the tangle. Crip had come down from the singing tree, and he now ran to her side and picked up a twig, but the lady was not yet won. She sprang up and flew swiftly down the hill, and Crip, flinging the twig away, followed in long running leaps across the lawn. He sang again, as he would keep singing till she gave him his answer.

For three days, from dawn to evening twilight, Crip sang his courtship songs. Not even in winter had my nutmeats served him so well. Taking no time to forage for natural foods, he sailed down to the feeding table, ate hurriedly, then fluttered to the roses, leaped up through the canes, thence to the branches of the nearest oak and on to the topmost twigs. His energies were the most amazing when I remembered the way he had collapsed in his last encounter with Red.

That he chose the oak by the roses was a good sign, meaning the lady loitered not far away. Now his phrases were proud and quick with an undercurrent of eager excitement, now low and gently pleading. Perhaps the one for whom he sang had moved a little nearer and had turned her head in quiet listening.

On the morning of April second, Crip, old and dingy brown, his right wing ugly in its stiff deformity, walked beside a mate of shining rufous russet, small and trim, a maiden come to her first nesting. They dug in the grass together, tossed the windblown leaves, and twice Crip gave his lady a possessive peck. Her meek submission told me of her youth. More often, the old thrasher paused to hold himself very still, lost in dreaminess, and to whisper faint breaths of song.

In his new joy, Crip had regained his old spirit. One day he caught Red under the roses and gave him a savage drubbing. Red's mate, Greta, had now laid her eggs and was not inclined to stray far from the nest. But let Greta come to the rose land and the young Mrs. Crip would send her flying. I was pleased to see that Crip and his wife would suffer no more intrusions from their thrasher neighbors.

At noon, Crip carried twigs to the roses, to begin the foundation of a nest. Even at his work he now sang tender whispers of a song. Proudly I watched our old crippled thrasher. He had not only come back to us, but had won out in a battle as old as the world. Conscious fulfillment he may not have known, but for me there could never be a more glorious spring.

Weasels Are Wonderful!

HELEN HOOVER

A FRANTIC SCURRYING AND SQUEAKING OF THE DEER MICE that inhabit the double ceiling of our cabin woke me early one spring morning. The wilderness dawn on the Minnesota shore of our Canadian-border lake was far too lovely to waste. I donned a robe and went outside. The morning sun sent long fans of light through the pines and across the fiddle heads of the interrupted ferns. A bright patch of sunlight lay full on the pale yellow flowers of the bluebead-lily in my garden. There was no sound except the gentle splashing of the lake.

Suddenly the squeaking in the roof was renewed. I looked up, and from a small hole under the eaves—a hole I should have thought too tight for a mouse—emerged the smallest of all living carnivores, the least weasel, *Mustela rixosa.* Licking the corners of its mouth with its cerise tongue, it ran gracefully down the wall of our cabin to the flagstones. Apparently it had just breakfasted on a deer mouse, and clearly the member of the weasel tribe had lived up to its scientific name, *Mustela,* from *mus,* a mouse, and from *tollere,* to pick up! It sat up almost at my feet, and examined me with that fearlessness and bright-eyed eagerness which are such attractive characteristics of all weasels.

This first encounter with the least weasel was also my last; and I have seen a long-tailed weasel, one of its larger cousins, only once. One day I went to call upon a lady who has a summer home near us. When I arrived she was standing in the middle of a flower bed, waving a pair of garden shears and screaming frantically. Darting around her feet, apparently intrigued by the fuss she was making, was a long-tailed weasel in its summer coat of brown. My neighbor still has not forgiven me for standing idly by until I had looked the weasel over thoroughly. Afterward I shooed away this "fearsome" creature! Others of the weasel tribe—in their white coats of winter fur—had given me glimpses of themselves as they darted about in the weeds, but I had despaired of ever getting a close-up view of one.

It was early summer when my husband and I saw a female ermine, or short-tailed weasel, *Mustela erminea,* then in her brown summer coat, going into a hollow log not far from our cabin. We refrained from investigating, as we are opposed to taking the chance of alarming any mother with young, especially a weasel, which will defend her babies with great courage. In times of danger, even the male may help carry the young weasels to safety. We watched patiently and were rewarded later on when the weasel crept from her nesting place, presumably coming out for a hunting lesson. The female ermine usually mates in early summer and does not give birth to her four to seven young until about ten months later, or in early spring of the following year.

All weasels are intrepid hunters. They stalk their prey with great persistence, aided by their keen hearing. If food is plentiful, they may eat only the blood and brains of the animals they kill. I have heard of onslaughts by weasels on hen roosts which left large numbers of the birds dead; but, as they sometimes hunt in two and threes, and prefer only parts of their prey, this may explain what is carelessly called "wanton killing." They dispatch their prey very quickly and like to take food home where they can eat it without interruption. In cold weather they often store meat for future use, occasionally making visits to their caches under the snow to make certain that it is safe.

Weasels are feared by all ground-nesting birds and are such excellent climbers that tree-nesting birds also fear them. Red squirrels wage constant war on weasels and chase after them like small avenging furies. The weasels do not stand to give battle, but lope away, the squirrel having no speed to match even the slower gaits of the incredibly swift weasel. Obviously, the weasel must always be on the lookout for attack, and it is noteworthy that it will run away rather than engage in useless fighting with an inferior foe. It defends itself with great courage, however, if cornered or trapped. This does not seem to bear out the statement that weasels are vicious.

Weasels are more feared than fearing, but may come to grief at the claws and teeth of the larger carnivores. The barred owl and the great horned owl, foxes, lynxes, bobcats, minks, and fishers, all harass the weasel in our northern Minnesota area. However, the weasel's agility and speed together are such a safeguard that its only real menace is man with his traps.

Weasels are valuable in controlling the numbers of the prolific rodents and will go into underground burrows in search of muskrats, woodchucks, moles, and rabbits. But they are particularly fond of mice, and it is this characteristic that led to my gaining such friendly relations with one female ermine that she now feeds unhesitatingly from my hand.

Late one fall my husband and I had a full-scale invasion of our cabin by dainty, big-eyed deer mice. We always have a few mice that come down from the ceiling to forage, and we always expect to have them. The mice were here long before we came and, I hope, will be here long after we have gone. We usually find the deer mice amusing and ingratiating, but when they skittered over the floor in such numbers that we were constantly in fear of stepping on them, it became nerve-wracking.

We decided that, if our neighboring weasels could be persuaded that our house was a good place to visit, they might cause the mice to move to other and safer quarters. We recalled that some weeks before our female weasel had come daringly near my husband when he was cutting suet for our bird feeder and had accepted from him a piece of the suet. Fresh beef seemed the best weasel food we had. We began leaving a bit on the step outside of our cabin every night. It was always gone in the morning; and we soon noticed an absence of deer mice in our home, except for the one or two that consider the place so much theirs that they will boldly come out on our kitchen counter to wash their faces before me while I wash my dishes.

One night we heard a furious series of squeaks outside the cabin door. Our female weasel, now regal in winter white, was expressing indignation and disappointment. I had forgotten her usual tidbit! This seemed as good a time as any to find out how she would react to the meat and to me, together, so I held her piece of beef on a fork outside the woodshed floor, under which she had dashed when I stepped out. She bared her teeth and hissed, but she finally snatched the meat and withdrew it into her place of safety. Then I offered her a piece with my fingers. She was hesitant about this—and *I* was hesitant, too. Her little teeth are needle sharp, and she is lightning fast. After several false tries, she snatched the meat from my hand with surprising strength and darted away. Weasels seem to move faster at night than during the day.

A few days later there was a tremendous racket outside. The blue jays screamed from the pines. The red squirrels chattered from the stumps. The nasal cries of the nuthatches were almost drowned out by the frantic *"dee-dee-dee!"* of the circling, diving chickadees. Across the snow came the weasel, leaping with such grace and lightness that she made me think of a small white plume rolling before a breeze. To me she may look like a fairy-tale animal, made of whipped cream with raisin eyes, a currantlike nose, and rounded shell-like ears; but to the small ones of the forest she is a dreaded hunter.

The tracks she left in the snow were instantly filled with pale blue shadows as the pale rays of the low sun slanted over them. Every footprint was clear; the front ones, with four evenly spaced toemarks preceding the little crescent-shaped pad; the rear ones, somewhat longer, with the four toemarks more to the side of the foot around the pad. In some tracks there were delicate hair markings in front of the toes. Her usual leap was about fifteen inches and often the prints of her hind feet overlapped those of her forefeet. I have observed leaps longer than three feet when she is in a hurry, and then she moves so fast that she is a white streak against the whiter snow, only the black tip of her tail showing clearly where she is. That touch of black seems to be nature's wisdom at its best, for presumably it will direct an attacking owl, lynx, or other predator on weasels, to the wrong end of its swiftly moving prey.

The more I saw of our interesting and beautiful neighbor, the more I wanted to see, so I decided to try to persuade our weasel that I was harmless. This took great patience—and some months of time. The weasel, like many carnivores, is essentially a creature of the night, and very shy. It is not easy to overcome its shyness, nor do I believe it should be overcome to the point where any wild thing loses its native caution.

The next time the warning clamor came from our birds and squirrels outside, I went out—well-clothed against a breeze and twenty-degrees-below-zero temperature. I sat down on the step of our cabin with a bit of beef on the toe of my boot. The weasel approached me with grave caution. She stalked me from all sides, moving low to the ground. She was so tensed for instant withdrawal that her wiry muscles quivered visibly. She disappeared into one of the entrances to her fine tunnel system in the snow, reappeared from under the shed beside the steps, slipped out of sight behind a storage box, and then came toward me from the rear. As I watched out of the corners of my eyes, she took a few experimental bites of the folds of my coat. The cold made it difficult for me to remain perfectly still, and she was gone in a wink if I so much as twitched. Finally she darted at my boot and snapped at the sole, then retreated a foot or two to wait for my response. When none came, she made several approaches, then snatched the meat and darted into her nearest snow-tunnel entrance.

In subsequent visits, as our little ermine gained confidence, I held the meat in the palm of my hand near the toe of my boot. I wore a heavy leather glove, which proved to be a wise precaution as she occasionally, in her caution, nipped one of my fingers. After a time I held my gloved hand in my lap until she ran fearlessly up my pants leg to get the meat. I had found it hard to realize that weasels weigh only two or three ounces, until she climbed weightlessly up my shirt front to have a closer look at one of my ears.

Our ermine is delighted with frankfurter and raw bacon, but she does not seem to respond at all to their unfamiliar scents. I hid bits of beef in my pockets and she very quickly nuzzled in to get them, but she did not seem able to find a hidden frankfurter or piece of bacon. Even when these were placed openly on folds of cloth she had great difficulty in locating them if they were not in her sight. If she did not discover the morsel in a few minutes, she refused to waste too much of her time and simply went away. All weasels have great energy, and there is never any sign of languidness about them. My weasel friend often lifts her head to listen when I am feeding her. Suddenly she may streak away from me, seeming to prefer the hunting of her natural dinner than the free meals that I have to offer.

Because the weasel gives few opportunities for close observation in the wild, its behavior is often described in generalities. My weasel exhibits some very unweasel-like traits, which leads to my conviction that weasels, like people, are highly individual in their behavior. In the first place, we have a few chickens, carefully protected by a weasel-proof screen—but our friend, to our astonishment, seems to be frightened out of her wits by the chickens! She circles widely to avoid the henhouse and when the rooster crows, she crouches, trembling, beneath my legs.

And our weasel *likes cookies!* I scattered some crumbs on the steps for the Canada jays, but she ate them. When I discovered her, she was still licking the step vigorously. Just to be sure, when she stood up to beg, I offered her some more; and she ate them right there in the open, something I had never seen her do before.

It is also said that the weasel is so dainty that it will go to great lengths to keep from soiling its feet; that it will even permit itself to be captured rather than walk through mud. I agree with their daintiness, but my weasel shows no hesitation about going through water or mud to climb into my lap for food. However, she wipes her feet carefully on my pants cuff before proceeding farther!

Each spring she goes away to attend to her serious business of motherhood, but we look forward to seeing her again each fall. Perhaps she will come in the harlequin coat of mixed white and brown that she wears as she is changing color from summer brown to winter white—standing up on our doorstep, her delicate front paws lifted, with her long, slender neck curved so that she may better view this huge and incomprehensible purveyor of her food.

Caliban

HENRY S. F. COOPER

ONE DAY IN JUNE, RACHEL, A SIXTEEN-YEAR-OLD, WAS walking on the hot paths of Central Park, New York City, on her way to my office. Her attention was suddenly caught by a small black object struggling in the grass at the base of a tree. As she came closer she saw that it was a young bird, a fledgling covered with down and pinfeathers. Its wings were spread, and it gasped for breath as it weakly tried to move forward by clumsy efforts of its wings and legs. The small creature was nearly dead of heat and exhaustion. Nearby lay the only refuge it had known—a battered and torn nest which harbored the dead body of one of its nest mates.

The girl's heart was touched with pity. She carried the bird to my office in her cupped hands. Thus Caliban, the grackle, came into our lives. We called him Caliban because he was such a homely little fellow and he was black as ink.

When Rachel brought the bird to me he was near death. In fact, I was sure that he was going to die. He lacked the strength to raise his head and he could not open his mouth. We gently opened his beak, then took some soft, moistened bread and pushed it down his throat with "thumb" forceps. We made a nest of cotton for him in a box, and when Rachel left my office with the bird I thought he had perhaps two hours to live.

Eleven days later, Rachel called me on the telephone. Caliban was alive all right. She had fed him a mixture of hard-boiled egg, biscuit, raw fruit, and cod-liver oil, and he had grown so big and his wants had become so numerous that he had been assigned the only bathroom in the apartment. Worst of all, her mother said she had to get rid of him. Rachel did not feel it safe to let Caliban go free in Central Park because he still was unable to feed himself, although he could fly after a fashion. Could I do anything to help? Fortunately I was leaving for my vacation the next day. I took him to Cooperstown, New York, with me.

The first morning I let Caliban loose in our garden. He immediately flew, and I suddenly realized that his flight control was not yet very good. He could only fly up and not at all down. He headed straight for the sky. It was only by the greatest piece of luck that he managed to catch onto the very top of the tallest tree in the neighborhood, and there he sat. Unfortunately, I had just fed him—so I had to wait about an hour to get him to come down. Then hunger got the better of him and he began to answer my calls. This time he did not trust his wings, but *climbed* down the tree by hopping from limb to limb.

He immediately worked his way into our hearts. He utterly and completely trusted us. When he wanted food he didn't think or hope that he was going to get it—he *knew* he was going to get it, and he got mad if he didn't. He was completely lacking in the fear that wild creatures seem instinctively to have of human beings. He would nestle in the angle of my elbow; and at first he seemed to like being stroked. Later he disliked being touched, although he otherwise remained fearless of us.

At first we let Caliban go free when we were about, but we put him in an old canary cage at night or when we were not at home. Gradually Caliban developed a great dislike for his cage. Whenever he was locked up he made the house ring with his complaints. On one occasion, however, when he became terrified at being caught outside during a thunderstorm, he flew to his cage like a frightened child and tried in every way to get in.

Gradually we let Caliban free for the whole day, only shutting him indoors in his cage at night where he would be safe from marauders. Soon he realized that sunset meant imprisonment. One evening, when I tried to catch him, he perched on our chimney top and nothing would tempt him to come down. From that time on we left him out both day and night, and we never discovered where he spent his nights. All we knew was that he disappeared at dusk and reappeared at dawn. In the early morning after his first night out he came to the kitchen door for a handout from our cook. He brought with him ten or twelve other birds that remained in the background and watched curiously while he was being fed. Afterward he flew away with them but soon returned alone. This was the only time that we saw him with other birds.

We came to believe the Caliban thought of himself as a human being. After all, human beings had attended to all his wants from his earliest memory. In fact, we thought it would have been illogical for him to think of himself in any other way. If he was in a tree or hedge he always let us know where he was by his peculiar croaking call. If he saw us from a distance he was very apt to fly to us and alight on the head of one of us, or on one of our shoulders. He especially enjoyed climbing all over us, pulling at our ears, the buttons of our clothing, or at shiny bits of jewelry that we wore. He was particularly fond of anything that glittered or was bright-colored, and he loved to tear matchboxes apart and scatter their contents on the ground. He pilfered cigarettes and cigars, and iced-tea time had a special attraction for him. The tall glasses, the shiny spoons and the ice, the sprigs of mint and the slices of lemon—all these proved utterly irresistible to him. After he had become tired of playing with these he would perch on the edge of a glass and try to take a bath in its contents, refusing to move even when the owner raised it to his lips. If the liquid did not suit Caliban's taste for either drinking or bathing, he would preen his feathers with it. Sometimes he used after-dinner coffee for this purpose.

He was very good at walking and would follow us around by the hour, particularly if we worked in the garden. Whenever we pulled up a weed he would rush in to grab any worm or insect that might have been exposed. He would often start to follow us on foot—and if the pace got too fast for him he would fly to one of our shoulders to ride. If he seemed to want company and saw us inside the house, he would fly to the window sill and tap on the glass with his beak. In the late afternoon, when he often got tired, he was quite apt to alight on my shoulder, snuggle up to my neck, and go to sleep. Just before going to sleep he would usually talk in a low voice, as if to tell me of the events of the day.

For about five weeks Caliban was our constant companion. It would be difficult to evaluate accurately the amount of pleasure he gave us. There was a sad side to it, too—it was obvious that he was adapted to human society but not to bird society. He lived a lonely life in this sense, always on the fringe of humanity—never completely with us, but never with his own kind. He also seemed rather indiscriminate in his fondness for human beings. During this period he

seemed to favor me over other people, possibly because I had the most to do with his care. Later on, however, he showed me no more attention than he showed to anyone else.

After my vacation had ended, I returned to New York. Caliban remained at our home in Cooperstown, but the next day he disappeared. We were fearful that he had become prey to a cat, but five days later, when we had about given him up for lost, a friend of ours told us:

"My next door neighbor was working in his garden this afternoon when a black bird alighted on his head and—would you believe it? —he couldn't get rid of him?"

We knew then that Caliban was still living. He had gone to dwell by the river bank about a quarter of a mile away. After that he began to range more widely. He seemed to want to be with people, and the more people the better. One little girl said that Caliban awakened her early every morning where she slept on a porch. When he arrived he alighted on her head and pulled her ears. A man said that Caliban spent a week with him, helping him in the garden and riding on his shoulder while he mowed the grass. Other people said that Caliban had joined them at a picnic about a mile up the lake—that he seemed to have had a good time and that he certainly gave them one.

At the lake front in the middle of Cooperstown is a park frequented by many people in the summertime. There is a stand there where one can buy hot dogs and soft drinks, or rent boats. Caliban moved there about the middle of August, stayed three weeks, and became famous. The owner of the stand wrote:

"My only regret is that I didn't have the camera handy when your bird was performing some of his cutest or boldest or sauciest acts—stealing a cigar out of the box and flying off with it to the park, pecking at ladies' nylons from under a park bench, preening himself in the soapsuds, tossing piece after piece of wrapped gum behind the ice-cream freezer, attempting to tweek a rose off a lady's hat."

After Labor Day people no longer came to the waterfront park, and Caliban moved to the business section of town. Here he went freely in and out of stores and stayed in one of them four days. He even went into the famous Cooperstown Baseball Museum.

Toward the end of September, Caliban disappeared. Perhaps he went south for the winter. If, on the other hand, tragedy overtook him as the result of his excessive trust in human nature—still his brief life was all to the good. For what bird ever became so famous? He was the talk of Cooperstown, the subject of several newspaper articles, and even the subject of a paper I presented before a learned group of scholars.

Caliban! We named you better than we knew. Seemingly part human—part wild—wholly neither—but living on the borderline between humanity and nature, it was only through the frailest thread of circumstances that you lived at all.

The World of a Chipmunk

ALAN DEVOE

AT FIRST, THERE IS ONLY AN enveloping darkness. Darkness and the feel of warmth against him as his tiny newborn body lies intimately with the bodies of his litter-fellows, and in his nostrils the primal smell of the inner earth, root-damp, grass-sweet, humid, and utterly enclosing. This is the initial life experience of the chipmunk. These are the first uncomprehended knowings that in the May of the year come to newborn *Tamias* (the steward, the prudent husbandman), lying blind and naked in the central chamber of the burrow, a foot or two underneath the blossoming bloodroots and yellow adder's tongue of the Outer World, but accessible only by a long and twisting tunnel through which no light can enter. Safety is here, in the friendly darkness: a dim contentment to pervade his uninstructed blood. This, and the already-stirring impulsions of instinct, of the hereditary unlearned lores which are the central wisdom of a little *Tamias* as much as of a hunting wolf or a migrating warbler or, not very differently, a chemically obedient milkweed that "knows" it must thrust its hairy stalk toward the hot sun.

In the quiet earth-darkness, blind and tiny, the baby chipmunk stirs and frets a little, and knows what he must know. He raises his infant muzzle, kneading and nuzzling the furry warmth that is the belly of his mother. He seizes upon a small teat and sucks a drop of chipmunk milk; and now an enormous peace, a quiet fulfillment, possess him utterly. He lies wholly tranquil now. There is a warmth, there is darkness, there is the smell of the enwombing earth, there is the taste of milk. He falls asleep.

This is the texture of the chipmunk's infancy, in the warm security of the grass-lined nest.

The weeks go by, and in the Outer World there is great change. Now is the season of tremendous happening, of the great annual thrust and drive and upward-rushing of the life-force in its myriad forms. The robins and bluebirds have nested now, the mayflies have danced their brief fantastic dance in the twilight, the woods and meadows have been caught up in an omnipresent tumult of greenness and aliveness and flowering and growing and singing. It is the time of the blue-winged warblers brooding; and the damsel-fly nymphs crawling from the brook water; and the young night herons, raucous and ungainly, making their first explorations of the mudflats and swamplands in the dusk.

It is nearly June. And in this time of metamorphosis and new life, of countless beginnings and maturings as earth draws toward its summer solstice, there has come change also to the chipmunk in his dark withdrawn birth-world. He has grown from the unknowingness of blind and naked infancy and is ready for adulthood. For many days now, since not long after his eyes opened, black and bright as little chokeberries, and his little squirrel-body took on the striated pelage that is the unmistakable coat of chipmunkhood, he has made explorations of his subterranean universe.

On swift scampering feet he has pattered, endlessly inquisitive, along the galleries of the burrow. He has explored that chamber, below the frostline, where there are mounded husks of hickory nuts, and that other chamber, reached by a long zigzagging route, where there are stored perhaps acorns and beechnuts; and he has been tempted to nibble at them, and so his weaning has come about. He knows now how to hold a nut in his adroit forepaws, twisting and turning it, and strip the husk from it with his sharp little incisors. He knows the uses of the pouches in his cheeks, and how they may be stuffed with foods that are to be carried from place to place; and he has acquired that curious and necessary chipmunk knowledge which tells him that when acorns are to be stuffed into his cheek pouches the sharp tips of the nuts must first be bitten off.

A little of all these things he has learned by experience, by trial and error, in his early explorings and investigations of the dark galleried world. But only a little. Mostly his knowledges have come to him as instinct. They have developed in him as his little lithe striped body has developed, willessly, without his taking thought of it. His acorn lore is as sure, and as uncalculated, as the instinct that prompted him a little while ago to suck the tiny milky dugs of his mother; or the instinct that a little later sent him pattering, curious and restless, through the galleries of the burrow; or the instinct that now in recent days has led him to engage in rough-and-tumble playings and frolickings with his brothers and sisters. These are the inheritance of his chipmunk blood. He obeys them. The sweet pungence of hickory nuts is meaningful to him, from the first; the scampering quickfooted gait he has developed now is not a privately decided thing, as a man's gait may be, but a hereditary and general chipmunk thing, inalienable from his blood, as a skunk's lumbering waddle is the changeless skunk way or a coon's heavy plantigrade plodding is the unreckoned and necessary movement of a coon.

To young *Tamias,* as to every other animal, the life experience presents itself as a series of external phenomena touching off spontaneous inner responses. In these last days of immaturity, now, the frolicking and anticking of his brothers and sisters arouses in him an excited urgency to tumble and tussle with them; and, as always, he follows impulse—"the subconscious faith of the animals"—and his education and development are carried one stage further. There are squeakings and chitterings and scamperings in the burrow now, and small furry body tumbling and wrestling with small furry body; and what is happening is that young chipmunk muscles are being made finally strong, and chipmunk coordinations made finally sure and quick, and the last preparation for life in the Outer World being effected.

Young *Tamias* has no knowing that this is so. The mind of a chipmunk is not a private mind. It is but participant in "the general intelligence of nature" (that *Mysterium Tremendum* ultimately no less inscrutable to philosophers than to chipmunks); and chipmunk destiny is forwarded by no private guesses, no deductive inferences, no shrewd concludings, but by the interior and unrealized impellings which forward likewise the destinies of negatively phototropic earthworms, positively phototropic bees, tactilely sensitive and obediently reflexive beavers when with unconscious and exquisite precision they fell a birch. The psyche of little *Tamias* is not made for thinking. No wild thing's is. It is made for feeling and acting. To play has a good feel; it fulfills an obscure desire. In the earth-darkness, under the tansy stems, *Tamias* plays.

The chipmunk looks nearly like his parents now. His squirrel body is almost six inches long, and his flattened furry tail almost four. The five black stripes that run from his shoulders to his rump are bright and sharp, as is the narrow little black stripe through his eye; and his short rounded ears are prominent on his tawny skull. His thick fur is warmly reddish and chestnut-colored now, clearest and warmest on his small rump and on his delicate little paws, and all his chipmunk powers that will fit him for the Outer World have come to their maximum development: the bright and watchful-eyed alertness, the sharpness of scent and hearing, the ingenuity of forepaws that are like little hands and that can dig a hollow in the sunbaked earth or hold delicately the smallest seed, the sharpness of twenty little chipmunk-teeth.

It is the time to go alone, to be an adult. The smell of his mother's fur has ceased now to attract him irresistibly, as the presence of light ceases in autumn to attract a wintering queen wasp; and the darkness of the burrow dimly oppresses him. There is a new impulsion now, urging him and tugging at his blood. It is the attraction of the sunlit world that lies outside the burrow-mouth—the free and windswept and sky-arched world where there are new foods to be found and hoarded, tree boles to be investigated, enemies to be outwitted and evaded, the unhampered and exultant life of an adult animal to be lived. On a summer morning, the young chipmunk patters to the burrow mouth, peeps out, and is gone. He has come to his majority.

The lives of all animals, from the greatest to the least, are ruled by four chief necessities. These are the necessities to feed, to have a lair, to breed, and to be wary against death. There are other ingredients, of course, in the life pattern; there is play, for example, and there is the dim half-drowsing resting, the obscure and relaxed hours of inactive and dreaming peace, that are a major part of living in the woods and meadowlands. But the four great necessities are paramount; and to these, as every animal must do, the small chipmunk comes to devote his adult attentions.

His feeding is enormous and almost omnivorous. Unlike the gray squirrels and the red squirrels, he is not impelled to extensive climbing in the treetops, to nibble at sweet elm seeds and maple keys and greening hickory nuts. Mostly he is a ground feeder. Restless, quick-footed, with fuzzy little tail straight out behind, he scampers along old stone fences, patters through the meadow grass, scurries and scuttles in the underbrush, his keen inquisitive little muzzle alert for the scents that mean provender. Grains of all kinds are welcome to him; seeds of a hundred sorts, berries, and nuts.

To the chipmunk, as to most animals that are largely vegetarian, the procuring of food presents little of a problem. He need not hunt for prey, as a hawk must; his diet lies everywhere around him. Only rarely, as the weeks pass and he makes his scampering rounds of the weed tops and the berry bushes, does he feel an inadequacy in his diet, a need for a taste that grain and berries do not give. When this happens, he takes to the treetops. There are birds' nests there, some with fledglings in them in the latter summer, and *Tamias* is able, when he wants, to clamber up to them as ingeniously as any red squirrel. He is as deft with an egg as with a nut. With the taste of egg yolk or the taste of warm blood in his little gullet, he is satisfied and returns to the ground again to resume his vegetarian feeding. Not often does his periodical carnivorousness become such a habit that he presents a peril to birdlife. It is a hunger that comes to him only rarely, like his hunger for grasshoppers and crickets, and like the recurrent appetite which may sometimes send him creeping softly into a nest of the little deer mice, to pounce on the litter and devour them as eagerly as though he were a weasel. Mostly *Tamias* goes peaceably, harmlessly, through the woods-world, stuffing his cheeks with acorns, squeaking and chittering and flirting his tail at the astonishments and excitements of the universe, preparing the seed hoards which have earned him his Latin name of steward.

Second only to feeding, as a major rite in his life, is the chipmunk's making of his burrow. It must be at once his storehouse and his refuge from enemies, and he has not been long an adult before he sets about its construction. In a secluded place—under a fallen log, perhaps, or in the shelter of a boulder—he begins to dig a hole. As he works, he throws the excavated earth behind him as a woodchuck does. Down sharply for a foot or so he tunnels, and then on a more gradual slope for a yard or two; and then, below the level to which the frost is likely to reach, the corridor is dug laterally. The chipmunk extends it yard after yard, making it only about two inches in diameter (an adequate accommodation for his own lithe little body, but readily barricaded against weasels); and presently he begins to work at ramifications that will be storage rooms. These he hollows and scoops until they are big enough so that any one of them can hold several quarts of seeds and nuts, and he may construct as many as three or four. In the root-smelling darkness, absorbed and furiously laboring little *Tamias* finishes the storage rooms, the long lateral corridors, the central sleeping place; and then the tunnels gradually upward to make the exit into the Outer World again.

Because this exit hole has been dug from below, there is no accumulation of excavated earth thrown out around it—no telltale sign which might let an enemy know of the burrow's presence. And so, when the chipmunk has come up through this unobtrusive orifice into the Outer World again, the instinctive wisdom of his ancestral chipmunk blood leads him to do an extraordinary and unconsciously very cunning thing, wise with that old earth-wisdom that is anterior to the intellect. He scampers to the original entrance hole, where earth perforce was thrown out as he excavated, and with swift dexterousness piles the earth into the hole again and scatters the surplus. Every sign of the telltale digging is obliterated, and the hole stoppered tight shut. As a final act of concealment, *Tamias* carries leaves and bits of grasses to the site and layers it over until every evidence of his work has been hidden. His burrow now has only the inconspicuous entrance which was originally its exit, and over this the tangle of weeds and underbrush will quickly grow a concealing screen.

Tamias does not know the why of what he has done—any more than an orb-weaving spider knows the why, or a dauber wasp when it paralyzes the spider for its young, or infant *Tamias* when he suckled in the spring—but the inherited behests of his blood have been fulfilled, and he has now an obscure peace of accomplishment, and nature has been wise for him.

All the rest of the summer the chipmunk's life follows now a not greatly varying pattern. Very early in the morning, before dawn, he awakens in his sleeping chamber and comes scampering to the door of the burrow and sets forth for his day's feeding. His universe is a smell of hickory nuts, a pungence of weed seeds and of dawn-damp earth to which his little muzzle is so close, an exultancy in the unrationalized awareness of his little chipmunk aliveness.

Nibbling, scurrying, searching, gnawing . . . this is his preoccupation. Occasionally there comes to his rounded furry ears the squalling scream of a hovering hawk, or there is detectable in his small quivering nostrils the rank odor of a fox or the thin musky odor of a gliding snake; and he darts then back to his burrow or to one of the shallower auxiliary burrows which he may have dug in concealed places nearby and among which he has established, by repetition, a quite regular route of travel. If it is to his main burrow that he has recourse for safety, he approaches it in a curious fashion. He rushes to it in high leaping bounds, almost such leaps, in miniature, as a white-tailed deer makes; and he is careful not to follow the same track that he followed the last time he came home. It is chipmunk tactic, natively instinctive, to ensure that with the passing of time he will not beat a regular and visible trail to the burrow's hidden entrance hole.

Feeding and being watchful against enemies: these are the chipmunk's central activities. For the rest, there is endless exploration to satisfy his curiosity; there is dozing near the burrow entrance or atop an old stump when he is well fed with seeds and the dreamy contentment steals over him that steals over all wild things when they are well fed and unpursued; and, not least, there are sometimes playing and singing.

The life-exultancy can well up in a small chipmunk even as in a caracoling deer or a ceremoniously dancing caribou; and now and then little *Tamias,* stirred by that clamorous gladness, may frisk and frolic and tumble in an exuberance of play. Hearing the sharp *"Chip!"* of another of his kind, he may answer; and from elsewhere in near woods or fields others may likewise make their little chipmunk utterance; and for many minutes together there may be a chorus of callings and answerings. Partly, in latter summer, it is perhaps what biologically is called a "pseudo-mating," like the performance of the spotted newts. But much of the while it is something else, something simpler. Animal life, even the least and littlest, like *Tamias',* has in it the element of a simple primal exultation.

On a day in the autumn the chipmunk feels a diminishing of his vitality. The coursing life force that has made him flirt his little tail and scrabble vigorously in the earth and chitter with his fellows has suddenly dwindled, with the coming of frost into the air. For several weeks now he has been filling his cheek pouches ever more busily, bringing back grains and seeds in loads of more than two tablespoonfuls at a time, storing them assiduously in his underground vaults until there has come to be a hoard of more than half a bushel. Instinctive chipmunk lore has served him again, in this gathering of his supplies; and he has brought into the burrow no berries or grains which may spoil from a long keeping. Now, with his granaries full and the sharpness of autumn in the air, he has felt the stealing over him of a growing lethargy. There is not the impulse, now, to be up before the dawn; there is no wanting to rush and scamper and chirrup and be endlessly inquisitive. There is a wanting only of quiet, and a love (as in infant days, six months ago in the spring) of the cool root-scented darkness of the under-earth. The blood says now: Be quiet. The drive of instinct says now: Hush, rest.

In the spring it will be time to mate. It will be time to wake, nibbling at grains and seeds stored prudently against that need, and time to scamper with all the rush and vitality of abounding chipmunkhood. But now it is the time to hibernate. It is the time for bats and bears and little five-striped beasts with flattened furry tails to have their winter sleep.

The chipmunk lies in his central sleeping chamber, curled into a ball, relaxed, motionless. Around him, as in babyhood, there is only the darkness, the smell of the grass-sweet earth, the enwombing silence. His breathing grows slow, slower. His heartbeat quiets. The winter has come now; and *Tamias,* the steward, the prudent husbandman, has done what he must do and known what he must know. It is very quiet here, dark and protecting. He sighs a little, shallowly, and enters into an enormous nothingness.

Geoffrey

PENELOPE WEIGEL

WITH THE LAST BITE OF THE FARMER'S AXE THE OLD apple tree quivered, and then crashed to the ground. From the cavity of the fallen tree a young screech owl, lone survivor of a brood of four, wobbled unsteadily into the sunlight to greet the surprised onlookers. We had stopped by the roadside to watch the farmer cut down the old apple tree, and I don't know who was more astonished, the farmer or my husband and I. Geoffrey, as we later dubbed the owl, was too young to fend for himself. We decided to take him home with us.

At first he was quite shy, and whenever we approached him he would ruffle up his reddish-brown feathers until he looked twice his size. The red "phase," or rufous plumage in the screech owl, occurs in both sexes without regard to age or season. After a few days Geoffrey seemed to lose some of his fear of us and began to strut around the house as if he owned it. My husband and I, both graduate students in biology, decided that the best place to study and photograph an unhousebroken owl was in our glass-enclosed back porch.

With the addition of a perch or two, Geoffrey's new home was complete.

Feeding a nocturnal bird posed a problem until Geoffrey became adjusted to his day-feeding schedule. At first whenever he was hungry he'd fly head-on against the glass pane of our porch door with an ear-splitting crash guaranteed to awaken the soundest sleeper. It was quite nerve-racking to stumble out of bed in the middle of the night and find a small owl sitting innocently on the threshold waiting to be fed. We solved this "night owl" problem by feeding Geoffrey pieces of raw horsemeat and kidney three times a day and just before we retired. To insure him healthy, well-formed bones we dusted the meat with a calcium compound. Using his strong beak and claws Geoffrey was able to tear the larger pieces of meat into those of swallowing size. Each time he bolted down a large chunk he would close his eyelids tightly as if this were necessary to aid in swallowing.

Later, Geoffrey was able to swallow a whole mouse, stopping only at intervals to catch his breath. The bones, fur, and other indigestible parts he disgorged in pellets. Experienced bird watchers always look on the ground for these telltale pellets when searching for an owl's roosting tree. Little did we know just what kinds of things the owl was picking up around the house until he coughed up an odd-shaped pellet while he was in the house one day. Besides the usual fur and bone, it contained, much to our amazement, a straight pin!

As the weeks passed by, Geoffrey became tamer and tamer. He would sit on our shoulders or the back of a chair while we read, and offer his head or beak to be scratched. When my husband and I came home in the evenings we gave Geoffrey the freedom of the house so he would have enough room to exercise his wings. He could fly nonstop from the kitchen to the living room, where his favorite perching spot was the top of a large picture frame. When he was not busy preening his feathers, he made a "walking" or hopping tour of our house. He presented quite a humorous picture as he scurried from room to room on his short wobbly legs. Because he was so small and trusting, we were continually afraid of stepping on him. The fact that we stepped over him, around him, and even occasionally bumped into him, did not bother Geoffrey in the least. He simply wouldn't budge an inch. As he hopped along the hall or squatted contentedly on the rug, his small form was hardly visible. So we began treating him like a piece of furniture. When he got in our way, we picked him up and moved him to one side. Geoffrey hated this affront to his dignity and clattered his bill angrily. Sometimes, if he sensed that we were going to pick him up, he might lift his feathery pantaloons and scurry away out of our reach.

Although the "wise old owl" is not half as intelligent as he is reputed, Geoffrey was able to learn a few things. One of our proudest accomplishments was to teach him to fly to our hands for food when we whistled. We conditioned Geoffrey to this by whistling each time we offered him food, and we never made an exception to this rule. Within a week Geoffrey had learned to associate the whistle with food and came promptly to us whenever we "called." My proudest moment was the day when I whistled and Geoffrey flew directly to my outstretched hand to take a piece of meat.

Perhaps our greatest wish was to get some good pictures of the owl in flight, to see exactly how he used his wings. For nature photography of this sort, my husband has converted a spare bedroom into a studio. To me, and perhaps to those not familiar with the requirements of a photographer, it looks more like a forest. Picturesque tree stumps and branches, nailed to supports, decorate the whole room. There are stumps decked with fungus, stumps with grotesque arms and holes, and worst of all, stumps with ants in them. It was on one of these that we photographed Geoffrey. Using the high speed electronic flash unit, with its speed of 1/5,000th of a second, every wingbeat and motion of the flying bird can be registered on the film. Geoffrey was not a willing actor, and it required great patience and much pushing and poking to get him to fly at just the right moment. Often he flew in the wrong direction. He was as temperamental as any prima donna and refused to act unless we first gave him some food. After the supply of horsemeat ended, Geoffrey's acting ability seemed to vanish with it. When he flew and landed on a stump, his third eyelid, or nictitating membrane, moved across his eyeballs from the inner corners outward. This membrane helps to protect a bird's eye from being damaged by twigs or branches when it alights in trees and shrubbery.

In the wild the screech owl's silent wings enable it to come upon its prey unawares. It is not a swift, streamlined bird and must rely upon stealth and surprise to capture its food. For this purpose nature has endowed owls with soft feathers that have fine, hairlike edges through which the air passes noiselessly.

Since we had previously decided that it was only fair to release Geoffrey when he was old enough to take care of himself, we felt that the time had come to let our pet go and enjoy whatever limited freedom a wild animal has. We took Geoffrey to a lonely, wooded spot. It was surrounded by open fields where mice are plentiful. When we tossed him into the air, he flew strongly to a tree and alighted in it, quite as if he had been doing such things all his life.

At home we no longer need the reserve supply of newspapers to put under Geoffrey's favorite perching spots; and our friends, who temporarily forsook us while Geoffrey lived with us, have returned. Yet it is difficult to say that our normal household and returned friends make up for those interesting hours we spent with this little screech owl.

The Desert Tortoise

LILLIAN E. MILES

ONE SUMMER MORNING A NUMBER OF YEARS AGO, OUT ON the southern rim of the Mojave Desert in California, a large desert tortoise ambled along the railroad tracks. The heat of the summer sun had dried the succulent roots upon which it usually fed; and so, according to the custom of its kind, it was migrating to the foothills where vegetation was more abundant and where it could more easily dig to water. A young man picked it up and brought it to Mrs. W. A. Crump of San Bernardino, California.

Mrs. Crump named the tortoise George and tried to find from books how he should be cared for. One book said that the desert tortoise lives on insects and requires no water, but George ignored the insects and showed a preference for the pool made by the garden hose. Also, Mrs. Crump found him eating the grass in the backyard; and she discovered that he particularly liked apples, carrots, and lettuce, and that he would eat cabbage if there was nothing else to be had. The desert tortoise is a vegetarian and likes to dig in the dirt. Mrs. Crump read that it hibernates, so in the fall she put George in a box, expecting him to go to sleep, but he stayed awake until Christmas. If he had been allowed to "dig himself in" he would probably have been hibernating by the tenth of October.

At first, George seemed discontented with Mrs. Crump's kindly but misguided attentions and tried to run away on many occasions. However, when an understanding was finally established between them, he settled down to a peaceful existence in the backyard. After George had lived alone for two years, Mrs. Crump acquired Martha, a female desert tortoise, to be a companion for him. Martha was smaller than George, but neither tortoise increased in weight or size while Mrs. Crump had them, other than the weight they gained before hibernating and the amount they lost during hibernation.

The tortoises had no visible ears, but they were actually sensitive to sound and came when called, often from a distance of a hundred yards.

There were small trap gates about the Crump's yard, built so their dog could come and go as he pleased. The tortoises also used them, by choice and not necessity, as they were remarkably strong and could tear a chicken-wire apart as easily as one could with a pair of metal-cutting shears.

The plague of dandelions in the yard ceased to exist for Mrs. Crump because the tortoises never permitted a single plant to grow. In summer they ate at about nine in the morning and five in the afternoon, and two apples and three carrots per tortoise were a day's rations. The desert tortoise does not have fully developed teeth, but his "gums" are the curved horny edges of the jaw, and they are razor sharp. He takes a nice round bite of carrot or apple and swallows it whole. He is not aggressive and never bites or snaps viciously as snapping turtles do.

Next to food, the tortoises enjoyed the spray of the garden hose. Martha, the female tortoise, got about two feet in front of the hose spray and dug a hole. She dug awkwardly but effectively, flipping dirt and mud up on her back. She waited until the water ran down and filled the hole, then she crawled into the pool and stayed there from thirty to forty minutes. George waited until she had finished digging, then he, too, ambled over and got into the water.

When not eating or bathing, the tortoises spent much time in their underground burrow, for, in spite of being desert animals, they did not like to be in direct rays of the sun. The tortoises showed a decided nervousness when placed upon a narrow box above the ground, but climbed an almost perpendicular hill, or even a few feet of chicken-wire, to reach food. Sometimes when no food was about they climbed anyway, seemingly for the pleasure of exploration.

It is rather unusual for desert tortoises to mate in captivity, but after George and Martha had lived together in the backyard for five years they mated. During the two weeks' mating season George walked much more rapidly than usual and carried his head high.

He was very aggressive and gave way to nothing. Once he found the wheel of the automobile in his pathway and pushed against it for half an hour before he turned aside.

The tortoises mated twice in nine years. Mrs. Crump's next-door neighbor had acquired a number of male tortoises and these animals, usually so quiet and peaceful, fought among themselves. One could plainly hear their shells clashing. Their object seemed to be to overturn each other. Whichever accomplished this won the fight. The victor paid no further heed to his vanquished foe, but walked away with his head in air, leaving his rival to turn back over as best he could. Contrary to popular belief, these tortoises usually can right themselves after being turned on their backs, but it requires time and a struggle.

The tortoises first mated in August. The following June, Martha laid her first eggs. For two weeks she ate nothing at all, while she prepared her nest in the sand. With her powerful front feet she scooped out a large hole slanting two or three feet back into the earth. It was shaped much like a Mexican water jar, smaller at the top and enlarged below. The nest faced east, toward the morning sun.

Martha laid nine eggs, and the laying required about thirty minutes. Beginning some distance down in the hole she laid her first egg, covered it with finely powdered dirt, and tamped it down with her hind legs. Working upward, she laid her eggs in a symmetrical row and covered each one carefully with about an inch of dirt. The eggs, shortly after they were laid, felt cool and were about an inch and a half in diameter, almost perfectly round, and pure white. They had a shell almost like a hen's egg.

When the clutch was laid, Martha walked away. Her maternal duties were completed. She never returned to the nest, nor did she take an interest in the baby tortoises when they hatched. The eggs were incubated by the warmth of the soil in which they were laid, and the incubation required from 105 to 120 days (three and one-half to four months), depending on the earth's temperature.

When Martha laid her first clutch, Mrs. Crump did not know how long it would take the eggs to hatch. Some people said thirteen months, others said one month. From time to time Mrs. Crump broke eggs to see if they were fertile, and found that the baby tortoises were developing. From the last egg laid, a baby tortoise emerged on the 105th day. That was several years ago and when I visited the

Crumps, he was still alive and well. At that time he measured three and one-half inches wide by five inches long, and at his rate of growth it would probably take him ten to fifteen years to reach maturity.

Three years later Martha laid a second clutch of nine eggs. Five tortoises hatched 120 days later. After the eggs were 110 days old they were dug up and placed in the sun, where one could see the live youngsters moving about inside the shells. Apparently the strong light and the heat disturbed them.

At birth the baby tortoises were about the size of a silver dollar. Their shells were lighter colored than those of the older tortoises and much softer, but within a year they were as hard as those of the adults.

As soon as they hatch the babies go immediately into the soft earthen nest their mother prepared for them four months before, and they do not emerge until spring. During hibernation, they eat nothing, and they live through their first hibernation on the residue of the egg yolk left in their bodies.

While the eggs were incubating, the adult desert tortoises were getting ready for winter. They ate almost continually and gained more than a pound in weight. Their movements became more and more sluggish. Martha did most of the digging of the winter cave. She dug with her front feet and kicked the dirt backward with her hind ones, throwing it fifteen or more feet in this way. George watched her and rested. When she had finished digging he went in and made the hole larger to accommodate his larger body. Their cavelike tunnel reached back under the house a distance of twenty-five or thirty feet. They used the same burrow each year but enlarged it occasionally.

They went into their hibernating den about the fourth of October, but moved in and out of it for a few days. They seemed to be weather prophets par excellence and were remarkably sensitive to changes, perhaps to barometric pressure, even before weather changes occurred. Approximately March fifteenth, they came out of hibernation. They weighed a pound or two less, but their health and appetites were unimpaired by their seven months' sleep.

The desert tortoise is the only tortoise native to California. Most people call them desert "turtles." Although they are related to the giant tortoises of the Galapagos Islands which sometimes weigh as much as three hundred pounds, one of the largest known specimens of the desert tortoise weighed around twenty pounds. No one knows how long they will live. A desert prospector states that he kept one for forty years, that it was full grown when captured and apparently in its prime when a camp marauder took it away.

Each of the Crump tortoises had thirteen center shell patterns on its back and about these thirteen center patterns were twenty-six fluted, shell-like scallops. Under the microscope each shell pattern was outlined by thirteen lines or ridges. Some people believe that one can tell the age of a tortoise by the number of lines surrounding the shell patterns on the back; but, of those examined, from newly hatched to full-grown, *all* had thirteen lines.

In captivity, the desert tortoise has a formidable enemy— the red ants, which bite the comparatively soft folds of skin about the neck, sometimes causing the death of young ones. Either in or out of captivity the automobile is a menace to them if they get into the street or roadway. It is not an uncommon sight to see one that has been crushed by a car whose driver failed to see the animal in time to avoid it. On the desert, coyotes and wildcats eat tortoises; and desert residents claim that tortoise shells often bear marks and scratches made by these animals. The desert Indians considered them a staple article of their diet, along with snakes and chuck-awallas.

Although wild desert tortoises face many natural hazards, in the Crump's well-fenced yard Martha and George had good prospects for a long and apparently contented life.

Our Friendly Tree Swallows

MYRTLE JEANNE BROLEY

NOTHING IN OUR YEARS OF BIRD STUDY HAS GIVEN US AS much pleasure as our friendly tree swallows. During the summer we live in a cottage at one end of a rocky island in Lower Beverly Lake, one of the lakes that forms the Rideau chain in southeastern Ontario, Canada. It is an ideal place for these graceful, swift-flying little creatures, since they love to flit back and forth over the blue water in their pursuit of the insects on which they feed.

We have had tree swallows in our nest boxes in April when the lake was still covered with ice and the winds were very cold. Occasionally a severe snowstorm blankets the area and the tree swallows then have a hard time finding enough to eat or a shelter. On such days our wide veranda will be a haven for hundreds of them, so chilled that they pay little attention to us as we come or go among them.

One day in late May I was shaking my dust mop at the back door. A white feather that I had picked up with it blew off. At once a swallow sped after this treasure and flew with it to her nesting box. A clamoring flock of tree swallows followed behind her. We were so amused at this that we hurriedly ripped open a feather pillow and got out more white feathers. It was surprising the way our little colony chased the flying bits of fluff. They were not interested in *colored* feathers, though, and sought only the white ones.

I noticed that a little female tree swallow, whose box was on a tree near the woodshed (into which we went very frequently), came quite close to me to retrieve feathers. Indeed I was sure she had begun to wait for me each morning around ten o'clock, the time when I usually tossed out building material to them. There she'd be looking out from the entrance hole or sunning herself at the side of her box. After a very chilly night I went out the back door at the usual hour; but instead of walking on to toss the feathers into the air, I held one up near the low roof, which screened me fairly well, with just my hand and the feather showing. The female tree swallow flew back and forth over my hand, then swooped down to take the feather, which she carried to her nesting box. She took two more feathers from my hands that morning, and soon she would fly to meet me to receive the offering. Others circled about, and soon there were several brave enough to pluck the lightly held plumes from our fingers.

It became a diversion for us and our friends to offer feathers to the swallows. We tied some on a string and were amused at the way the birds struggled to get them. Of course, we did not let them try too long but fixed the feathers in between the strings so that they could get them easily.

All of our swallows swarmed about us when we tossed up, or held out, white feathers. It was fun to toss some of these on the water when it was still. The birds swooped for them so swiftly, yet never collided or bumped each other. It is true there were often fights when a feather was being taken to the nesting box—other birds endeavored to rob the proud possessor of the feather until the feather was pushed or carried through the entrance hole.

Sometimes my husband would offer a really large white feather and watch the commotion that the swallows made over it. It was too large to go through the small nest-box entrance hole easily, and the swallow had to work it around until it finally got it into the best position. All this time the other tree swallows were trying to gain possession of the feather. We stuck one of these plumes firmly into the ground and were amazed at the way the birds, often three and four at once, worked to pull it out.

Meanwhile, I had been working with my friendliest bird. She had growing young in her nest, which she and her mate fed assiduously. She had grown used to me standing by her box while she went in and out. Then I put my fingers around the one-and-a-half inch opening and after a little hesitation she rushed in with her load of insects.

After a while I put my fingers half over the entrance hole. This would make it necessary for her to push at my fingers to get in, and I was astonished that she did. She would even sit on my thumbs to rest before forcing her way past my hand into the nest box. Soon both adult birds were going in and out as if my fingers were part of the box. They allowed my husband and daughter to act as bars or perches, too.

Noticing that the parents were carrying dragonflies to their hungry brood, we caught some and offered them, still alive, of course, to the female. She took them and fed them to the young, and the male also grew bold enough to take them. Flies that we offered them would usually be eaten at once by the adult birds, and I fed them to the birds later, while incubation was in progress. The female would just stretch her head out of the box, take my offering, and eat it at once. The male usually came out of the nest and sat on his perch.

The next spring we arrived at the cottage after most of our tree swallows had arrived. A few kept coming in, though, and one morning I said to my husband, "You know, all the boxes are filled, but not one of the birds acts like my friendly pair of last summer."

We did not band the birds. To do so it is necessary to catch them in a net as they leave the nesting box, and we found this made them nervous and unfriendly. At places where birds go into a live-trap after food and are banded and released, they will often return to the trap again and again. Netting them just isn't the same. As we wanted our birds to be tame and fearless of us, we left the banding to people who went into areas away from their homes to do so.

The second day after we had arrived at our summer cottage was wonderfully mild and sunny. We were seated on the veranda when suddenly a tree swallow winged in over the lake and settled on the railing near us. He caroled his rippling little song, then flew over and sat on my husband's shoulder.

"That must be Tamey," I said (this was the name we had given our cooperative little male), "and we haven't a box for him."

"There's one that I have just put together," said my husband. "It isn't painted but I guess he won't mind that." He hurried off to get it. When he came back with it in his hands, the swallow flew over and settled on the perch as if he knew this was for him. I took the box while Charlie went for the camera. Tamey, for it was indeed he, looked in the nesting hole; hopped to the top; went back to the perch and then, while I still held the box, went right inside to examine it. When Tamey came out, we hung the box in place on

a post near the veranda, and he went in and out of it several times before flying off. Very soon he returned with a little mate and the two took over the house. Whenever we went near the post on which the box hung, one of this pair of swallows would settle on our hands or our arms, as if they knew that this was the one repayment for providing them with a home that we most desired. They would sit on my husband's head for minutes at a time.

Tamey took flies from us at once, but the little female was more shy. We offered them other insects, too. They ate some; and others they took from us, then flew out over the lake and dropped them into the water. The fuzzy tent caterpillars Tamey did not like, and it amused us to give them to him and see him fly out over the water and drop them. He would grab them well in the center and drop them from quite a height. One of the other tame swallows grasped them just by the tip as if it did not care to handle them at all.

One very chilly morning I broke up the white shell of an egg and tossed it outside. Later on I glanced out and saw several of our tree swallows busily picking up bits of the shell and eating them. I called my husband, who was as surprised as I. He got more shells and ground them finer so that the birds could pick them up more easily. We did not know at that time that purple martins will also eat eggshells.

After the brood leaves the nesting box, it does not return to it. The young are able to fly well at once and to catch their own food. Some bird books say that a second brood is raised, but we have not seen this happen in our group. Of course, if something goes wrong with the first clutch of eggs, the bird will lay again.

In late summer and early fall, tree swallows gather in thousands and sit on fence wires, trees, and bushes, or skim over our meadows and fields. When colder weather arrives they migrate south, still in these large flocks. On a chilly morning we often see the roof of our guest house, which is out on a lake point, covered with the little creatures; and we realize they are taking a last look around before heading south.

Cottontails in My Garden

FRANK F. GANDER

ONE AUGUST MORNING AS I WALKED OUT INTO MY California garden, the talkative notes of a covey of quail sounded from the shrubbery. The birds were moving toward the spot where they knew I would be spreading food for them. A fence lizard near the path took from my hand a mealworm that I offered it, and as I came near the lath-house, I met a friendly cottontail. This rabbit was almost grown and had been living in my garden since it first came in as a tiny, fluffy baby, so it was accustomed to me and did not fear me. I stopped to watch it for a few moments and saw that it was feeding on the plants of the area, eating a little of first one and then another. In a short time, within my nursery, it had sampled plants from every continent.

After the cottontail had satisfied its appetite, it started to hop past me along the path, which at this point was less than two feet wide. For just a second it hesitated about coming so close; but it came on, turned its head and sniffed at the cuff of my trousers as it passed, and then hopped out of the shadow of the lath-house into the full sunlight. Apparently this was too warm for comfort, for the rabbit soon turned around and came back past me along the path. Just in front of me and not six feet away, it stretched out full length on a patch of baby's-tears (*Helxine*), which grows in a moist, shaded place. It nibbled a few leaves from the plant, then grew drowsy, and with half-closed eyes soon seemed to be sleeping.

As this rabbit dozed so trustingly before me, I thought of other cottontails whose lives had touched mine down through the years. How different had been our relationship from this present friendly one! The first cottontails I can remember were those I used to see along the country roads near Wichita, Kansas, when I was a small boy and my father used to hitch the horse to the buggy and take the family out for a drive on summer evenings. It was at Wichita, too, that I first saw a rabbit shot, and by the time I was twelve years old I had joined an older brother in coursing rabbits with greyhounds.

The quail in my garden broke into my train of memories with their impatient calling; but the rabbit in front of me dozed on, so I continued to watch it. Thinking over the various experiences with cottontails in the past, I realized that I had probably hunted them more in California than in all other states together, for here I have spent over half my life. I had done some shooting to get specimens to be preserved for scientific study in a museum and some, too, to protect my garden.

Whether or not my thoughts about hunting rabbits were sensed by the little creature in front of me, it would be impossible to determine; but something caused it to get up, yawn and stretch, and move on. What a pleasure it had been to watch it and to watch the various other activities of rabbits in my garden! How glad I felt now that I was no longer at war with them, but had learned to watch them with friendliness instead of running for a gun every time I saw one.

Many things I have learned about cottontails, too, by watching the ones in my garden. I have learned that they are great samplers and seldom eat much at a time from any one plant, but move about, eating a little here and a little there. Much of what they take is waste material—grasses, pimpernel, oxalis, and similar weeds; and also the fallen blossoms of many plants, including the native white sage and many exotic species. Sometimes they do not wait for the flowers to fall but eat them off the plant. I have watched them eating California poppies, horned poppies, Chinese balloon flowers, and hibiscus blossoms in this way. In addition, they eat some seeds, taking these off the plant or picking them up off the ground. They seem to be especially fond of the seeds of the annual wildflower called "golden girls" (*Chaenactis*), and they also eat the seed heads of some grasses.

Of course, they sometimes annoy me greatly by eating plants that I treasure; but I have learned to protect all young plants with cages of wire netting of one-inch mesh, until the plants are large enough to withstand the depredations of rabbits. Plants that never get that large must be protected continuously or must be kinds which rabbits do not like. Yet I would not banish rabbits from my garden, for this garden is a naturalistic one and needs the activities of birds, rabbits, and other small creatures to complete it. Cottontails seem to belong here.

Cottontails, I believe, would make themselves at home in anyone's garden, for they live throughout the length and breadth of our land. When driving in the evening or early morning, one can seldom travel many miles in rural areas without seeing cottontails along the roadside, for this is the most widespread kind of wild rabbit in the United States. However, there are others. In brushy areas of the Far West can be found a very close relative, the brush rabbit; and in swamps and marshes of the southeastern states live the swamp rabbit and marsh rabbit. The tiny pygmy rabbit lives only in a very small area, principally in Idaho. The jack rabbits of the prairie country west of the Mississippi River and the snowshoe rabbits of the high mountains and northern states are hares, and differ from rabbits in several ways.

With jack rabbits and other hares, the young are born well covered with hair, and with their eyes open. They are able to hop about from the first. With cottontails and their close relatives, however, the young are blind at birth and practically naked, so that the mother prepares an excellent nest for them. Cottontail nests that I have seen in Kansas, Texas, and California were quite alike—each was a small bowl-like depression in the earth, lined with dry grasses or leaves; and this in turn was lined with fur which the mother cottontail had pulled from her belly. When the mother is away from the nest, she leaves the young covered with a blanket of this same fur, and over this may spread dry grass or leaves. This last layer brings the top of the nest up to a level with the surrounding ground so that it is well concealed.

In Kansas, late in the summer of 1921, I surprised a mother cottontail nursing her young in such a nest, in a weed patch. She had pushed the covering blanket to one side and was sitting over the brood of young while they reached up and nursed. Startled by my approach, she disengaged herself from the young, hopped from over them, turned back and made a quick pass at the fur and grass blanket to pull it over the nest, then fled in terror. So frightened and rattled was she that she ran into a poultry wire fence. Before she could get her wits about her and escape, I grabbed her and, to my surprise, found she was a young female not yet fully grown. The condition of her nipples verified that she definitely had been nursing babies, and thus I first learned that a young doe cottontail might produce offspring in the same year that she herself had been born.

The nest that I saw in Texas was discovered by dogs, but they had not disturbed it when a group of us caught up with them. It was much like the Kansas nest, except that, since it was in a wooded area, leaves instead of grass formed the top covering. This mother rabbit was chased by the dogs and ran up the sloping trunk of a large liveoak and hid in a hollow limb. The dogs followed her up the trunk but could not get to her in the hollow where she had hidden herself.

Two nests I found in California were on grassy hillsides and almost identical with the Kansas nest in appearance. I found one as a house cat was raiding it, and the other I discovered only because it had first been found by a large gopher snake (*Pituophis*) that was making a meal of the young rabbits. One other time I saw a gopher snake catch a young cottontail. In the chaparral one spring, I jumped a little rabbit that was still in the fluffy baby stage. It scuttled across a small clearing, and as it came to the bushes on the opposite side, a gopher snake seized it and quickly wrapped himself about it to kill it.

Snakes of many kinds are known to eat cottontails, which also are preyed upon by many other animals. Hawks, eagles, and owls catch rabbits of all sizes; and in the Southwest, the roadrunner occasionally catches very young rabbits. All predatory mammals from the weasel to the wolf and lynx feed on rabbits extensively. Opossums and skunks also eat some broods.

Young cottontails seem to be most vulnerable to attack when they first leave the protection of the nest. They scatter then, each fluffy baby frequenting its own small area. The mother keeps track of each one for a time and visits them to let them nurse. One spring I was out in a wild area when I heard a low sound that I did not recognize. Carefully peeking over the intervening bushes, I saw a baby rabbit come out of a tangle of brush and run to its mother. The mother sat upright and was alert for danger, but her back was toward me. The baby rushed up to her and started nursing. From this position, both could spring into flight readily if some foe appeared.

The first litters of the season arrive very early in the spring—in the southern part of their range, as early as the first of February.

Successive litters follow on into summer as long as green food is available. Mating for the early litters occurs about the first of the year in my part of California; and at that time, the bucks do considerable fighting. Sometimes I find scratched up places in my garden with rabbit hair scattered about, and I know that two bucks have been in combat. Occasionally a somewhat similar "sign," usually with some remains of the rabbit, shows where a predator has taken a cottontail. The need for the cottontail to have many broods is apparent when one considers the numerous animals in fur, feathers, and scales that eat them.

Man, too, is an important enemy of the cottontail, but the ones of my garden have changed me from a foe to a friend. At first I did not welcome them and fought them vigorously; but, in the spring, cute baby rabbits came in from the chaparral and looked so little and helpless in a hostile world that I could not bring myself to add to their troubles. Soon they grew accustomed to me and became tamer day by day, as they also grew in size. Now these friendly little creatures are safe with me; and I should miss them, indeed, if they were to disappear from my garden.

Irrepressible Nuthatch

LOUISE DE KIRILINE

THE AMAZING THING WAS NOT THAT SHE CAME BUT THAT she stayed. For to my knowledge, no other redbreasted nuthatch, except she and her present mate, have remained in the Loghouse Territory (our bird study area at Pimisi Bay in central Ontario) more than a winter and a spring. After that they usually vanish, and not one of more than twenty banded nuthatches has ever returned. Furthermore, she achieved an unusual performance for one of her kind; and I think that this story will be a first record published for North America.

But let me introduce her properly! On December 17, 1952, a day of cloudy skies and frost in the air and six inches of snow on the ground, she arrived unaccompanied by anyone but a flock of black-capped chickadees. I suspect that she met these gay commuters somewhere back in the woods and that she could not resist joining so carefree a company. But when they arrived at the feeding station at the

Loghouse and the chickadees swarmed on to the feeding sticks and hollowed-out coconuts, and began eating of the foods served there—lard pudding, peanut butter, and suet—our nuthatch held back in astonishment. Never before, I am sure, had she seen such strange contraptions, and if the chickadees had not been pecking at them she would never have recognized their contents as food.

She perched in the white spruce; and from this vantage point, her body extended in the longest line from her stubby tail to her up-turned bill and flickering her wings lightly, she gazed down upon the chickadees with keen interest and said: *"yep-yep-yep!"* But before she could do anything else, the chickadee flock departed upon the next lap of their routine tour and she with them.

When she appeared upon our scene her plumage was slightly worn. It is true that the females of the species seem to be more sub-dued in their coloring of blue-gray and rust than the males. But unless the shade of their crowns is seen, shiny black in the males and a soft blue-gray in the females, the sexes cannot be distin-guished, especially a few months after the annual molt. Just after the molt, all red-breasted nuthatches look strikingly bright and colorful, but various degrees of wear soon rob them of their good looks. Only the fledgling can be distinguished by its plumage, with certainty, from its elders. But, in addition to the fluffy and pale feather-dress that adorns it before the change into the first winter plumage, the young bird often wears black spots or small lines on the chin and on the white eyebrow stripe.

It is different with the leg color of the red-breasted nuthatch. In young birds just out of the nest it is very light greenish-yellow, by comparison distinctly lighter than in the parents. In the old birds I have examined in the hand, it has varied from light olive-green to very dark, almost black. Although the evidence is still far from conclusive, it is possible that leg color is related to age in this species.

Assuming that this is true, our nuthatch was young, because her legs were light green. In view of her coming at that very time, and alone, this was important. Had she hatched in the summer of that year she might never yet have had a mate. The exciting thing was that already three males were daily visitors at our feeding station. They had arrived during November, one by one, all without mates. One of them had light green legs, the second, brownish-gray, and the third, almost black legs. I had banded all of them with aluminum bands before the lady appeared; the first one wore a gold and the third a blue band, while the second one was uncolored. Thus she produced a promising situation for answering my burning questions: Do red-breasted nuthatches, like the white-breasted nuthatches, normally live paired the year around? How do they go about getting paired?

The next day she had successfully overcome all prejudices against food and feeding places that did not look natural to her. Every time she came with her entourage of chickadees she ate voraciously as if in dire need of quick restoration of lost storage fat. Neither this day nor the next were there any signs of an encounter having taken place between her and anyone of the three bachelors. All four came and went at staggered periods, each with their separate flock of chickadees.

On the fourth morning it happened. What extraordinary luck that I happened to see her alighting on the wire! She sat, hunched just a little, pointing her bill from side to side and aiming to take off for the nearest suet stick, when *plunk!* Uncolored Male alighted on the same wire two and a half feet away from her. The jolt startled her. No sooner did she catch sight of the male than she dashed at him, her wings beating the air almost as fast as those of a hummingbird. Obviously, her design was not to fight him, but to sit in the spot where he sat. He flew off, thus reacting to her move as the situation required. Again she flew after him in the same manner, in and out of the thick branches of the white spruce. Twice more she sat herself where he sat, and twice more he gave way to her. As a finale, she perched high above the world on the tip of a branch of the white spruce. There she pointed her bill rhythmically from side to side and lifted her wings high vertically above her back, flapping them up and down in time with the movements of her bill. If she said anything during this demonstration I was too far away to hear it.

I did not see any more displays until shortly afterward when she and Uncolored Male came to the feeding station together. He alighted on the suet stick first, upside down, fed, then bent his head far back and gazed in the direction where she was, uttering soft notes: *Tetetetete!* I looked at her and there she was, pivoting slowly from side to side like an electric fan in action, while she pointed her bill toward him and shivered her wings as she answered him with the same soft notes: *Tetetetete.* Thus she dispelled all my doubts of their happy union.

For several reasons her behavior was interesting. First, because she, not the male, took the initiative, although it is known that in some species the females may undertake the first pairing gestures very early or just before the nesting season actually starts. Second, if, as it appeared to be, this was her first meeting with one of the bachelors, she did no choosing but opened procedures with the first and the best that might become her mate. How she recognized him as a male is a third question. Did she, as we do, know his black crown as his badge of masculinity? Perhaps, knowing him only for a nuthatch, she simply flew at him to see what he would do. Very often, during off-season, males are inclined to evade the females; but a female might have stood up to her and by pose and gesture asked her what she meant by trying to dominate. After her initial move, she confirmed the male's attitude by two more "attacks" and, finally, she performed a "victory" ritual on the branch of the white spruce.

Once paired, the couple became a close unit. I agree fully with Viscount Grey of Fallodon, who wrote:

"The birds that mate for life and remain together throughout the year evidently get a high degree of satisfaction from each other's company. . . ."

Undoubtedly this was true about my pair. It was constantly demonstrated by their mutual concern about each other and close attendance upon each other; by the female's pretty attitudes before her mate, with wings a-shivering as a prelude to coming courtship-feeding; and by their unceasing conversation amongst themselves—*tetetetete.*

One day when the pair was feeding at a stick, a chickadee tried to dislodge them. Uncolored Male ominously raised himself to his full height on stretched legs, clinging precariously to the stick with the tips of his claws. High above his back he lifted his fully opened wings and in this pose he pivoted in a half circle back and forth, like a ballerina on tiptoe. The striking display he thus attained of his feathers and color patterns and the amazing enlargement of the midget nuthatch soon robbed the chickadee of all desire to interfere.

On January 5, 1953, the little female went into one of my bird-banding traps. I put an aluminum band on her left leg, and a green band on her right one. Thus she acquired her name—A for aluminum, G for green—Aggie.

Early in March, Uncolored Male began to sing, The song of the red-breasted nuthatch is far from impressive, musically. It is a continuous, weak-sounding, one-note *we-we-we-we-we,* that can hardly be heard more than fifty feet away. But there is a quality in this wee tonal effort and in the manner in which it is given that make it remarkable. There he sat, Aggie's mate, atop the tall white spruce. He held his body in a straight horizontal line and grasped his perch with legs well apart while he swayed rhythmically from side to side, the notes pouring freely from his slender wide-opened bill in all directions.

It was not a territorial song he gave in the sense that other birds advertise their territories, for he was far from the spot which, I later found, the pair had selected for their nesting. But apart from the nest area, the nuthatch also established a secondary territory which he guards and defends with utmost vigilance. This is an irregularly circular space in the midst of which his mate has her being and which, therefore, moves along with the birds. Nor does he, like many other birds, need to make himself conspicuous in order to attract the opposite sex, since long ago he acquired his mate. For that very brief period in the spring during which the nuthatch sings, I think that he performs mostly from pure enjoyment and blissfulness even though other elements, like appeal to his mate or the edification of other nuthatch males, may play a role.

A few days later, Uncolored Male fed his mate before me. Aggie was half-crouched on the wire, with her neck stretched forward and her bill pointing slowly from side to side. With very small movements she shivered her wings rapidly. The male at a feeding stick grasped a morsel in his bill, flew to the wire, hopped toward her in a businesslike manner, and popped it into her bill. At that moment he acquired a new name, Hop-hop-hop. She, having swallowed his spousal offering, flew to the stick and joyfully began gorging herself on lard pudding. Sometimes courtship-feeding is not a need but a ritual.

A week later the male sat on the very tip of the dead white birch. It was an overcast morning in the middle of March, with a chill wind blowing from the east and eleven inches of snow still on the ground. But there he was, obviously in a state of ecstasy, pivoting back and forth, lightly flicking his wings, and singing at the top of his small voice. Then I discovered the hole above which he serenaded, six inches below him. Only just started, it was nothing but a mere indication of beginning hole-boring marked on the white bark. The next instant Aggie clung to the spot and began working diligently.

In cavity-nesting species, the hole-boring period is usually an arduous time filled with work and little play, and only toward the end of it lovemaking comes to the fore. Only on that account can I explain Aggie's reserve when, a few days later, I met the pair midway between the feeding station and the nesting place. As the male tried to advance toward her, all his body elongated, pointed and extended forward, she turned away and would not suffer him to approach. His amorous attempt thwarted, he retired to a nearby tree and here, his head stretched toward her and his whole body swaying violently from side to side with wings vibrating rapidly at his sides, he suddenly passed over from his continuous *tetetetete* into a high-pitched, meaningful, trilled note and held it for a long second. The next instant both birds were gone in the direction of the nest. How beautifully and smoothly nature can relieve and divert the high tension of an unfulfilled desire!

Until the end of April I had too few moments to watch the pair and I saw little of them. Once, finding no pitch smeared around the hole I felt sure that the nest was abandoned. Then one day I found the pair in their favorite feeding place not far from the nest tree. Obviously, it was a recess during incubation and Aggie was traveling about from tree to tree. She picked little food by herself, as her mate kept feeding her with inexhaustible solicitude. From time to time he interrupted his services and mounted the nearest treetop whence, assuming his customary pose of musical abandon, he sang to her his sweetest songs, *we-we-we-we-we.*

I followed them to the nest and was surprised to find that, with eggs evidently being incubated, no pitch had yet been applied around the doorway. Hitherto, eggs in the nest and pitch around the doorway had been almost simultaneous phenomena in all the cases I had watched. In fact, I had become accustomed to regard pitch as the only sure sign of occupancy in the early stages of a nesting.

But a week later, when every sign and calculation indicated that the chamber within was full of newly hatched babies, gumdrops glistened around the nest opening for the first time. The male came with food and with a graceful flourish disappeared directly into the small aperture. An instant later he flitted out; in his bill he carried a tiny white fecal sac, which he carefully put away on a twig. Aggie followed him closely. As she flew after him low over my head, she gave a song composed of a string of soft, clear, utterly musical notes, an astonishing and never-before-heard performance by a red-breasted nuthatch female.

While they were gone, the gum around the entrance to their precious infants gleamed and sparkled in the sun, like eyes can sparkle in the refraction of light. For eyes in nature, whether live or imagined, as they may appear in a pattern or as light strikes an object or a substance, seem to have a discouraging effect upon would-be troublemakers.

On June fifth, Aggie and her mate conducted their brood of fluffy children to the feeding station for the first time. The youngsters were fast adapting themselves to conditions outside their secluded hole nest. By trial and error they were learning to recognize food, pecking at stuff like their parents did and ever so often getting a good piece of "meat" quite on their own. A few days later, father brought four of them to the birdbath. It was a hot day. He followed his habit—hop-hop-plop—and then abandoned himself to a series of vigorous splashes and duckings, the spray flying. The young ones sat in a row on the edge of the bath. They put their bills into the water and with great energy and aptitude went through the movement of ducking and wing-shivering without getting a single drop of water sparkling over their plumages. Only after a good deal of "air-bathing" did the full ritual gradually dawn upon them. Before they were little more than two weeks out of the nest, all were independent of their parents. Anyway, Aggie had long since ceased bothering about them, but the significance of this remained to be discovered.

The time passed and the pair was still around, rugged-looking and worn, but curiously without signs of getting into heavy molt. One day early in July, to my surprise I perceived Uncolored Male atop his dead birch above the old nest hole, going through his usual ritual of wing-flicking and bill-pointing as when he was at the height of nesting. Then he flew in and out of the nest—and I thought he did that just from old habit. But, no, a few days later the signs became too obvious to doubt the true state of affairs. *Aggie and her mate were raising a second brood in the same nest in the same season.* There seems to be no other record of a red-breasted nuthatch ever having raised a second brood in the same season, although, obviously, it can and must have happened before. Its European counterpart, *Sitta europaea affinis,* is said to have "one brood usually, but exceptionally two."

On July twenty-second, exactly four months and seven days after our nuthatches had delivered their first excavating peck on the entrance into their nest-to-be, I watched their last son launch himself upon his first flight. He was sitting in the opening, calling with his scrapy little note, *yan-yan-yan,* to his brothers and sisters already hidden in the tall trees a hundred feet away. He pushed himself far out. Of a sudden he was airborne, successfully bucking a fifteen-miles-per-hour side wind. He landed safely in the crown of a birch eighty feet from the nest. And the repeated calling from juvenile throats told the parents and me the precise location of four young birds that had just left the nest hole.

There is not much more to tell about Aggie, except that she kept on feeding this last brood long past the customary two weeks. Naturally, the youngsters, now a lot fatter and heavier than she, continued to pursue her as long as she serviced them until, finally, the molt wrung from her all her available energies.

Uncolored Male disappeared at this time, and I am certain that nothing but death could have forced this separation from his mate. The former bachelor with a blue band on one of his black legs, having lost his partner a few weeks earlier, still came to the feeding station. I missed that meeting between him and Aggie, when their courtship must have begun. But the moment I heard again the pretty mutual note, *tetetetete,* I knew that nature, once more, had appropriately adjusted two nuthatch lives.

Jumping Phantoms of the Desert

ALFRED M. COOPER

ALMOST ANYWHERE IN CALIFORNIA'S COLORADO DESERT you may encounter a curious mound made up of a collection of burrows somewhat resembling those in a prairie-dog city. The animals living in these warrens are among the shyest on earth, and you may live near them for years and never see one.

These beautiful native kangaroo "rats"—they are really not rats, but are related to the pocket mice—are noted for two things: they are the "jumpingest" of all small mammals, and they have a positive genius for getting about the desert without being seen. While cruising about they may leap in single bounds that carry them eighteen to twenty-four inches over the ground. The desert kangaroo rat, about the size of a chipmunk, has soft cream-and-tan fur, a very long tail with a little white brush at the tip, long hind legs, and tiny forelegs.

Some years ago I made an effort to get well acquainted with a number of desert kangaroo rats in the wild. I found this to be quite a job. Where a wild chipmunk would come to eat out of my hand within three days or less, it took me six months to get chummy with a wild kangaroo rat. Since then I have cut this time down to as little as one week and have tamed thirty-six of these little fellows that live near my desert home.

If you happen to be in desert country for week or so, try your hand at taming a kangaroo rat. You will find this a fascinating pastime. Proceed in this way.

Find a warren somewhat removed from any dwelling. Be sure that it is actually inhabited by noting that the burrow mouths have been freshly brushed out by the inmates. (The kangaroo rat uses its powerful jumping legs for kicking fresh earth outside, cleaning the entrance each day.) Never take a dog with you on your trips among them.

Select a likely-looking burrow entrance and leave a few crusts of bread or nut kernels about a foot from the hole. Repeat this at other warrens in your vicinity and do this chore in the evening. Do not act surreptitiously, but talk to the hidden kangaroo rats in a matter-of-fact tone.

Continue this routine for four evenings, and don't expect any tangible results during this period. On the fifth evening, just before sunset, feed again at the same burrows and walk away. This time, however, stop about twenty or thirty feet away and stand motionless. After a time—usually between two and five minutes—the little kangaroo rat will "show" for an instant, then he will duck below again. A few seconds later he will reappear, pick up a crust, and stand looking at you. In the same casual tone, speak to him again. This will probably scare him half to death, and he will dive back into his hole. Remain motionless and continue talking to the little fellow and within a minute he will come up for another look, and perhaps pick up another piece of bread crust.

That's enough for this first direct contact with the kangaroo rats. Next evening, repeat the proceeding and note that he shows himself sooner and probably will carry all of the tidbits below while you are talking to him. Don't just stand there, a silent, sinister figure, but *talk!* Let the kangaroo rat associate your friendly tone of voice with your motionless, harmless body and some eatables that are a real treat to him.

On succeeding evenings repeat this process, but each evening move a bit closer to the burrow entrance. Before long the kangaroo rat will accept you, your voice, and the nice food as inseparables, and will permit you to hunker down within three feet while he stores away the food you have given him.

The following night don't feed him at all; but on the following evening, hold an exceptionally nice nut kernel near the opening and call for him to come up and get it. This is the crucial test. Hesitating, and with much backing up and coming forward, the little kangaroo rat finally will overcome his fears and accept the morsel from your motionless hand. He will do this ever so gently, closing those tiny forepaws on the kernel; then, as you release it, he will seize it firmly in his needlelike teeth and dive below.

From here on it is just a question of how much more time you care to give to this kangaroo rat and to any others you may have tamed. If you wish, you may go much further. After a few more days you can approach a group of warrens, call out, and every kangaroo rat in the vicinity will appear at his burrow entrance. When you begin feeding one, another will slip up to you, and then several more. Before long they will jump on one of your knees or a shoulder. Finally, when you call, the more venturesome will run to meet you, coming across the desert floor with long leaps, those long tails tapping the sand at each jump. Six feet away, the leader will stop dead, eye you for a moment, then at your word will take off in a most amazing leap and land on your shoulder.

You can win the complete confidence of a kangaroo rat only by restraining any impulse to seize him or in any way interfere with his liberty to come and go as he pleases. Also, you will discover that these creatures that you have got acquainted with will respond only to *your* voice. If any other person approaches their burrows they will not even show themselves. However, if you later care to bring guests to see them, they will accept your word that the visitors are all right, although they will not go near these people.

The rather involved procedure I have outlined is essential if you really wish to get acquainted with a kangaroo rat. Of course, you could trap him; but he quickly dies in captivity, and in a cage he is just another unhappy creature that has lost its liberty. The real fun is in getting acquainted with him at close range while he is free to come and go as he pleases.

You will find the kangaroo rat to be an extraordinarily clean little animal. His fur feels much like sealskin. All those I have tamed are free from fleas or other vermin and are sleek and healthy. After a time you come to note definite differences in them, as to coloring, size, and other characteristics.

These distinctions are so marked that you soon recognize particular kangaroo rats, even though they may move to another warren. Then you naturally begin naming them; and after the first dozen you find yourself running out of diminutives, and resort to such names as Skeezix, Skippy, and Butch.

During the mating season (February and March), you will find your friendly kangaroo rats all scrambled up. You may discover Skippy a quarter mile away from home, but he will respond at once to your voice. In the spring the young are kept concealed until they are weaned, after which they quickly learn to come to you for nutmeats or bread crusts. They are tiny, with bodies the size of your thumb, but already they have the very long tails and much of the jumping ability of their parents. They also build separate little warrens of their own, with tiny burrow entrances identical with those of the full-grown adults.

The kangaroo rat has many natural controls, and it is not surprising he is slow to become friendly with humans. The desert fox considers him a tidbit, the owl and hawk strike from the air, and the rattlesnake searches for him underground. He is even wary of airplanes passing overhead. When he senses the approach of an enemy he dives below, then sets up a steady drumming with a jumping leg against the ground, either as a warning or, perhaps, as a gesture of defiance.

His warren consists of an intricate labyrinth of passageways. His principal natural food is the bean or nut of the ironwood tree. These, and any food you give him, he stores underground, burying the eatables in the sand. He must conceal his food supply, since his companions will steal from him and from each other, whenever the opportunity affords.

He has one "cute" but, from my viewpoint, rather unpleasant characteristic. Even after becoming acquainted with you he may suddenly dive into his burrow and kick a quantity of sand and gravel into your face before you can dodge. If you were a real enemy he would thus continue kicking until the mouth of his burrow was closed. In winter he similarly closes up all burrow openings facing toward a cold wind.

Despite the number of creatures that prey on him, the kangaroo rat gets along pretty well. He can move with blinding speed when above ground, and he is rarely far distant from a burrow mouth. Underground, he can sense the intrusion of a snake and can often keep out of its way. If a fox attempts to dig him out he has only to move into a distant part of his burrow while the fox is wearing himself out at the entrance.

In four years of observing thirty-six wild kangaroo rats I have never "lost" a single individual. However, since this is about their normal life span, some of the older ones I know are now beginning to show signs of age. They make interesting pets, but only if permitted to remain in their wild state. Kangaroo rats are harmless and destroy nothing of value. Best of all, you may cultivate their acquaintance with no fear that you will render them less capable of taking care of themselves.

Pelican Portraits

PERCY L. DEPUY

Once, long before I had seen a white pelican in flight, I decided that pelicans were homely; however, I have learned that they have their moments—moments of great beauty. Those are usually the occasions when the birds are seen in flight together in sufficient numbers to give an impression of grandeur. Large flocks of white pelicans stopped off at Squaw Creek National Wildlife Refuge in northwestern Missouri during the years I was refuge manager there. This afforded me an opportunity to study these birds.

I saw some of them at their best one morning the first autumn I spent at Squaw Creek. The sun was just edging its way above the Missouri River bluffs behind me as I drove my old pick-up truck down the road from refuge headquarters. In front of me, a blanket of fog hung over lakes, swamps, and woodland. At some points, the fleecy mist was piled into thick clouds, obscuring the landscape.

Above other spots, it formed only a thin veil, exposing vistas of mystic beauty.

The sun's slanting rays transformed this scene into a pink and white fairyland. A bit of lake shore about two-hundred yards ahead of me had a backdrop of tall green cottonwood trees. It seemed to become an enchanted isle where fairies might be expected to dance and play, provided one had the imagination to see them. Then, *presto!* the fairies appeared! Forty or fifty big white pelicans sailed out from behind a screen of fog and majestically flew across the enchanted isle in a single straight line, like dancers crossing a stage. Sunlight, gleaming through the chiffonlike mist, seemed to cast a pearly aura about each snowy body and its pair of flashing pinions. In less than five seconds, the large birds had passed from sight behind another fog screen but the picture still lingers in my memory. The sun drove the mists away within half an hour, and this seven-thousand-acre waterfowl sanctuary looked like any other expanse of river floodplain except that it had more than the usual amount of muddy lakes and marshlands.

Later that morning, I saw several fleets of pelicans getting their breakfast. Pelicans have fish for breakfast, fish for lunch, and fish for dinner; if they eat snacks between meals, they have fish then, too. These birds have a system for catching fishes which is a remarkable example of cooperation—they stage fish-drives.

That morning, they were divided into companies of one hundred or two hundred birds. Each company formed itself into a long skirmish line with the birds ten or fifteen feet apart. Then they advanced, swimming in a company front, probing the water with their immense bills as they went. This dipping probably netted some fish, but that is not all that it did. It produced a lot of splashing which sounded like a herd of horses fording a stream. The fishes, frightened by this racket, were driven ahead of the skirmish line into shallow water near the shore. There they were largely at the mercy of the birds, and considerable numbers of them must have been scooped up. Those huge bills, and the built-in dipnets (gular pouches), dangling beneath their bills, may not add to the pelican's beauty, but they are mighty useful parts of their natural equipment.

We of the refuge staff estimated that there were four thousand pelicans on the refuge that fall. They stayed for about a month, and removed at least a ton of fishes from our lakes each day they were present. However, there were so many fishes in the lakes that they needed to be thinned out to give those remaining a chance to grow. Thus, the pelicans rendered the human fishermen a service, although fishermen are not always willing to admit it.

When a pelican launches itself into the air, it is quite a feat. That first old bird I got a good view of, while it was taking to the air, was swimming on a barrow pit when I came along and frightened it. First it accelerated its swimming until it was going as fast as it could; then it started flapping its wings to gain additional thrust, gradually lifting its body as it gained momentum. After its body had cleared the surface of the water, its wings took over more of the job of propulsion but its feet and legs continued to assist. For the next fifty or sixty-five yards, it kicked the water after the manner of a boy propelling a scooter down the street with one foot. The pelican used both feet, bringing them down together, which gave it a rocking-horse motion. Its feet left a trail of dapples four or five yards apart on the water, marking its line of take-off. Finally, after I had begun to wonder if the bird were ever going to make it, or if it would end up by tumbling back into the lake, it lifted into the air.

There were lots of visitors at the refuge that fall. One Saturday morning, a busload of junior high school youngsters with two of their teachers appeared at headquarters seeking permission to tour the refuge area. I accompanied their expedition. Lonely blue herons patiently waited for fishes to swim within striking distance of their spearlike bills, and flotillas of ducks or coots slipped smoothly through the water. These drew interested comments from a few of the youngsters, but they really came to life when we sighted a compact raft of about two-hundred white pelicans. The birds were riding at anchor about a city block out from shore.

"They look just like a snowdrift floating on the water," remarked one little girl.

Then the bus approached too closely to suit the birds and the whole raft exploded in a pandemonium of frenzied activity as it took flight. The large number of ponderous bodies and the big black-tipped wings beating the air brought the youngsters crowding to the near side of the bus amid a chorus of rapturous "Ohs!" and "Ahs!" It was almost as though a fleet of glistening white yachts under full canvas was sailing out of the lake and upward over a grove of trees.

Our white pelicans have one prize number on their repertoire. It might be called their "grand march"; certainly it is their masterpiece of showmanship. They presented it four or five times during their sojourn at Squaw Creek that fall. The first time I saw the grand march was on a golden afternoon in September when bright sunshine beamed down on almost waveless lakes. Tall sunflowers loaded with yellow blossoms lined the levees along which I drove and dickcissels called from their perches on barbed wire fences.

During the course of my travels that afternoon, I came upon several people fishing from the levees. I stopped to ask one man if he was catching anything. Then I noticed that he had apparently forgotten all about his fishing. He stood intently staring at the sky. Wondering what he saw that interested him so, I stuck my head out of the cab and stared too. After my eyes had become accustomed to the light and distance, I saw what at first appeared to be a swarm of gnats. Suddenly I realized that they were not insects, but birds a long way up in the air.

I drew my binoculars out of their case and focused them on the creatures. Silhouetted against the blue dome above were perhaps five hundred birds soaring on motionless pinions. Their stubby white bodies, huge bills, and black-tipped wings told me they were white pelicans. Each bird was circling to the right, then circling to the left as though absorbed in playing its part in some solemn ritual. The ceremony was apparently one that required its participants to take themselves far away from earthly interference to a retreat where the air was pure and the perspective wide. Up where they were, they could see dozens of miles of the broad Missouri River and hundreds of square miles of countryside in Nebraska, Kansas, and Missouri.

Below them, the little town of Mound City, Missouri, snuggled against a green hillside. Its inhabitants were going about their daily tasks, most of them unaware that one of nature's finest shows was in progress, perhaps a mile above their heads.

Twice during the next hour, I paused in my patroling to watch the grand march and to wonder. Like a Milky Way composed of living white stars, the flock hung there, with each individual bird gyrating about a relatively fixed center. The sight gripped me, even though I was viewing it from three miles away.

Each time that I have seen the grand march since that September afternoon, I have wondered about the motive in back of it. What is it that drives these creatures to forsake their homes on the water and hitch a ride on an updraft for an hour or two of seemingly purposeless soaring in the wild blue yonder? Is it a play instinct? Or, is there tucked away somewhere within the pelican's brain an inherent love of the grand and the dramatic? Whatever their reason, it cast them in the role of the beautiful, and it is one of the most exquisite and wonderful sights in all the out-of-doors.

The Masked Bandits in Our Home

DOROTHY HATFIELD

TWO MASKED BANDITS OPENED THE SCREEN DOOR AND stepped into the living room of our Texas home, looking slightly mischievous and not at all sinister, as bandits should. They weren't interested in loot normally desired by most bandits; they were in search of my sugar bowl! Our bandits were Frankie and Johnnie—two raccoons.

We'd had Frankie and Johnnie, a male and a female from the same litter, since my husband brought them home to our three-year-old daughter one evening. Then they were tiny balls of fur, so young they hadn't yet learned to walk, and their black masks and tail rings were still pale.

We first fed the baby raccoons milk from doll bottles, using the same condensed-milk-water-Karo formula that I gave my little girl when she was a baby. It must have been satisfactory because the little "coons" began to grow. We then switched from the doll bottles to baby bottles; and, as Frankie and Johnnie grew older, they learned to lap milk from a saucer.

The diet of our pets was kept, as nearly as possible, in accordance with the diet of wild raccoons. My husband caught crawfish, minnows, grasshoppers, and other insects for them. In the trees of our yard, they could find acorns and catch insects. To this natural diet, we added fruit, milk, meat, and occasionally sweets, for we discovered they loved candy, sugar, and Coca-Cola.

Seedless grapes were a favorite with Frankie and Johnnie and they peeled the skin away before eating them. Grapes seemed to be the food most frequently washed by the raccoons. Why we never knew.

My husband and I had successfully raised pet raccoons before and the old story about them washing their food before eating it had been disproved. None of our pet raccoons was that fastidious, but they would wash their food if we placed it in a pan of water. Although Frankie and Johnnie had a basin of water always available for food washing, they would, often as not, eat without washing it. Nearly everyone who knew of our pets would ask us if Frankie and Johnnie washed everything before eating. We told our friends that this old story was an exaggeration, according to our experience.

From the beginning, we decided we would not restrict our pets' movements. They were never chained nor kept in a pen, but were given freedom to roam as they pleased. While very small, Frankie and Johnnie were content to sleep in a box inside the house, but before two months passed, they preferred to climb the oak tree by our front door, then get on our roof where they slept nestled under the eaves.

Nocturnal by nature, the coons napped during the day (about like a house cat) and played at night. Often we could hear the raccoons on the roof, purring and playing, tumbling and boxing like two kittens. Frequently they would stop playing and plot a raid on my kitchen. They would open the screen door with their claws and sneak inside the house. If we heard the door slam, we knew the bandits had made another raid. It took our pets no time to distinguish the flour canister from the one containing sugar. They learned where the refrigerator was located (and its contents), and just what maneuvers were necessary to swing open the food cabinet doors. Needless to say, we soon learned to lock the screen doors, to have "coon-proof" latches installed on the cabinets, and to keep in mind that our two bandits were, at all times, ready to "get into something."

Mischievous but intelligent, raccoons make stimulating pets. We had no trouble taming Frankie and Johnnie; and they were so good-natured our three-year-old daughter, Shirley, played with them as she might have played with kittens or puppies. Although the raccoons were unsuspicious of us, they were instinctively distrustful of strangers, especially people who seemed to fear them. I've had many guests become frightened upon the entrance of our pets, though they never bit any strangers. Our pets, for some reason, became friendly much more rapidly with strange children than with adults, and they brought a number of children much happiness.

Frankie and Johnnie loved every minute they were allowed to spend in the house. They snooped, investigated every crevice, felt and patted everything. Little black paws would wiggle under chairs, in the bookcases—everywhere. My jewelry box was a treasure chest of enjoyment for them. They would take my earrings and roll them between their paws, beady little eyes all the while beaming at the glittering wonders of civilization. Coins, bobby pins, anything they could pick up and hide were missed only to turn up in some illogical place later on. Shirley's stuffed toys suffered numerous attacks, her marbles were hidden, her dolls scratched.

Not all of their antics were pleasing to me, however, if I might have created that impression. As puppies chew shoes, and kittens tear stockings, our raccoons ate my favorite ivy plants, licked from the sugar bowl, chewed up my brooms, hid my earrings, and, in general, raised havoc in the house if left alone. Intelligent, sensitive to the tone of the voice we used, they knew just what they could do to avoid a scolding or what would bring one on.

As Frankie and Johnnie grew, they deserted our roof for a hollow log in a nearby pasture, not far from our home. From then on, we saw our pets only at night. We had kept the raccoons only five months and regretfully we knew they were growing away from us, relying on their own resources, instead of ours. We felt, though, that no matter how much we missed our pets, they belonged in their natural habitat. They had, while living in our home, brought us our share of enjoyment and supplied us with enough conversational material to last for years.

The frequent night visits slackened and weeks passed without a visit from our pets. We reconciled ourselves to the fact that, at last, they had reverted to the wild. We adopted a stray house cat in the hopes we could forget, as gracefully as possible, our Frankie and Johnnie.

A few months after they had reverted to the wild, I heard the screen door rattle in a familiar manner. I rushed to the door, hopeful, and there stood a large raccoon, resplendent in its silky winter coat. I called to it and finally it stepped into the house, high-strung and wary. It was Frankie, the male coon, and once inside, he headed straight for the kitchen and stood up by the refrigerator. His wild life hadn't erased the memory of how convenient it was to go to the refrigerator and beg for a handout. I fed my pet, and after a while reluctantly opened the door and stood watching, a big lump in my throat, as the coon melted out of sight. Since then, Frankie has returned many times, at least once a week, but he is always alone. We don't know what happened to Johnnie, the female. Perhaps she mated with a wild raccoon.

Our "Minnesota" Barred Owls

RACHEL D. TRYON

THE SWIFT AND SILENT FLIGHT OF A BARRED OWL IS A miracle of grace and agility. A large bird, rather awkward-looking when it is perched on a branch, it will glide through dense woods so that not a leaf moves with its passage. If you examine the area through which it has flown you simply cannot see where there has been room for the four-foot wingspread and the heavy-looking body to pass. Its appearance of heaviness, caused by its thick, fluffy feathers, is deceptive, for it weighs slightly less than two pounds.

Our Minnesota home is on a ridge between two lakes. One of our windows overlooks one of the lakes and the top of a steep, wooded slope, so that the tips of some of the trees are at our eye level. The main branches of others, especially one large bur oak halfway up the slope, are just in front of the window. From the window, we watched a pair of barred owls bring up two youngsters. All the while they were apparently oblivious of our presence.

The accepted idea that all owls are exclusively nocturnal is, of course, not true. Authorities say that the barred owl sees better in the daytime than at night and that they also hunt more in the daytime. Our observations bore this out. Our pair hunted from the old oak, fished from a cottonwood tree that leans over the water, and sat for hours right in front of our window in a pouring rain during the day. They also fed their young, hooted, called, and cackled in broad daylight.

From our human point of view, barred owls are poor housekeepers. They are messy and careless about their nests and are not very particular about their place of nesting. They probably prefer a dry, hollow tree; but when one is not available, an old squirrel's leaf nest or an abandoned nest of a crow or a hawk will do. Hollowed-out and patched with a few additional twigs, the barred owls may line the old nest with pine needles.

Red-shouldered hawks and barred owls seem to have an affinity for each other. They use each other's nests and even, in one amazing instance, laid eggs in the same nest. We have not observed any such chumminess, though there are red-shouldered hawks every summer in our vicinity.

Barred owls usually lay two or three eggs. These are white, not glossy, and on the surface feel a little rough. We could not see the eggs of our particular pair, but the parents hatched two owlets. The nest was a hole in the old cottonwood, fifty feet up from its base. The nesting hole was over the water and was completely inaccessible to us. But we could watch the comings and goings of the adult owls from the first part of April until the first part of June. During this time, while one owl was on the nest, the other perched nearby and stared about; or it slept, preened its feathers, or occasionally uttered its characteristic eight hoots, *"Who cooks for you! Who cooks for you-a-a-all?"*—the *"you-a-a-all"* sliding down the scale despondently.

One morning at breakfast we noticed a squirrel chattering, sitting on the trunk of the old cottonwood very near the nesting hole. Suddenly one of the barred owls appeared silently out of the woods, flew directly at the squirrel, and knocked it quickly and neatly off the tree. Then it returned to the tree and sat for a long while preening its feathers or gazing all around. Since the young owls were in the nesting hole, we did not see them in their first white, downy stage, which lasts about three weeks. Nor did we see the youngsters come out of the nest. But on the afternoon of June 5 we came home and saw a young barred owl facing us in the bur oak. It was very gray, very fuzzy, quite solemn, and extremely unsteady on its feet. When it raised its wings, as it did periodically, and staggered a few steps along the horizontal branch, it displayed what looked like a pair of ruffly white panties that hung from its waist to its ankles. It also had a disconcerting habit of leaning forward a little and moving its head in a circular, clockwise motion, its face toward the front all the time, as though its head were mounted on a cam shaft. It seemed about one-half to two-thirds the size of the adult and had no tail feathers at all. It was probably about four to five weeks old.

One day, to our delight, we saw the parent appear with a mouse in its beak. It put the mouse in the baby's beak and flew off immediately without waiting to see how its offspring would manage the mouse. The young owl was not perturbed, however. It lowered the mouse to the branch on which it stood; put one of its yellow claws on it to steady it; then, suddenly, swallowed it in one enormous gulp. Afterward, the owl shuddered slightly, blinked, and resumed its solemn stare. The next time that the parent owl came to the tree it was getting dark so that we couldn't see exactly what happened. But the two owl heads stayed close together for some time in a position which suggested that the adult was feeding the youngster. The time between these feedings was three and one-half hours. We know there was no feeding between these times for one of us kept watch constantly.

Two days later, on June seventh, there were two young owls side by side in the same oak. One of them, I thought, looked slightly more unsteady than the other. One of the parents brought a large piece of some kind of animal intestine and fed it to them by tearing off small pieces and doling it out to them, each in turn. The next day their menu consisted of fish, a medium-sized one, administered to them by the parent owl in the same way. Fishes, frogs, crawfish, and lizards, besides mice and other small mammals, comprise a good deal of the barred owl's diet. There must be quite an advantage to the adults in having the nest near a lake. Several times we saw a parent owl fly down to the shallow water at the shore to pick up something. Incidentally, we never saw one of our owls chase a bird —though, of course, they do occasionally eat small songbirds and small owls.

As often as we saw the young being fed, we never saw one of the adult birds eating. We were interested to read that barred owls, like some other birds of prey, are likely to have "feeding nests" near their breeding nests, where they can consume their prey undisturbed by the always-hungry young ones.

It is vocally that the barred owl really runs riot in its expression. The *hoo-hoo-hoo-hoo, hoo-hoo-hoo-hoo-a-a-ah* is the standard call, but in each of our parent owls the pitch seems to be different. Which is the higher-pitched, the male or the female, we do not know. Some authorities say that the male is the bass and the female the treble. While we imitated them one night, one flew right in front of us and landed on a post very close by. In checking on the call of this particular owl, we found that its treble call had a pitch of about the G above middle C during the main part of the call. The bass call was considerably lower.

Often in the evening and sometimes in the middle of the night, there was a great to-do in the yard: various kinds of hoots, queer shrieks, and laughing noises. One of the most entertaining of these is the one which starts low and goes gradually up the scale, *oh-oh-uh-uh-ah-ah-eh-eh-ee-ee-ooooah,* the last part sliding down like the ending of the regular eight-hoot call. After the young were able to get about freely there were family calling sessions by the adults. One would start, and its mate would begin even before the first had finished; and then they would go through their entire repertoire of hoots, shrieks, squeals, and catcalls. It sounded as though they were disagreeing violently on the proper method of teaching the children, which were usually perched close by.

Before this, while the youngsters were still exercising their wings and walking gingerly about on the branches of the bur oak, we heard and eventually identified three calls that were different and new to us. One was a plaintive *ah-eee,* with a rising inflection. To our surprise we discovered that it came from the old owls, for what purpose I don't know, except that it seemed to be connected with their parental responsibilities. Another call was obviously a warning from the parents to the young. Whenever I walked near to a tree where one of the youngsters was sitting, I heard a short but soft *whoo-whoo* that had a muted quality, unlike the eight-hoot call which is rather strident at close range. The third call came from the young owls. It was a prolonged hiss or wheeze, perhaps, ending in a sharp squeak, *s-s-s-s-s-s-s-s-ik,* a rising inflection at the end. We felt sure this was a hunger signal, for it increased in intensity whenever the parents came near. An owl's sense of hearing is very acute, and it certainly needs to be to detect this wheeze at any distance from the young owls. Another call, *e-e-e-e-e-e-eek,* sounds like an outgrowth of the squeaking hunger call. One must add to all these notes the weird scream that the barred owl sometimes gives. This is not quite so terrifying, however, as the maniacal shriek of the great horned owl, which makes one's hair stand on end; nonetheless, the barred owl's shriek is an eerie cry.

Regardless of its weird assortment of calls and cries—its colorful vocabulary—we can recommend a pair of barred owls as top-notch, around-the-clock entertainment.

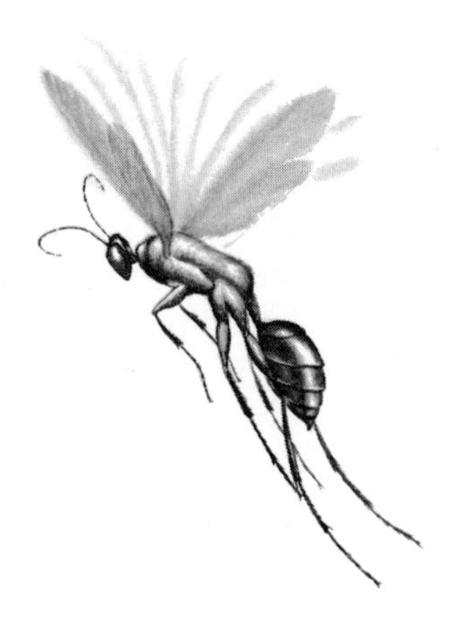

Mrs. Sphex

EDITH R. McLEOD

SHE WAS DAINTY AND SLIM, ALL IN BLUE, WITH A TINY waist—you might truly say wasp-waisted—and she had brownish-black transparent wings. I named her Mrs. Sphex, but you will not find her in the city directory, for she was a threadwaisted wasp, belonging to the genus *Sphex*. Her body, about nine-tenths of an inch long, was a dark, metallic steel-blue. From her head protruded two rather short, curved antennae.

When I first noticed Mrs. Sphex she was flying about a foot above ground, back and forth and around and around over our driveway of finely crushed rock. What was she doing, I wondered, or what was she hunting for? I sat down and watched her. She began to dig industriously. I quietly edged closer and squatted down near her. With great rapidity she dug away in the finely crushed rock and the dust of the drive, removing the tiny fragments of rock from the hole she was digging. Presently she abandoned it and hurried here and there, starting holes in various places, only to abandon them shortly. I could understand why. In one spot the surface was too hard and packed; in another she seemingly encountered a large pebble—a boulder to her, undoubtedly—and had to give up. One spot she tried was too sandy, for the dusty fine sand kept falling back into the hole as fast as she scooped it out. She finally returned to her first choice where she spent about a half hour excavating.

So engrossed was she in her work that she paid no attention to me as I inched nearer and nearer until my face was within a foot of her. She did her excavating by lugging each rock fragment out in her mandibles (mouth parts) one at a time, flipping it back between her legs far enough to be well clear of the entrance to the hole. The pebbles built a little mound around where she was working. Down again, head first, after another load, then backing out, she seemed to take the fragment from her mandibles with her forefeet, and flip it between her long supporting back legs to the distance of an inch or two. So rapid were her movements that it took me some time to figure out how she did it. Finally she had dug so deep that she was out of sight, but she continued to come backing up repeatedly, carrying out a piece of tiny rock each trip. The tunnel sloped a bit, facilitating her removal of the debris.

Finally she stayed inside the hole for eight or ten minutes. Evidently she was packing the walls of the nursery to be, for I knew by this time that she was preparing for the generation that was to follow. When she came out this time she flew away over the fence.

She was gone about five minutes and then, about fifteen away, I saw her coming. She was flying low and laboriously, but when she reached the drive she alighted and half crawled, half flew toward her burrow, lugging a cutworm two or three times larger than herself.

At this point catastrophe overtook Mrs. Sphex. With a sudden swoop a house sparrow made a lunge at her and grabbed the cutworm. Mrs. Sphex probably escaped being grabbed herself by letting go of it in time. She fluttered around a bit, stunned by the misfortune, then back she flew over the fence.

It was nearly twenty minutes later before she returned, carrying another cutworm. The first time she had been gone such a short while that I believe she had the cutworm already located, stung, and anesthetized, but this time it was different. She evidently had to make quite a hunt before she found another.

She grasped its head in her jaws and struggled along, straddling the long body of the cutworm, sometimes dragging it, sometimes flying. Now I understood one of the uses for her long legs.

She passed her tunnel and laid the cutworm a yard away, it having been paralyzed by a sting from her. Then frantically flying and crawling about she tried to find the hole. When she did she descended and did a little more work, carrying out a few more pebbles. By this time there was a mound of pebbles about her nest.

Then she couldn't find her cutworm. She knew approximately where she had put it down, but there was much running around before she finally stumbled over it. Grasping it by the head and straddling the body, as before, she dragged it to the entrance of the hole. As the hole of the nest was only big enough to admit her own body, I surmised that she was going to have trouble going down with that fat cutworm, but she didn't. Still straddling it she went down head first, dragging it with her.

She stayed within for ten or fifteen minutes, during which time she evidently laid an egg in the body of the paralyzed cutworm. In that condition it would still be fresh and nourishing for the baby wasp's food when it hatched out. Many insects provide food for their progeny in this way. The larva and pupa (chrysalid) stages all take place down there in the nursery, and not until the insect is a mature wasp does it leave the nest.

It was at this exciting stage that my husband came home for lunch. Some husbands find lunch on the table, but the husband of a naturalist may find his wife lying on her stomach in the driveway watching an insect. I motioned him away, and he good-naturedly sat down on the rock wall and waited to be allowed to pass.

Lunch was a little late.

After laying the egg Mrs. Sphex came up and quickly began carrying gravel back down the hole, one piece at a time. Soon I could see the back of her body as the hole was gradually filled. Each time, after depositing a piece of gravel, her body gave five or six jerks. Why? I wondered. When the hole was filled enough so that I could see her head, I saw that after laying the pebble in place she butted it several times with her rather large, flattened head, to pack the pebbles firmly in place.

In about ten minutes the burrow was filled. She mounded the top a bit—to allow for settling, perhaps?—then she did a puzzling thing. Backing away, she turned around and with her hind legs kicked and sprayed dirt and sand over the nest, much as a dog kicks out a flower garden with his hind feet. I assume that she was instinctively covering up all traces of her handiwork so that hungry enemies could not see where she had placed her nest and would never know of the choice morsel she had stored a few inches below the surface.

The Roadrunner

FRANK F. GANDER

IF YOU TRAVEL MUCH ON THE HIGHWAYS OF ANY OF THE southwestern states, sooner or later you will see him—that strangest of birds of the region, the roadrunner or *paisano*. Often you may meet him along the roads of thinly settled regions where he likes to race with the occasional passerby on horseback. But our modern automobiles are too fast for him, so he wisely shuns the highways used by speeding cars or crosses them hurriedly when occasion demands that he do so. It was, of course, this habit of running along roads that caused the early settlers to call the bird "the roadrunner." Spanish-speaking people have given it the name *"el paisano,"* the countryman.

Quite a fair-sized bird is this runner of the roads, nearly as large as a small hen but more slenderly built and with a very long, expressive tail. The over-all coloring appears rather dull at a little distance, as each feather is mottled, the center being iridescent black that glistens green or bronze on the back and wings, and purple on the neck, and this is margined by soft brown and gray. The brown is most pronounced on the breast, while the lower underparts are plain gray. Long feathers on top of the head may be elevated in a crest; and usually when this crest is raised, a patch of bare skin is disclosed, extending back from each eye and shaded from light blue to white and then to orange.

One of the oddest characteristics of the roadrunner is its feet, which have two toes turned forward and two backward. This seems strange when compared with most birds, but it is a feature of all birds of the cuckoo family, to which the roadrunner belongs. It is in a group known as ground cuckoos, and there are additional kinds in Mexico and southward. The straight, strong beak and long tail are also family characteristics.

This tail of the roadrunner is very useful to him. It is as expressive as a semaphore. It is slowly pumped up and down to express indecision, and occasionally it is wagged from side to side. It may be thrown up and forward until it almost touches the back of the bird's head; or it may be carried straight out level behind, as it usually is when the bird is trotting along a road or running. It may be snapped open and shut like a fan when the bird is nervous, and it makes an excellent rudder to aid in making quick turns when its owner is darting about after live prey.

Much of the prey of the roadrunner is very active. In wild desert areas this bird feeds principally on lizards, and in cultivated areas mostly on grasshoppers; but practically any kind of small animal life is acceptable to it as food. In addition, it eats a very few grapes and small wild fruit at times. A roadrunner that I prepared for preservation in a museum collection had the recognizable remains of ninety-eight grasshoppers in its crop, together with four of the very sour fruits of the lemonade sumac, *Rhus integrifolia.* Birds living near me at present feed largely on grasshoppers throughout the year, except in late summer when young lizards are abundant everywhere. Then they spend much time in pursuit of such prey. At any time they are alert for lizards, and several times I have seen them catch these active creatures in my garden.

One roadrunner that I was watching at close range came suddenly over a large rock that had screened its approach, and then dashed forward and caught a fence lizard. The reptile seemed to be killed or stunned by the grasp of the beak, as it did not struggle, and the bird soon swallowed it. I saw another roadrunner in wild pursuit of a whiptail lizard, which finally escaped by hiding under a rock—but not until after it had lost its tail. After the lizard had hidden, the roadrunner went back and ate the tail that it had broken off its intended victim.

Only once have I seen a roadrunner eat a snake, but they are known to do so quite commonly. The actual capture of the snake was screened from me by bushes, but as the roadrunner raised its head I could see a patch-nosed snake wiggling in its beak. The bird beat its prey against the ground to kill it, and then swallowed it, head first. As the snake was almost two feet long, this took a minute or two. Roadrunners are known to eat many kinds of snakes, including rattlesnakes.

Not only does it eat rattlesnakes, but also such creatures as tarantulas and other spiders, scorpions, and centipedes. It also eats mice and other small mammals, including baby cottontails, and small birds and their eggs whenever it can get them. It eats snails greedily, and whacks the mollusk against a rock or other hard surface to crack the shell and remove it before swallowing. On occasions, some carrion is eaten. I watched one of these birds pick up and swallow a shrew or small mouse that it found dead on the ground. It is not an uncommon experience for museum collectors to have roadrunners visit their camps to eat the discarded carcasses of small mammals and birds that they have skinned for specimens.

Roadrunners are quite apt to visit anyone camped in their territory, for they seem to have much curiosity about the activities of humans. Three years ago I bought an acre of uncleared brush land, and when I started construction work on it, the roadrunners made many trips daily across my acre. By the time the young one left the nest, the parent birds had become quite accustomed to my presence and moved freely near me.

One day as I was sitting quietly, the young roadrunner came close to me as it ran to meet its mother which was bringing it a mouthful of grasshoppers. Suddenly seeing me, it was startled and fled back to a clump of sumac. The mother was not frightened, so she called to the young one and went to it and fed it. Apparently learning from the example set by the mother, never again did this young bird show fear of me but moved around me with as little concern as did the old birds.

From these observations and others, I concluded that roadrunners learn more readily than do some birds. This was shown also by their hunting methods. When hunting grasshoppers, the roadrunner would move openly through the grass and weeds, head held high, and looking alertly from side to side. Every few steps the bird would flick its wings open and shut. It very obviously seemed to be trying to startle the grasshoppers into betraying their presence by movement. Once discovered, grasshoppers seldom escaped the quick stabbing bill of the roadrunner.

When a cicada started singing, however, the bird changed its hunting technique at once. This cicada is a small species which sings from low perches in weeds and brush. As soon as the roadrunner heard one of them, it would crouch low and slink along through the weeds as stealthily as possible, watching ahead to try and locate the singer. Very wary are these insects, and sometimes they took flight before the roadrunner was within grabbing distance. But the bird was successful often enough so that it never failed to stalk one that started singing nearby.

During a hot spell in late fall, I had just turned on a sprinkler in my garden when I saw the male roadrunner coming along the path. He was panting from the heat, with his beak open and his wings held well out from his body. When he reached the sprinkler, he pulled himself up tall and slim, flattened his feathers down tight against his body until he looked much like a chicken caught in the rain, and then he stepped in under the sprinkler. For nearly a minute he stood there with the water pouring over him; then he stepped out, shook himself once, and was thoroughly dry. My first thought was that this was a very foolish way to take a bath; on second thought, I decided that the roadrunner was not taking a bath, but just cooling himself a bit. Since then I have seen roadrunners wallowing in the dust like quail or chickens, so quite likely they do not actually bathe in water at all. They drink water, however, when they have the opportunity, even though many of them live in very arid regions where for long periods no water at all is available.

The following year, a pair of roadrunners raised five young; and these appeared in my garden one by one over a period of about three weeks, so that the three oldest ones were very much on their own by the time the youngest one appeared. From this I knew that their mother had followed the conventional roadrunner way of starting to brood as soon as the first egg was laid, and had laid her eggs singly, with three or four days' interval between them. I did not look for the nest but assumed that it was like others that I had seen—a bulky structure of sticks, lined with finer material, often with broken bits of dried cow dung, and placed rather low in a dense or thorny bush.

Just when the youngest one was getting old enough to catch much of its own food, the old male was hit by a car and badly injured. His legs were not broken, though, and he got into the brush where I could not find him. I never saw him again.

In the fall, the mother and five young hunted together, and that is the only time I have seen six grown roadrunners foraging together in one field. Apparently the female did not feel the urge to drive the young from the territory as the male had done the previous year. By the first of the year the group had disbanded, but there were still many roadrunners about. At times there would be as many as three of them calling from the hills around my garden. This "song" of the roadrunner is somewhat like that of the cuckoo, but louder and coarser. The bird sits on a rock or other perch with his tail hanging down; then he inflates his crop with air, presses his beak down against it, and straining, forces out his weird calls.

All through the spring months there was much calling. In the chilly early mornings, I would see one or more of the birds sitting on some high point where they could catch the first rays of the sun. With their backs to the east, they would lift their wings and raise their feathers so that the warm rays could penetrate right in to the skin. When they were warmed up, they would begin their calling.

Roadrunners also have another call, a low *dut* accompanied by a rolling of the upper and lower bill. These birds were around continuously all that year, but no young came into my garden.

One bird, a male, has grown quite tame. It came and watched me one day while I was screening compost, and as there were many white grubs in the pile, I tossed these out to the watching bird. It ate an incredible number of them; walked away for a short distance and stood quietly for about half an hour; then came back and gobbled up another mess. From this start, and further tempted by offerings of mealworms, this bird was feeding from my hand in less than two weeks. Whenever it came near me it crouched down low and made little grunty noises, just as I had seen the young birds do when coming to the parent to be fed.

For days it followed me so persistently that I could hardly get near birds of other kinds; although before this, individuals of several other species had been so tame as to feed from my hand. They all mistrusted the roadrunner and scolded it wherever it went. When it was not following me, it was perched up in my oak tree trying to catch the goldfinches as they stopped there on their way to the birdbath. It even got up on my canary's cage and nipped that poor creature on the wing. I decided that the roadrunner was just a little too friendly, so I stopped feeding it. Soon it was ranging widely and passing through my garden only at intervals of several days. Now it was again an interesting neighbor, no more perfect than are my human neighbors, but doing so much that is useful that I can forgive it the occasional deeds of which I do not approve. May the the time never come when I shall no longer find the strange tracks of the road-runner along my garden paths.

Pelorus Jack—
A Dolphin Diplomat

CYRUS CRESS

THERE WAS A REPORT GOING AROUND THE STRAITS OF NEW Zealand's South Island telling of the return, in spirit, of Pelorus Jack, the famous "pilot" dolphin of the last century.

Jack's spirit—fisherfolk said—had housed itself in a scaled down version of the original. The "reincarnation" was a bottlenose dolphin less than half the length of the great thirteen-foot Risso's dolphin, renowned the world over as "Pelorus Jack" and for more than thirty years ships' pilot and keeper of the French Pass area.

For some time this new, unnamed emissary of Neptune's court had taken a self-assigned beat along a strip of Marlborough coastline. The popular belief was that he had attempted to carry on the task of meeting passing boats, continuing a mammal form of marine diplomacy that had endeared the original Pelorus Jack to the hearts of thousands.

Any marine engine noise was all that was needed to summon the little dolphin from its den in a small, rocky cove. The friendly "fish" (not a fish, but a mammal of the whale family) met small outboard boats with the same enthusiasm as he did the larger coastal vessels that ply the waters between White's Bay to the northeast of Blenheim and Port Underwood. Sunday fishermen said that the dolphin would follow their boats for hours, gamboling and playing, then wait patiently, until the fishing was over, for the return trip. Most of the people who were acquainted with the pocket edition of Pelorus Jack felt that it had been separated from its fellow herd members and, being of a gregarious nature, had begun, as Jack had, to seek human companionship—even to the extent of scratching its back on the side-planking of boats; accepting handouts of fish; and doing an occasional good-humored dash among startled swimmers. But try as it might the newcomer to the straits would have a difficult assignment if he were to achieve the record established by the most famous of all sea "critters," Pelorus Jack.

The great dolphin's natural habitat was the North Atlantic. There his species, Risso's dolphin (*Grampus griseus*), were hunted for their oil. Risso's were considered easy marks, and whalers had been known to herd them like cattle into shoal water, where the gregarious beasts were harpooned without difficulty.

Pelorus Jack had disassociated himself from his family flock to live the life of a lonely hermit. Most unusual of all, he seemed to love steamships—especially those that carried passengers; and the passengers found Pelorus Jack an interesting recluse. He had the rare combination of personality plus a dressed-up appearance that made him the Beau Brummell of all water animals. He sported a blue-white coat, tinged with purple and overlaid with yellow. Brown edges outlined the opal colors and formed piping that added a formal note to his attire. Over the top of his uniform a collection of scratchlike markings interlaced to form a kind of network. The maze of marks mystified observers, but most believed that they were the result of tussles with Jack's favorite food—cuttlefish; but more than likely they were caused by the circular suckers, armed with claws, of the giant squid.

Because of his activity and continual movement, there was no opportunity for anyone to make a close examination of Pelorus Jack. It was taken for granted that he was "Jack" and not "Jill." The exact history of Pelorus Jack's life in the South Island straits isn't known, but it is generally accepted that he began his famous "pilot" act in the 1880's and continued his strange association with steamships until April, 1912, after which he disappeared.

His meeting with all steamers passing through Pelorus Sound, whether by day or night, in stormy or fair weather, was a self-appointed task. Why he spent his hours cavorting around the bows of ships trading between Wellington, Picton, and Nelson, which at that time made almost daily crossings, is not known. All that is known positively is that he carried out his missions for more than three decades. Jack seemed to have a single purpose in life: that of spreading the welcome mat on the salty water of French Pass. Folks on the ships said that the great white dolphin had a large measure of sociability, and he seemingly believed in what people said about him.

The dolphin's haunts were close to the winding waterways about the entrance of Pelorus Sound. At that point the mountainous northern tip of New Zealand's South Island breaks into a collection of capes and headlands. Within the sheltered waters the sea is continually calm, and sea birds dot the ragged coast that extends well over three hundred miles. The entrance way to the sound is a stormy place, buffeted by constant winds. It was the stormy channels that Jack chose as his watch.

As a diplomat, Jack had no peers. He seemed to sense that travelers on the packets were eager to catch sight of him. He was expected, and he always arrived. He most often came in sight slightly south of the Chetwode Islands and above a twisted lump of land, poking seaward, called Alligator Head. His entrance was spectacular—a foamy dash, highlighted with a series of leaps which oftentimes took him clear of the water. After his display of exuberance and good will, the dolphin would head for the bow of the vessel and continue at that position for several miles. While at his post Jack never bothered with tidbits the customers on deck provided. It was as if he considered his duty as pilot through the rough waters his first concern.

Pelorus Jack's visits were so reliable that more than a few ships' captains made it their routine to announce over the megaphone that it was possible for them to call the great Risso's dolphin by simply blowing a few short blasts on the steamer's whistle. When the ship made its way into Pelorus Jack's district, it was a sure bet the little "whale" would join the ship.

After staying with the vessel for a time, Pelorus Jack would leave his friends. He always seemed reluctant to go, but always left the ship at Clay Point, or Ana-toto as the place was called by the Maori natives. At that crooked finger of land Jack left his delighted public and went home. Where home was remained a mystery. The Maoris believed Pelorus Jack to be their long-lost sea god, Kaikai-a-waro, a great warrior of noble blood who had returned to New Zealand in the form of a dolphin. It followed, in the old tales handed down by the Polynesians, that their deity of the sea made his home in a spacious cave carved by the spirits of the water. The Maoris in their stories of Kaikai-a-waro made mention of qualities and virtues found in the white dolphin of French Pass. After seeing Pelorus Jack, it was easy to believe he was more than just a plain sea citizen.

Though Jack seemed to have unmeasured amounts of good will to offer his friends on shipboard, some people failed to respond in kind. One outstanding case deals with a now unknown passenger who crossed the straits on the S.S. *Penguin,* a small coastal ship which Jack knew well. The pilot dolphin had made his usual approach, performing his leaps and "sashays," then fell to the more serious chore of guiding the ship and playing around the bow. Hardly had Jack taken up his position when a rifle cracked from the deck. The passenger had fired upon Pelorus Jack. The supple dolphin left the *Penguin's* side and was never seen again from that vessel. Many people refused to travel on the *Penguin* in consequence of the malicious attempt on the friendly dolphin's life. Curiously, some years later, the S.S. *Penguin* was broken on the rocks not far from where Pelorus Jack had been fired upon, and a number of persons on board lost their lives. The attempt on Jack's life from the decks of the *Penguin* was not the first, nor was it to be the last. Other stories concerned whalers' designs on Jack's slick hide. Other people seemed spiteful, as if for some strange reason they couldn't stand to see a wild thing so natural, so unafraid, and apparently so happy.

Finally, in a desperate attempt to save Jack from the hands of assassins, a conservation law was passed protecting him and all of his species from the guns of the malicious and the whaler's harpoon. Pelorus Jack was again unique. He was the only individual dolphin that had inspired the writing of a law for his protection. The proclamation appeared in the New Zealand Government's *Gazette* of September 29, 1904, to the effect that during a period of five years from that date it would be unlawful for any person "to take the fish or mammal of the species commonly known as Risso's dolphin, *Grampus griseus,* in the waters of Cook Strait, or of the bays, sounds, and estuaries adjacent thereto." To do so was punishable by fine of not less than five pounds or more than one hundred.

Jack stayed around for eight years after the law was passed. But in April, 1912, with a tally of more than thirty-two years of constant service, the dolphin diplomat vanished. Jack's disappearance from the wild waters of the Antipodes was as mysterious as his coming.

Prohibiting Taking of Risso's Dolphin in Cook Strait, &c.

Ranfurly

Governor.

ORDER IN COUNCIL.

At the Government House, at Wellington, this 26th day of September, 1904.

Present:

HIS EXCELLENCY THE GOVERNOR IN COUNCIL.

WHEREAS it is enacted by section five of "The Sea-fisheries Act, 1894," that the Governor in Council may from time to time make regulations, which shall have general force and effect throughout the colony, or particular force and effect only in any waters or places specified therein, for, among other things, prohibiting altogether for such period as he shall think fit the taking of any fish, and may by such regulations impose a penalty for breach of such regulations:

And whereas it is desirable to prohibit the taking of the fish or mammal known as Risso's dolphin (*Grampus griseus*) in Cook Strait and the adjacent bays, sounds, and estuaries:

Now, therefore, His Excellency the Governor of the Colony of New Zealand, in exercise of the hereinbefore-recited power and authority, and acting by and with the advice and consent of the Executive Council of the said colony, doth hereby make the following regulations:—

REGULATIONS.

1. DURING the period of five years from the date of the gazetting of these regulations it shall not be lawful for any person to take the fish or mammal of the species commonly known as Risso's dolphin (*Grampus griseus*) in the waters of Cook Strait, or of the bays, sounds, and estuaries adjacent thereto.

2. Any person committing a breach of this regulation shall be liable to a penalty of not less than five pounds nor more than one hundred pounds.

Alex Willis

Clerk of the Executive Council.

Following his departure, or death, his friends on the Picton-Nelson steamers found the trip through French Pass a dull journey as compared to the days and nights when excited passengers would point from the railings and shout, "There comes Jack!" Some made special trips and kept a steadfast vigil in their hopes of seeing him again, but he never reappeared.

Today people still talk of Pelorus Jack, the pilot dolphin. They wonder and will always wonder what internal drive spirited the big sea animal through storms and moonless nights to the sides of ships. Why did he meet them? How did he know they were coming? Did he *hear* the approach of the ships—the vibrations in the water caused by their engines and propellers? And finally, why did he disappear so suddenly—where did he go? The Maoris seem to have the best answer. They say that Kaikai-a-waro, the warrior chieftain, is only resting in his spacious cave carved by the spirits of the water and will one day return. Everyone hopes so.

In the meantime, folks have taken to the little bottlenose dolphin, with hopes that he will carry on Pelorus Jack's good work.

Snobber—Sparrow De Luxe

EDWIN WAY TEALE

IN VINELAND, NEW JERSEY, ONE SUMMER PEDESTRIANS were astonished when an English sparrow darted down from the branches of trees, alighted on their shoulders, and peered intently into their faces. Housewives were equally amazed when the same bird flew in at their open windows. It fluttered about, examined their rooms, and flew out again. The mystery grew for several days. Then the following advertisement appeared in the *Vineland Times-Journal:*

"Lost. Tame female English sparrow. Reward. Call 1291J."

That advertisement brought about the return of a remarkable pet. It also revealed a boy-and-bird companionship which was as interesting as it was unusual. The boy was Bennett Rothenberg; the sparrow, Snobber. They were visiting the boy's uncle near Vineland when the bird became lost.

The boy and the sparrow lived on the eleventh floor of a great apartment building across from the Planetarium, on Eighty-First Street in New York City. The bird was never caged. It was free to come and go. At will, it flew in and out of the apartment window more than 130 feet above the street and the Planetarium park. Each night, it slept on top of a closet door left ajar near Bennett's bed.

On rainy days, the sparrow made no effort to mount upward along the sheer cliff of brick and glass to Bennett's apartment window. Instead, she rode up on the elevator! Flying in the front entrance of the apartment house, Snobber alighted on the shoulder of the elevator operator, Frank Olmedo. When they reached the eleventh floor, Olmedo rang the bell at the apartment and when the door opened, the sparrow flew, like a homing pigeon, to the boy's bedroom. One summer during a month when Bennett was away at a summer camp, Olmedo cared for the bird, and the two became fast friends.

It was in the spring of 1943 that Bennett, then fourteen years old, found a baby sparrow in Central Park. He carried it home and installed it in an empty robin's nest in his room. With the aid of a medicine dropper and a pair of tweezers, he fed it at hourly intervals. On a diet of flies, bits of worms, water, and pieces of egg-biscuit, it grew rapidly. It gained weight, and the whitish fuzz on its body developed into scores of strong and glossy feathers. A snobbish tilt of its beak when it had had enough food gave it its name.

The boy taught Snobber to fly by placing it in low trees, offering food, and chirping to it. The sparrow learned to recognize his chirp and would fly up to the apartment window from the trees below when Bennett called. To the uninitiated, all sparrows seem to chirp alike. But not to Bennett. He recognized Snobber's chirp in a tree full of sparrows. By the sound, he could tell whether she was angry, curious, or excited. When they went for walks together, they often seemed to be carrying on a conversation, chirping back and forth, as the sparrow darted ahead from tree to tree. On reaching Eighty-First Street, Snobber flew on ahead and waited—like a dog—at the entrance of the apartment house for Bennett to cross the street.

A friendly bird, she often was much in evidence when the boys of the neighborhood were playing games. In the middle of a baseball game, she sometimes alighted on the shoulder of the batter or settled down directly on the baseline to attract attention. At other times, when the boys were flipping playing cards in a local version of "pitching pennies," Snobber would dart down, grasp one of the cards in her bill, and fly away with it. Any small, shiny object instantly aroused her interest. When she found a dime on Bennett's dresser, she picked it up and darted this way and that, flying until she tired. Two marbles in a small metal tray on the boy's desk kept her occupied for a quarter of an hour at a time. She pushed them about with her bill, apparently delighted by the jangling sound they made.

Her interest in bright-colored objects prevented Bennett, one fall, from keeping track of the position of Allied armies by means of colored pins on a large wall-map. No sooner did he put up the pins, placing them carefully to show the location of the lines, than they would disappear. He would find them lying on his bed, the dresser, his desk. Snobber, fluttering like a flycatcher in front of the map, would pull out the pins with her bill. Redheaded pins seemed her first choice with yellowheaded pins coming second. She became so interested in this game that she would perch on Bennett's shoulder, or even his hand, while he inserted the pins. Then she would pull them out as soon as he had finished his work. When he substituted tiny flags in place of pins, her interest rose to an even higher pitch. In the end, Bennett had to give up his efforts, and the game ended for Snobber.

One August, in Central Park, an eminent ornithologist of The American Museum of Natural History—a scientist who had journeyed as far away as equatorial Africa to observe bird life—was surprised to see something entirely new to his experience. A sparrow darted down, perched on a boy's shoulder, and began to eat ice cream from a cone. The sparrow, of course, was Snobber, and the boy was Bennett.

Ice cream, pieces of apple, and small bits of candy were delicacies of which the bird was passionately fond. Boys in the neighborhood shared their candy and cones with her when she alighted on their shoulders. As soon as she saw a piece of candy, she began to chirp and flutter about. Bennett and a companion sometimes played a game with her for five minutes at a time by tossing a piece of cellophane-covered candy back and forth. Like a kitten pursuing a ball, Snobber shuttled swiftly from boy to boy in pursuit of the flying candy.

Along Eighty-First Street, pedestrians were often as surprised as were the people of Vineland to have a sparrow swoop down and alight on their shoulders. The reaction was varied. One woman jerked off a fur neckpiece and swung it around in the air like a lasso to ward off the supposed attack. Several persons made a grab for the sparrow. But, always, Snobber was too quick for them.

One summer day, an elderly gentleman, stout, near-sighted and wearing a derby hat, was walking down the Planetarium side of Eighty-First Street reading a newspaper held close to his face. In his left hand he clutched an ice cream cone from which he absentmindedly took a bite from time to time. Snobber was perched on the lower limb of a tree. She cocked her head as he went by; she had sighted the ice cream. Swooping down, she alighted on the cone and began nibbling away. Just then the man put the cone to his mouth abstractedly to take another bite. The cone bit him, instead! Or, at least, that was the impression he got when Snobber pecked him on the lower lip. Unable to believe his eyes, he peered nearsightedly at the cone and bird. Then he began to wave the cone in circles in the air. Like a pinwheel, the cone and the pursuing sparrow whirled above his head.

Seeing the commotion, Bennett ran across the street to explain and to catch Snobber. But in the process he accidentally knocked the cone from the man's hand. Thinking he was being set upon from the air and the ground simultaneously, the nearsighted gentleman clutched his newspaper in one hand and his derby hat in the other and sprinted, puffing, down the street. At the end of the block, he stopped, turned, shook his fist, and hurried around the corner.

Indoors, when Snobber got hungry she perched on a seed box as a signal to the boy. Two of her favorite foods, aside from seeds and bits of biscuit, were cornflakes and maple sugar. She got greens by eating pieces of leaves from time to time. If the sash were down when she wanted to fly out the window, she dashed about the room in a special manner that Bennett learned to understand.

As might be supposed, the sparrow, when outside, had difficulty at first in picking out the right window among the vast number that pierced the masonry of the great apartment house. Once, after Bennett had chirped to her with his head out the window he was called back into the room. When he looked out again he was just in time to see the sparrow come flying out of a window on the floor below. As a guide for Snobber he tied a ribbon to the iron bar of a window box outside his bedroom. Before dusk, Snobber always returned to the apartment. The only time she spent the night outdoors was during the days when she was lost near Vineland.

From the beginning, Bennett determined that if Snobber ever wanted to go free he would not try to restrain her. The train trip to Vineland, that first summer, was one of the few times when she had been locked in a cage. The ride was bumpy, and she disliked it, chirping most of the time. Bennett spent his time during the journey explaining to interested passengers about the sparrow in the cage. At his uncle's farm, Snobber was ill at ease. She had never seen a rocking chair before, and the unstable perch it provided when the boy was sitting in it disturbed her still more.

On the second day there, she dashed from an apple tree in pursuit of two wild sparrows, flew too far, became confused, then hopelessly lost. Four days later, when Bennett recovered her through his advertisement, she was several miles from his uncle's farm in the direction of New York City. She recognized the boy in an instant and flew chirping to his shoulder. A small American flag in the window of the house where she was found resembled the ribbon tied to the window box of the apartment house and may have influenced her in choosing that particular place. When chasing among the trees with wild sparrows of the Planetarium park, Snobber seemed to prefer Bennett's companionship to that of any bird. She was always slightly suspicious of other sparrows. When she took a dust bath with others of her kind, she always stayed on the edge of the group. If one of the birds became too familiar she charged it with lowered head and open beak. Bennett once brought home a young sparrow to keep Snobber company. She refused to have anything to do with it. He then placed a canary in the bedroom as a playmate for Snobber. When he returned to the room to see how they were getting along, he found her holding the hapless bird by the bill and swinging it around in the air. The next day she lured the canary out on the window ledge and then chased it away down the street. After that, the boy ceased trying to find a bird companion for her, and Snobber became content to let matters rest as they were.

Her first spring, although she had not mated, Snobber was overcome by the impulse to build a nest. Tearing up a robin's nest and a song sparrow's nest that Bennett had in his room, she used the material to create a nest of her own. She was busy with this task for days, sometimes flying about the room with straws fully a foot long. In the nest, she laid two eggs. Neither hatched and one later rested on cotton batting in a small box in Bennett's room. It bore on the lid the notation: "English Sparrow Egg Laid By Snobber."

When Bennett was doing his homework, during the winter, Snobber often perched quietly on his book or on the desk beside him. And, at night, when the boy was sleeping in his bed, the sparrow was lost in slumber on the top of the closet door, its head tucked in its feathers. Often, it slept perched on one leg. At such times it had the appearance of a ball of ruffled feathers, with one leg sticking down and its tail sticking out at right angles to the leg.

As soon as it was daylight, Snobber awoke. Bennett didn't need an alarm clock. He had Snobber. She hopped down, perched on his head, and began tugging at individual hairs. If he didn't wake up, she often snuggled down near his neck for an additional nap herself. If he disturbed her by moving in his sleep, she pecked him on the chest. As a consequence, Bennett often kept moving back toward the far side of the bed until, when he awakened, he was lying on the edge and the sparrow was occupying most of the bed.

On the floor of Bennett's bedroom, there was a shiny spot six or seven inches in diameter. This was where the sparrow took her imaginary dust baths. Alighting at this spot, she squatted down, fluffed up her feathers, turned this way and that, and went through the motions of taking a real dust bath by the roadside.

Like Mary's famous little lamb, Snobber sometimes tried to follow Bennett to school. He rode to and from classes on the subway. Winter mornings, he always tried to leave the apartment house without the sparrow seeing him. But the bright eyes of the little bird missed little that was going on. Several times, just as he was sprinting a block from his home, he heard a lively chirping behind him and Snobber fluttered down on his shoulder. Twice he had to explain to teachers that he was late for classes because a sparrow had delayed him! At the school he attended, however, both teachers and pupils knew all about Snobber. In fact, whenever Bennett got an extra good grade, his classmates had a standing explanation: *Snobber had helped him!*

I Lived with a Black-Tailed Jack Rabbit

HENRY PAUL JACKSON

WE LIVED IN A HOUSE IN SOQUEL, CALIFORNIA, THAT WAS mostly glass, and the rabbit's name was Harveya. Of course, it was Harvey when she was given to me, a baby probably less than a week old, abandoned or lost in a farm field. Friends doubted I could raise her, but after Harveya grew up they agreed with me that she was one of the nicest pets one could have. I was very proud of her.

If I seem to boast in telling how I saved her life, housebroke this beautiful little wild creature, and almost domesticated her—forgive me, for my desire is to share with others my wonderful experience with an animal that, at least in the country where I lived, was usually considered, along with the many cottontails, a pest.

By good chance there was a doll bottle handy, and Harveya co-operated at once by taking the nipple and emptying it of half-diluted and warmed homogenized milk; shortly she would take seven bottles at a feeding three times a day. Then I recalled that rabbits love carrots. I added carrot juice to her diet, and she grew rapidly. (She would not eat carrots.) Amazingly, her ears grew faster than her body! And for a time I wished I had called her "Ears." When she was only about half-grown, the ears were much longer than their mature length of six to seven inches. I remembered how the young calf is "all legs" and yet becomes proportionate in size when it has grown. So did Harveya, in the full form of her kind, with beauty of line and of movement, from the tip of her black-topped tail to the silky, nearly translucent black-tipped ears that she could turn, semaphore fashion, independently in different directions, and which seemed to be able to catch a whisper, or high notes, most easily.

When Harveya was a small hare, I had to housebreak her. This seemed impossible until I noticed that she urinated after the sixth bottle. Accordingly, for several feedings, with the sixth bottle, I brought her to a sandbox, which she would use at once. One day, to my surprise and delight, she went to the box on her own; and then I knew the problem was solved. It must be said, however, that as she had the run of the house—a glass enclosed area of a thousand square feet—she left some droppings outside of her box, but almost always in the immediate vicinity, at least on the paper surrounding it.

From the first I permitted her to sleep where she wished, and she chose to stay beneath my bed. Thinking that the floor was too cold, colder even than the ground where a jack rabbit sits, I gave her a thin but firm pillow, which she adopted. But one day I could not find her, and thought someone might have left a door ajar to the outside. While sitting on the couch I happened to glance up. To my surprise, there sat Harveya on the shelf at the end of some books. Like a bronze statue she sat, her ears erect, nearly touching the shelf above. That night she didn't return to my room, so I took her pillow to her. For about three weeks the bookshelf was her favorite resting spot, night or day. It was interesting to see how she got up so high: she would jump to the couch, then to a pillow, and then to the first shelf. About this time she was inclined to scratch on the pillow or on a vacant place near it to make her "form" (in the wild, a slight depression in the ground). When she discovered she could not scratch out a place, she would finally straighten out the pillow with her teeth and settle down. This scratching out a form then practically ceased.

Finally came the day when, with her ears raised, she touched the shelf above. Evidently, she did not like this. One night, instead of bounding up on the shelf, she remained at the corner of the stone platform that was the base of the large, three-cornered fireplace where she sometimes sat. I carried the pillow to her, and ever after this was her favorite spot to sit when I was at home.

By this time Harveya had traveled more than five-thousand miles with us in our car, on the same pillow, on the rear seat or lying on the back of the front seat. She attracted attention wherever we went. She loved to ride in the car if she had her pillow, for this seemed to give her a feeling of safety. She stretched out on it like a dog and remained perfectly contented. Her box was always near her on the seat, and she never soiled the car.

She had learned to drink early. She was so amusing when she stood on her hind legs and put her paws into my free hand to brace herself while sucking on the bottle that we babied her long after it was necessary. Learning to eat, though, came slower. First she nibbled grasses and then only when I poked the end of a blade into her mobile mouth. Finally she sampled and liked rabbit pellets that we bought for her at a pet shop. Later, we discovered that she liked "quick" oak flakes, apple, and, especially, dark bread, toasted and dipped slightly in skim milk. The last of these, usually with carrot juice and in small amounts, became her "goodnight" treat. She ate daintily and invariably left part of it, returning to it later.

When she was first sampling solid foods, to our amazement, she seemed to try everything. After she discovered that some solids were tasty, she ate raffia off the Chinese chairs, wood from the fireplace, paper boxes, and even clothing, with a threat to the rugs. One night, while we were traveling with Harveya, she was left to roam about our room in the motel. I had hung my favorite pair of slacks over a chair in the motel. In the morning, I discovered that my slacks were full of holes! The holes were of various sizes, all made by Harveya. For a few moments I thought of abandoning her; but there she sat, with her innocent, hopeful expression which, since she had no voice (excepting a heavy *Phfft!* used only when she was angry), indicated she was waiting for her morning bottle. Of course, I forgave her. Fortunately, this was the end of her sampling of articles other than edibles; but her natural curiosity over everything about her was one of the things that made her so interesting to us.

From babyhood, Harveya washed her fur as a cat does, but she was several weeks old before it was so completely or thoroughly accomplished. She even washed her tail, which showed us her great flexibility of body. She finally finished by cleaning her ears, and this had to be seen to be believed. She pulled each ear down, with her feet, and did not not release the ear until she was quite satisfied with her handiwork.

In her flexibility, her various postures were as unexpected as they were interesting or artistic. Her usual or conventional one, of course, was sitting with her slender front legs close together. Her large brown eyes in her narrow little head were inconspicuous in contrast to the ears. Her ears she held erect so long as she was alert—thus she commonly sat on her fireplace pillow awaiting the breakfast call, for all the world like a jurist silently passing judgment on her world. As soon as she saw activity in the kitchen, which was visible from her seat, she moved to a place near the refrigerator, where, with her front legs usually withdrawn, she settled down, apparently, until the toast was ready. But she seldom actually insisted—she just placed herself in a strategic position where her motionless silence was expressive, pathetic, and successful! Only if I was seated, or if there was an exceptional delay, did she scratch or pull lightly on my trouser cuff.

After her morning clean-up, she relaxed, with her ears dropped and scarcely discernible against the shoulders. But she only seemed to be asleep. At the approach of a strange person, or if she heard an unfamilar noise, she was away like a flash. She bounded to a box on the floor of my clothes closet, where the door was always left ajar so that she might nestle deep in the old slacks (which she no longer chewed), with only her pressed-down ears visible. There she remained until her sense of danger was past. But if no untoward incident occurred, noon time would find her stretched out in her most intriguing position. One day a friend of mine—also a friend of hers—was sunning himself on the sun lounge, a place preferred by Harveya. When Harveya decided she wanted the place, she took his shirt in her teeth and gave it a shake. When he got off the lounge in response to her urging, she settled on the couch, her rear feet stretched out and her head and ears down, a picture of contentment.

When she was small I would let her outside on her own, and she would return through the open door in about an hour. But one day I paddled her lightly with a piece of paper for some indiscretion, perhaps for jumping onto the dining table or an open bed. Intelligent as she was, she soon learned by this method of punishment what she shouldn't do. The next day, when I let her out to run a little, she stayed out for forty hours! It was a moonlit night, and far and wide I roamed, searching for her; but I did not find Harveya.

That evening, as I sat at the dinner table with guests, I heard Harveya scratch at the sliding door to the patio. I opened the door and Harveya came up to me. I was overjoyed at her return. She lay down at my feet for me to pick her up, which I did with pleasure! Soon she came to the refrigerator, and assumed her asking position. I got up from the table to get her some milk; and she followed me, standing up on her hind legs, to the amusement of my guests. I am sure that she was as glad to be home as I was to have her. I might add that every one of us enjoyed our dinner after that. I know that my appetite was restored.

Harveya liked to play. In the evenings, she pulled at my leg, hopped away, then half turned as an invitation for me to chase her, and the romp was on. A large sofa was heaped with pillows across the center; while I clapped my hands, swinging from one side to the other, she learned to leap back and forth over the barrier. This was varied by a flying jump to the huge upholstered chair, down and around, in and out of corners, on and under furniture, and then back to the sofa again. When she was tired she would let me know about it. She would slap at me with her hind feet as if to say, "That's enough!" If I insisted on romping, she turned in her tracks, with a speed and dexterity that was incredible, and kicked at me with her hind feet. This was usually accompanied by an amusing sidewise wiggle of her haunches. Then, with a rapidly beating heart, which I could see pounding the sides of her lithe body, she was willing to be caressed, although she permitted this at any time. As I stroked her, especially about the base of the ears and down her back, she relaxed in obvious satisfaction. She jumped on me, at times, and stayed near me, but did not fawn as a dog does. She never scratched me.

The possibility of letting her have a family of her own has, of course, been discussed; and if there are ever baby Harveyas I hope to have success in domestication of one or more of her offspring. From my delightful experience with Harveya I can truly say that if anyone will take the time, they, too, may develop a charming and loyal pet from one of these little hares with the big brown eyes and the long ears.

My Conditioned Chickadees

LOUISE DE KIRILINE

FROM THE BEGINNING IT WAS NEVER MY INTENTION TO tame the black-capped chickadees that came to our Canadian feeding station. In my opinion, taming spoils the true character of the wild creature that is tamed. But when, about fifteen years ago, one of the chickadees near our Loghouse on Pimisi Bay showed an unusual disregard for my nearness, and indicated a willingness, without a great deal of persuasion, to come to my hand, I decided that this association would be wholly the responsibility of the chickadees.

I never regretted this decision. What the chickadees have since shown me of their elfin character, what they have taught me of their feelings and reactions—all was done in an atmosphere of untrammeled liberty for them. There was only the seed—the magic sunflower seed. The seed pulled away the fear that at first separated them from me. It built a bridge of harmonious relationships between us and established the only kind of foundation, I would say, upon which a true appreciation of nature's creatures is built. Whatever compulsion that the seed may have exerted at the start, in forging the bond, vanished later and was of no account.

As I said, there was at first one particular chickadee. This one I called Peet by reason of a special note he gave as he approached me. Most of the other chickadees also gave this note in the way of an alert, which had the effect of catching the attention of the other birds as well as of me. But Peet the second, who came into existence a good many years later, was not given his name for the same reason. He got his because he, of all the chickadees of my closer acquaintance, most resembled the first Peet in character and consequently influenced events in the same way. Both lived in the forest around our house; and being at home is very important in directing the behavior of birds in particular, and of other creatures, too. Both chickadees possessed that innate quality of enterprise that creates pioneers and which, in effect, was the root and origin of the good understanding that came to exist, at times, between the birds and me.

This is how it came about.

Our chickadees had never in their lives, as far as I know, seen a sunflower seed. The first time I put a few of them on their dinner plate, most of them did not recognize the seeds for anything except something strange. But Peet, and that was the first time I distinguished him, pecked at the seed. He took it and turned it around in his bill. This was important. In some way it imparted to him the condition of the kernel. Was it a good seed, a thick seed, a light seed, a poor seed? Whether he could hear it move inside the shell as he shifted it about, or somehow judged its weight, I never knew. But he and the other chickadees nearly always discarded a bad seed, and sometimes, also, a good one.

Having made the test, he flew to a tree. There he put the seed under both of his feet and held it fast against the branch. This is the way all chickadees and, I believe, all titmice handle a seed. And because they *know* this, without needing to learn it, it is an instinctive act. He split the seed open by elfin, hammering blows upon it with his bill. When he did not succeed in opening it the first time, he turned it around and tried another spot. It cracked, and he pulled open the shell letting the fragments fall to the ground.

Peet usually ate the kernel, but sometimes he stored it. This happened in times when there was much food available and comparatively few chickadees to share it or, to put it in other words, when the food supply was a little heavy in the environmental balance. Nearly always autumn was the best time to store things away. But there were other times, too, except the breeding season, when the chickadees stored their surplus rations.

With great care Peet selected his storing place in the wedge between two twigs, or in a curled piece of bark, or in any convenient fissure where it could be securely tucked in. Often after having deposited the seed, he pulled it out again, flew off with it, searched for another place, found it, and pushed in the seed. *There!* At some time during his countless inspections of every twig of every tree in our woods in his great quests for food, he, or somebody else, found the kernel again and ate it.

Now, when I offered Peet a seed in my hands, he took it after only a slight show of hesitation. This gave me to understand that the sunflower seed had rapidly won high favor with him. With increasing assurance, Peet performed the act again, and then again.

The other chickadees looked on. I knew that they were curious and afraid, interested, and hungry. I knew because some of them lifted the feathers of their black caps, and smoothed them down again. Others opened their bills without uttering a sound, and still others made chewing motions with their bills and tongue. This chewing had really nothing to do with their eating, or wanting to eat, because they did it, not from anticipation, but from not being able to eat at that particular moment when their timidity overruled their hunger. A few more courageous chickadees became so aroused by the sight of Peet plucking so much good food from my hand, that they made daredevil flights to halfway between their perch and me, then head-over-tails flew back to the perch, often with cries of real or mock fright. Each such attempt brought them a little closer to their goal—the seed—until finally they snatched it and carried it off with great speed and rejoicing.

This was the way that the two Peets became the "key birds." Thus, unknowingly, they worked upon the inclinations of their chickadee followers, inducing them to repeat their own successful acts to the advantage of all concerned.

When this stage was reached, the chickadees began to learn things in connection with me and the seed. They found new and convenient ways of seizing the seed, no longer from my own hand only, but from my pockets or from my lips as they alighted blithely on my nose or eyeglasses. At times when the seed and I vanished into the house, some of them clung to the edge of the eave or an icicle and looked in. Some, like suspended marionettes, hovered at the window when they saw me inside. Some followed me from window to window, alighted on the sill, sat, looked in, then pecked at the pane, chagrined that they could not reach me. My immediate response to these charming sights and sounds was, of course, to go out and give them a seed. Gradually, they learned that these activities of theirs usually resulted in the reappearance of me and the seeds. And from then on I had only to move away from the window to have the chickadees fly directly to the door, where, sure enough, I appeared and they got their due reward.

By this time the chickadees began to connect me with the seed so closely that the seed and I became, in their eyes, one object. This led me to wonder how exactly did they know me? What in my appearance made them distinguish me with such consistency that they came volplaning down to me from sixty-foot treetops the instant they glimpsed me; that they flew under roofs and inside of houses to find me, and even into my car before I left or at my return from a trip? All of them were by no means so adept at recognizing me. But there were Peet and half a dozen of his followers whose capacities in this respect seemed to have few limits.

In order to find out more about this interesting behavior, I traveled in a boat out on the nearby lake at various distance from the shore. Chickadees are reluctant to cross open spaces, even on land; and they do so willingly only in places that they are used to flying across, or those that they cross in a flock. Even then, a faint-hearted one, when only halfway across, may turn back, or drop down to shrub or tree cover. In spite of this, Peet came to me over the open water, a distance between 150 and 200 feet. Intrepidly he launched himself upon these flights, sometimes in a good wind that blew his tail sideways, a sweet and touching little figure, alone in midair. When he arrived finally at my boat, he pitched on my head or came to the tip of my finger. Having received his seed from me, he made the return trip flying low and direct to the safety of the lake shore. Most of the other chickadees never came any farther away from shore than twenty-five to fifty feet, becoming prey to all kinds of distractions, such as chasing a companion or pecking at some food.

Only a few matched Peet's flights over the water. But beyond these distances from shore, I might as well have been invisible; they appeared not to see me, although, with a bird's sharpness of eyesight, it is most unlikely that they could *not* detect me.

One day I lay down for a nap on the floor under the roof of the open porch—a warm and sunny place. If I thought that I would be well hidden from the chickadees I was quickly put to shame. Peet came, perched in my hair, looked for seed in my hand, and found it. After Peet, several others came and did the same. My noon-hour sleep was ruined, but I really did not mind. It was an interesting discovery to find that the chickadees recognized me, even when I was lying down, and not in my usual upright posture.

After this I did everything I could to keep the chickadees from distinguishing the outlines of my person. I crouched, and I covered myself over, to see what would happen. The chickadees were not deceived. They had always seen, or did see, enough of me to shatter my most painstaking efforts at hiding from them. Then I remembered how songbirds see and recognize hawks and owls, whether these predators are in flight or perching. I could only conclude that the chickadees recognized me in the very same way, no matter what I wore, or whether I was upright, or lying down. The picture the chickadees had of me was that of a whole figure, much simplified perhaps, if we could draw it exactly as they saw it, but nevertheless a highly adequate and appropriate picture. All the same, even the infallible chickadee can sometimes err, as I have seen them do, when the large gray form of a Canada jay reappears after an absence and suddenly throws its soundless short-necked shadow across the chickadee heaven. And with the fright of the hawk deep in their hearts, the small birds sit perfectly still, in a "deep-freeze" pose, wherever they are, or they may scurry for cover.

I was never able to feel that the chickadees really knew me personally. Any man that came up our path to the house was to them a seed container, also. When I stood beside the stranger, the birds *preferred* to come to me, but only until my companion offered them a seed. After that, their preference for me quickly vanished. Many birds are able to distinguish one person from another, as we have learned from the fascinating accounts of Dr. Konrad Lorenz and other specialists in the study of animal behavior. The difference between the environments in the learning of the wild birds of these experimenters and of mine may be this—that these people lived in heavily-populated communities where it was necessary for the birds to learn to distinguish one person who fed them from a multitude of indifferent ones. I live in the wilderness. There are not enough people to make it rewarding for the chickadees to know us apart.

In the time that I knew Peet the First, I owned a blond muskrat coat with a dark collar. The first time I appeared among the chickadees wearing this coat, the effect on them was spectacular. They flew away with every sign of distress. They refused to come near me. They went into a mobbing scene, as they often do at the sight of a dangerous predator, with loud scolding, wing-flicking, short flights from twig to twig, and chasing of each other, which they did simply because they were too excited to contain themselves. Their noise and excited movements attracted every other bird in the vicinity, all of which fussed over the objectionable human creature that stood before them wearing fur.

What exactly these irate midgets took me for is difficult to say. I must have reminded them of whatever fur-bearing animal they were used to seeing—weasel, mink, or, possibly, muskrat. But obviously they were overdoing the thing. There is a peculiar tendency in birds to become overly impressed by an object that in some way exercises an exaggerated stimulation on their senses. No doubt, in that coat I was a gross exaggeration of a predator to the chickadees. They never got used to it, and I was always unacceptable to them whenever I wore it.

Tree-Dwellers of the Tropics

ELIZABETH INGLES

A LOUD REPORT SPLIT WIDE OPEN THE QUIET OF THE tropical night. In a few moments another shot, much nearer, sent me hurrying to the window to listen. Any unexplained shot is terrifying, especially after dark, but here on Barro Colorado Island, Panama Canal Zone, where guns are absolutely taboo, a rifle heard at night arouses instant speculation. Are poachers stalking the unwary animals of our sanctuary? Will our graceful, half-tame deer fall before the weapon of some native jack-light hunter? Such thoughts went through my mind as I listened for further sounds in the still night. The next shot was really close. Grabbing my flashlight, I quietly went out the cabin door and hurried through the clearing toward the place at the edge of the jungle from which the sound came. In an instant there was another volley. Now, without obstructing cabin walls, I was able to identify the "shot." It was the racket made by almendro nuts falling on the corrugated iron roof of the pumphouse. Some animal feeding in the tree was dropping the nuts or shaking them from the branches.

The night was beautiful. A waxing moon faintly lighted the clearing. The tall silhouette of the almendro, or wild almond, stood out from the forest wall, but the animals in the tree were not visible. At last, in the beam of my powerful flashlight, I saw the small forms of night monkeys moving over the branches. I had seen caged night monkeys in the Panama City market, but this was the first time to my knowledge that the species had fed near the clearing. Years ago a family of night monkeys had lived in a hole in an old tree near the laboratory. Casual visitors to the Barro Colorado might have tapped on the gray trunk beneath the nest and been rewarded by seeing a sleepy little face peering intently down at them. Termites, rains, and winds finally completed the destruction of the nest tree. Now we see the animals rarely, for night monkeys are strictly nocturnal. They sleep during the day in a tree-hole nest. In the evening, stretching, perhaps yawning, they gaze with their big black eyes from the nest hole into the gathering dusk. To them the night is familiar. While the other species of Island monkeys are settling down to rest, the night monkeys are taking over the tree trails for their own use.

The night monkeys in the almendro tree are one of four kinds of monkeys living on Barro Colorado Island. The tall almendro tree is but one of many forest giants that with smaller trees, palms, shrubs, tree ferns, and bromeliads, orchids and other epiphytes, make up the tropical evergreen forest which, except for a clearing of perhaps six acres, covers the Island.

Barro Colorado Island in the Panama Canal Zone was set aside by the United States Congress in 1923 as a tropical research laboratory. Before the canal was built, it was a forested hill beside whose red cliffs the pirate, Henry Morgan, camped on his cross-country march to the ill-fated city of old Panama. When the waters of the mighty Chagres River were impounded to form Gatun Lake in the building of the canal, the hilltop became an island of nearly six square miles. To this island, which is now a part of the great Smithsonian Institution, scientists travel from all over the world to study the plants and animals that live here. They have published many hundreds of books, popular articles, and scientific papers on their studies. Yet the forests of Barro Colorado still contain many unsolved scientific problems. Each new study suggests others. Perhaps the surface is hardly scratched. For example, practically nothing is known about the life history of the Canal Zone night monkeys, the noisy little visitors to the almendro tree.

The night monkey is about the size of a tree squirrel. It has a soft gray coat and a nonprehensile tail that terminates in a small brush. Like those of many other nocturnal animals its big, solemn, black eyes appear far too large for its small size. Night monkeys are said to make ideal pets, especially for people who must spend the daytime working away from home.

At night it is alert, ready to play, and is an affectionate and interesting companion. I think the animals that looked down from the high branches of the almendro tree—wide-eyed and unblinking—were a family group, probably the parents and last season's offspring. Certainly, in spite of all the noise they made, there were not more than three animals in the tree. The species is not believed to travel in troops like the capuchins and howlers. This family "talked" among themselves while they ate, uttering soft whistling noises, something like *"whew-whew!"*

Often from the porch of our cabin, some thirty feet from the wall of the jungle, I watched squirrel monkeys, or squirrel marmosets, running through the trees. With the howlers and capuchins, they take over the tree trails by day. There are no spider monkeys on the Island, although two species are found elsewhere in Panama.

Unlike the tropical trails along which the humans walk, the tree trails of the monkeys are not cut by a machete. Nor are they marked to my eyes. To the monkeys the markers must be clear, for each day they seem to follow along the same branches, climb up the same long swinging lianas, and jump from the same trees. The soft gray- and brown-flecked coats and bright eyes of the squirrel monkeys give them a deceptively friendly, innocent look. Judging from the close-up view I had of several of them in a cage in the Panama City market, I would say that in captivity they have nasty dispositions. They bared their sharp little teeth and their cries were more belligerent than plaintive. Their hard little faces were unappealing and unfriendly.

In the forest, the squirrel monkeys I watched seemed to be very quiet. However, other observers report that they chatter to each other while scurrying through the trees and often call in high-pitched, squeaky tones. From a distance, they resemble squirrels. They are reported to travel in small bands, but I never saw more than a pair at a time.

Although they make the tree trails their own, they do not travel them with the grace of the capuchin monkeys. Here again they are more like squirrels. With the exception of the great toe, their toes are claw-tipped. This is useful in certain types of climbing, but does not give the animal the purchase upon a limb so necessary for truly arboreal life. Scientists who have studied squirrel monkeys report that they eat a variety of food. They like star-apples, wild figs, seeds, and blossoms. Probably they eat very little meat, except possibly insects. Captive animals liked grasshoppers and cooked meat but showed no interest in raw meat that was offered them. On Barro Colorado, squirrel monkeys do not appear to be nearly as numerous as the capuchin and howler monkeys. Perhaps they prefer to live in small trees at the edge of clearings and to shun the deep forest.

On Barro Colorado there is plenty of deep forest, hanging lianas, and shrubby tangles. From such a habitat as this, one hears each morning the roarlike barks of the howler monkeys giving blatant welcome to the new day. From a distance the loud reverberating voice of *Mono negro,* or "caraya," as the natives call the howler monkey, is extremely impressive. When one is standing below the tree in which a clan is resting, the deep growls, which in unison become a loud roar, are wild and terrifying. Yet there is something about a howler's face, seen at close range, that is very appealing in spite of its large size. We seldom were able to approach the howlers very closely. Their numbers on the Island appear to have decreased since the days when Drs. Frank Chapman and C. R. Carpenter made their interesting studies of their behavior. Perhaps the monkey yellow fever, which recently swept north from South America into Panama, Costa Rica, and Nicaragua, took its toll among the Barro Colorado howler clans as it did elsewhere. It is hard to know. When death comes to a tropical forest dweller, there are many other animals ready to pick its bones.

Although we saw howlers often and heard them every day, the troops were not large, and the animals seldom came to the edge of a clearing.

When observed in the dense woods they are usually high in the largest trees. The monkeys did not move away when they realized that they were being watched, but jumped up and down, shaking the limbs and often breaking and dropping small branches toward the observer. One day the large male leading the band climbed lower and lower down the tree toward a group of people watching from the trail. His black face was wrinkled in a scowl, his teeth were bared. All together his attitude was defiant and hostile. We were intruding on his privacy. After all, this wonderful forest is his home! Who can blame him for resenting the stares of the curious?

Howler monkeys travel through the trees slowly and cautiously. Unlike the capuchins I watched, they never made long jumps, but progressed carefully from the terminal branches of one tree to the terminal branches of the next. When necessary the prehensile tail is used as an anchor to keep the animal from falling from the branch on which it is sleeping or to catch a branch or vine in case of a fall. Often the band is led by a large male in his prime. The young males and females follow. Mothers carrying their babies come last. When the young are very small their mothers carry them on their breasts; as they grow older they learn to ride pickaback.

In the Barro Colorado forest there is ample food. The crop of almendro nuts in February was excellent. There were many figs and other fruits and plenty of young, sweet leafbuds. All of these are eaten by howler monkeys. This species is largely free of enemies on the Island. Its large size and arboreal habits save it from ground-dwelling predators large enough to do it damage, although the young may be killed by ocelots. Here, howler monkeys, as elsewhere, are probably heavily infected with botflies. Probably man is the howler's greatest enemy, but no man hunts on this island sanctuary.

Why should an animal so greatly blessed with abundant food, congenial family life, few enemies, and pleasant surroundings find it necessary to send its agonizing roars into the quiet of the dawn or into the still calm before a tropical storm breaks in a torrent of rain over the espave tree in which it rests? But roar it does, perhaps simply because it must. Even though the numbers of howler monkeys have diminished, there is no more characteristic sound on the Island than the deep voice of *Mono negro.*

The capuchin monkeys are the comedians of the forest. They travel through the trees with gay abandon, jumping carelessly from one tree to the next. To the onlooker they seem to be playing a game of tag or follow the leader. Often a band of about fifteen follows a tree trail within a hundred yards of our forest-side cottage. Sometimes they come much closer. Once I saw a fine male travel through the low shrubs at the forest edge, climb to the top of a small bush, stand erect and scratch his sides and belly vigorously with both his hands. Occasionally the more adventuresome of the band leave the protective cover of the woods to cross the clearing on the ground and eat the sweet fruits of the star-apple. This tree is isolated from the forest and grows within thirty feet of two cottages and directly over the path to the laboratory.

When the deep-throated, gobletlike blossoms of the balsa tree bloomed, the capuchin monkeys made early morning and late evening trips to the trees. Climbing out on the limbs, they squatted beside the blossoms. Then taking the flower in both hands they lifted it to their mouths. Sometimes they leaned over and buried their faces in the pale yellow blossom. Perhaps they were drinking water that had accumulated in this cup, or eating pollen, or insects that were caught there. The capuchins are more carnivorous than the other Island monkeys. They like insects, birds' eggs, and young, small arboreal rodents, and possibly bats. The bulk of their food is vegetable, including figs, star-apples, manzabis, tree leaves, and nuts.

Late one afternoon, a troop of capuchins climbed through the tree beside the inlet where a number of visitors were gathering beside the launch in preparation for leaving the Island. The monkeys had no fear of the noisy humans below. One beautiful male climbed down the branches overhanging the water within fifty feet of the group of people on the dock. He stared curiously. As he advanced down the branches he broke off all dead twigs within reach and threw them into the water. He made no attempt to throw the twigs at the observers. It seemed to me that he dropped the twigs simply to hear them splash in the lake below, or he may have been showing off. The large iguanas that habitually rested in these trees jumped with great splashes into the water when the monkey got within reach of them.

The native boys on Barro Colorado call the white-faced capuchin monkeys *Mono cara blanca.* On the mainland the species is rare because the natives hunt them for food or sell them as pets. On Barro Colorado, capuchins are numerous. Unlike the howlers which travel comparatively short distances, the capuchins seem to move widely over the Island. They have set routes over which bands of fifteen to twenty-five, scattered out for a hundred yards or more, run easily over the branches or climb swinging lianas. Almost every day the monkeys followed the tree trail near our cabin to eat in the almendro tree. Then for five days we did not see them. Apparently the desire for different food or something else unknown to us led them to follow another of their arboreal highways. We missed the show they put on daily. We were glad when we again heard the familiar chattering and noise of breaking branches. Our capuchins were again following the tree trail that terminated at the almendro tree.

A visitor from the North familiar with the unhappy faces of zoo monkeys is quite unprepared for the beauty and charm of these wild primates in the jungle. Here the destructive and selfish interests of man do not threaten their safety, and they move with confidence and freedom over the serpentine lianas or through the spreading broad-leafed trees that make up the forest arterials of their tree trails.

Jeff

ALEXANDER SPRUNT, JR.

ONE OF THE MOST REMARKABLE ASSOCIATIONS OF A WILD bird with a human being came to my notice in 1952. There have been records of the taming of wild mockingbirds, pelicans, ducks, thrashers, and others, but I had never heard of anyone, anywhere, with a "pet" sooty tern.

One September day, I left Key West, Florida, on the *Fort Jefferson,* a boat owned and operated by the National Park Service. I was bound for the Dry Tortugas, where I planned to make a two-weeks' study of fall bird migration. The captain, Joseph Santini, had on the stern of the boat in a wire cage a young sooty tern. Naturally, its presence there produced questions, to which I received some interesting answers.

On a July day in 1952, a frigate bird, which is sometimes predatory on other birds, swooped low over the sands of Bush Key, Dry Tortugas, and picked up a young sooty tern from the enormous nesting colony there. Either its hold on the youngster was insecure, or the struggles of the tern were such that the frigate bird lost its grip. The little tern fell from the frigate bird's clutches and dropped into the moat which surrounds Fort Jefferson, on Garden Key, Dry Tortugas. The incident was noted by Park Service personnel, and Joe Santini rescued the waif. He took it to his quarters at the Fort, and from then on, the remarkable association developed.

When we were journeying there on the boat in September, Jeff, as Santini had named the tern, was liberated from his cage while we were still some eight or ten miles east of the Tortugas. Jeff flew away over the water and disappeared from our sight. Santini told me that the tern had made three or four trips with him, by boat, to Key West; but he had never before turned him loose so far from his home on the Tortugas. That evening, at about seven o'clock, while we were in Santini's quarters, the tern came to the door and called for its supper of minnows! For the next two weeks I saw a good deal of Jeff, and learned more about him—or her. Every day between about five thirty in the morning and late afternoon, Jeff arrived at various times outside Santini's Fort Jefferson quarters and announced his arrival with a high-pitched, two syllabled whistle. The first time that he came while I was there, Santini said to me, "Now *listen,* and let's try him out."

"Jeff," he said in a natural tone of voice. Instantly the tern called back to him with a high-pitched two-syllabled note. Santini again spoke the bird's name, and the bird again replied. Then Santini turned to me, and said "You try it!" I said "Jeff," in a natural tone, but the bird did not reply. Then Santini said "Jeff"; and again the bird called. Each time—and we tested the bird over and over—it responded to Santini but not to me. We were invisible to Jeff at the time; therefore it must have distinguished Santini's voice from mine.

Then Santini said, "Open the icebox door and shut it." I tried it. Every time it heard the door shut, the tern called! Santini usually kept minnows in the icebox for Jeff, and he fed him thirty to forty of them every day. Apparently the bird had learned to associate two things—the sound of the door of the icebox shutting and the minnows that Santini usually fed it shortly after it heard the door close. While I was there, half a dozen times a day the bird would arrive, announce its arrival, and await results. Sometimes Santini would be there; sometimes he would not. At no time could *I* do anything for Jeff—he responded only to Santini! Twice, Santini and I went "crawfishing" out beyond the end of Long Key Reef. Sooty terns flew about the boat, all looking alike; and now and then Santini would call, "Jeff!" Often there would be no response from any of the birds; but at other times one of the terns would leave the circling birds and alight on our boat. It was Jeff!

This was a wonderful experience. I left the Tortugas on September twenty-third, after a two-weeks' study of the fall migration of birds there. At the time I wondered what Jeff would do—would he stay on the Tortugas with Santini, beyond the time when most of his or her kind deserted the Tortugas for their fall and winter wanderings? Nobody knew. But the night before I left Fort Jefferson, Jeff had not come, all that day, to Santini's quarters. Nor was he there the next morning when I left for Key West. Santini piloted me on the *Fort Jefferson* the sixty-eight miles eastward to the Key West Naval Base. He seemed distraught and worried, and I knew why. He radioed from his boat back to the Fort three times, and each time he asked, "Has Jeff come back?" The reply was always the same: "No, he hasn't."

We hoped that Jeff would return in the following spring, but neither Santini nor I ever saw him again. We hope and believe that Jeff went wandering away with his own kind, and that each spring he comes back to the Dry Tortugas to mate and nest among the thousands of sooty terns that for a few months each year blacken the white sands there.

Fence Lizards in My Garden

FRANK F. GANDER

ONE SUMMER DAY WHILE NOONING UNDER AN OAK TREE in my garden near Escondido, California, I amusedly watched a male fence lizard that strutted about atop a large granite rock near me. Raising his body on straightened and stiffened legs, with his back arched and his throat puffed out, he bobbed grotesquely about. The bright blue of his throat and the two bands of blue along the sides of his belly showed nicely; his back was dark gray with flecks of blue-green showing here and there, and along either side were indistinct gray lines. Occasionally the lizard would interrupt his display to move to the edge of the rock and snap up small flies that had drawn near. Several of these were hovering about in the shade of the tree; and whenever one came near the rock the lizard got it—not once did he miss.

Flies and other insects constitute most of the food of the fence lizard, but they do not eat just any insect that comes near. Instead, they show much discrimination in selecting their food. They ignore most bees and wasps, but occasionally an adult male lizard will take a bee if he has opportunity. They eat some ants, others they do not touch, although they will eat any pupae greedily. I have watched a fence lizard stand beside a moving column of ants and deftly snatch the pupae from the ants as they carried them along. Apparently some ants are quite distasteful to these lizards. On one occasion, an ant had attached itself to a mealworm which I had tossed to a lizard. The lizard ate the mealworm, ant and all. Instantly the actions of the little reptile became comical. He blinked his eyes, held his mouth wide open, and put one forefoot up against his throat.

Altogether, he acted like a person who had taken a bite of food that was too hot.

When ants are winged, or in their flying stages, they do not seem so distasteful to lizards and are eagerly captured by them. The lizards eat flying termites, too; grasshoppers, and moths of many kinds, small caterpillars, some beetles and their larvae, aphids, and many other kinds of insects. Spiders and small scorpions also are included in their diet. Occasionally I have seen a fence lizard eat the blossoms of wild snapdragons and the fallen petals of roses. Plant food may be of some importance to them early in the year when insects are not very abundant.

Usually, the adult fence lizards in my garden begin to come out of hibernation about the end of January. Young of the preceding season do not hibernate but are active on sunny days throughout the winter. Even with the thermometer at 50° F., if the sun is shining these little lizards will be lying out on the rocks. They continue to grow all through the winter, and most of them are nearly grown and ready to start reproducing by early summer. The young males are very active and aggressive; and though the older males are larger, they have to engage in frequent battles to protect their territories and their mates from the younger males.

When two males are fighting, they circle warily about each other, each trying to grab the other by a forefoot. If this hold is secured, the lizard that has gripped the other then flips over on its back. This throws its opponent clear over itself and it lands with a thud upside down. The thrown lizard never seems to be hurt by this maneuver and may eventually win the fight. If opportunity offers, a fighting lizard will grab its foe's tail and try to snap it off, but I have never seen one succeed in doing so. This, it seems to me, indicates that lizards may have some control over the ease with which their tails are broken.

Fence lizards establish territories much as birds do, and they dispute over boundaries in much the same way. Strong or especially aggressive males may have several mates, each controlling her own small portion of his larger territory. The females are smaller than the males and are usually a lighter color, but both sexes change the intensity of their coloring so frequently that sometimes the female of a pair will be darker than her mate. Most adults are very dark when they first become active on cool mornings, perhaps because this dark hue absorbs more of the sun's rays and thus helps them to warm up faster. Some dark individuals have spots of dull red on the back.

While a lizard's color may vary greatly at different times, there is also some variation between individuals. Two females that frequented the same cement-block wall were slightly different in size. The larger one was always light gray, while the smaller one was quite dark. These both belonged to the same male, and all three of these lizards became very tame. They would come into my hand to take mealworms; and if I sat in a chair near them, they would come and climb over me in hopes of being fed.

Many lizards about my garden have become tame enough to feed from my hand, and I have found them exceedingly alert and interesting creatures. Repeatedly they have shown me that they recognize the whole of me as an individual, and when I offer a mealworm in my hand, they look into my eyes before accepting or declining the bait. Those that refuse to come to me usually turn away so that the tail is pointing at me and then vibrate it very rapidly. I have never been sure of the significance of this act but have seen it in more than one species.

Fence lizards recognize the dangerous creatures in their environment just as readily as they distinguish those which are acceptable to them as food. One day I tossed mealworms one at a time where they would be equal distance from three creatures: a male fence lizard, a female granite spiny lizard, and a bird—a California thrasher. Neither lizard had any fear of the much larger bird and would even snatch mealworms right out of its beak if the thrasher were not alert to prevent this. Yet I have seen these same lizards seek safety when they saw a roadrunner, a large cuckoolike bird that eats lizards, approaching fifty feet away. Both the thrasher and the roadrunner have rather long legs, long tails, and long beaks; but the lizards do not confuse the two birds. One is to be feared; the other is not to be feared. Nor do they show fear of any of the other birds around my garden, except the jays. Jays often hop after lizards, but I have not seen them catch one. Roadrunners, however, feed on lizards regularly, and so do sparrow hawks, or kestrels, but sparrow hawks do not come into my garden.

Probably some fence lizards are eaten by house cats, skunks, opossums, and such creatures; but these prowlers are active mostly at night when lizards are snugly hidden away in small crevices. A few hibernating lizards and small ones may be discovered and eaten by shrews. But, next to the roadrunner, the most serious threat to the fence lizards in my garden are striped racers and king snakes. Both of these snakes hunt lizards. One day, I watched a fence lizard that was, in turn, watching a foraging racer. The lizard was the same shade of gray as the granite rock on which it was perched, and it remained completely motionless as long as the snake was near. Fence lizards also fear some others of their tribe, such as the whiptails and alligator lizards, which eat smaller lizards.

Each female fence lizard lays several clutches of eggs during the summer, and the earliest broods of young may be half grown by the time the last ones hatch in the fall. The eggs are somewhat larger than navy beans, oval, leathery-skinned, and when first laid appear creamy-yellow from the color of the yolk within. They are laid in earth which retains some moisture and also gets warmth from the sun. Time of laying depends upon the weather. In some years the first eggs may be laid as early as May. Baby fence lizards first appear in my garden in late July, and others hatch at intervals until about the end of September.

In 1955, the first matings that I saw were on March 28. There was much chilly weather after this, during which the lizards were hibernating, and I could not determine just when the eggs were laid. As I have observed to be usual with most lizards at the time of mating, one female was already quite distended by the size of the ova she was carrying. For about a month I saw her occasionally on warm days and noticed that she was getting heavier and heavier, and then I failed to see her again. Possibly a roadrunner caught her, for during this same period her mate lost his tail.

This dropping off of the tail is a well-known phenomenon common to most lizards and may frequently be the means of saving the lizard's life. Any predator grabbing the lizard by the tail will be left with only that wriggling appendage while the lizard escapes. The lizard then grows a new tail. Rarely, a lizard is found with a forked tail, caused by some injury.

Fence lizards live over much of the United States and are also called swifts or scaly lizards. They are much rougher than many lizards, as each scale, down the center, has a keel that extends out into a spiny point. Fence lizards feed largely on insects. They are quite useful and deserve our protection, but they also merit our sympathy because of the interesting role they play in the animal and plant community.

My Greater Sandhill Cranes

DAYTON O. HYDE

DARK AGAINST THE GOLDEN OREGON SUNSET THE CRANES came, in stately silhouette. The eerie, darkening pines seemed to reach up at them as they passed with measured beat, four greater sandhills with their necks outstretched, dignified, solemn, effortless, cleaving the warm, sweet meadow air with leisurely grace. My saddle horse, young, green, and nervous, snorted at their passing shadows, monstrous and distorted, racing across the meadows. The cranes set their wings, talking among themselves, and banked about in a slow, easy circle. What lonely marsh had homed them for this day; what watery sequestered draw had fed them, echoed with their strident, challenging cry? Suddenly they were upon me, churning the air with noisy, braking wings. My terrorized colt plunged, squealed, and ducked his head. For one wild moment, I had joined the cranes, arms outstretched, solemn, effortless, while my horse careened off crazily into the gathering gloom. One crane pecked at my shoelaces, another tweaked my ear lovingly, another speared at the brim of my battered hat, while the fourth, unconcernedly, bowed an invitation to the dance.

These four young greater sandhill cranes are pals of mine—at times. All four were raised one season from a single pair of pinioned breeders that were the result of an experimental sandhill crane breeding research program I began in 1953. It was a program of need, forged in the fires of sorrow. I lived then, as I do now, in one of the last breeding strongholds of the greater sandhill crane. For years they were the harbingers of my spring. I remember that year —the days of scanning empty heavens, eyes burning with the brightness of the cold, crusty snows. Suddenly, from so high above as to be imperceptible, a strange croaking floated down upon the valley; then, small specks appeared, like light ashes caught in some strange, endless vortex of the winds, a mobile of the gods, circling, croaking, flapping, soaring. Suddenly they had come home; now the snow softened and the cold was forgotten; the empty stillness of the winter burst with the boisterous calling of the dancing sandhill cranes.

But it was a year of sorrow. I watched a lonely female feeding quietly in the marshes near her last year's nest. She did not join the dancing but wandered soberly alone, scanning the heavens for a mate that never came. Out of thirty-four greater sandhill cranes that had migrated the fall before, only eight had returned.

I had never before been concerned for them; like many others, I had accepted them as a part of the natural scene, something that would never vanish. Like other people, I hadn't realized that the great flocks of cranes which arrived in the spring were not really *Grus canadensis tabida,* the greater sandhill crane, but *Grus canadensis canadensis,* the little brown crane. These smaller cranes nest in the Far North and have not been threatened as have the greater sandhills, the Florida sandhill, and the Cuban sandhill, which have been driven out of most of their natural ranges by the advance of man. Lawrence H. Walkinshaw, in his book *The Sandhill Cranes,* placed the last strongholds of the greater sandhill as Oregon and Michigan and estimated their numbers at about from thirteen hundred to eighteen hundred.

Determined that the greater sandhill should never disappear from my scene, I pondered my best course. What could I do to be of some help? Could I establish a controlled breeding flock before their need was desperate?

Such a program had, of necessity, a slow and cautious beginning. Out in our meadows, while I worked rescuing the nests of Canada geese from high water, I found a flooded nest of a sandhill crane, built on a drifting island in a canal. It had floated up with the rising water, but was entangled in barbed wire and soon to go under. Valiantly, the hen stuck with her nest, but soon she was forced to seek the bank. I soon had one of the eggs in an incubator. This egg produced our first sandhill crane, the first of many.

Basically, our program had four facets: incubation and rearing techniques; the development of feeds and medication; breeding techniques; and, most important, the development of methods of production that would enable us to adjust artificially produced cranes to the wild. Constantly through the next years, we kept trying new methods, striving to simplify and to better. Not until three years later did our research come to the end of its first full cycle with the breeding of our captive-hatched birds. For the first time we were able to assimilate our facts and come up with some findings that may make the future of the cranes brighter.

In our trials and errors, we found that, while we have been able to hatch cranes successfully in incubators, the most successful method was the old-fashioned use of a bantam hen of good size and proved worth. Managed wisely, the bantam foster mothers hatch the goose-sized eggs perfectly, help interest the newborn crane chicks in food, and are an important soothing influence on them. As with many young birds, the young cranes have little interest in food for several hours after hatching. We use crushed earthworms to start them eating. The food is offered to them with our fingers or in forceps, in bright light. A good bantam hen is invaluable for a difficult chick, since she picks up a worm, offers it to the chick, drops it, taps the ground beside it, clucks lightly to it, and very often starts the chick eating. Using a hen as an aid, we have started many young cranes with no trouble.

We now give each bantam but a single crane egg to hatch. There is usually a three-day difference between the time a sandhill crane lays and incubates her first egg, and the time she lays the second. Thus there is usually a three-day difference between chicks and for some reason, the older chick refuses to tolerate the younger. Time and time again, in my observation of wild cranes, I have seen the hen leave the nest with two downy young, to find only one with her at the time of my next observation. I have long suspected that the predator involved was the older chick, and recent research convinces me of it. Any assault by the older chick upon the younger, even at the age of two days, produces in the younger chick a panic that sometimes lasts for an hour after the older chick is removed. Struggling blindly to escape, the young crane beats itself against any obstacle. In one such panic, a young chick fled across a twelve-foot stream, found a small crack in the fence, and ran several hundred yards through a meadow. Still running and exhausted when caught, it had clearly no intention of returning.

In this very manner, crane chicks in the field may be lost from their parents. I do not mean to imply that sandhills never raise two chicks in the wild, but I do believe that this antagonism of the elder chick toward the younger may seriously limit their production. Broods of two growing young have, in my observation been almost a rarity, yet the majority of crane nests contain two eggs. Dr. Walkinshaw, in *The Sandhill Cranes,* states, "Of 27 pairs of cranes in Calhoun County, Michigan, 15 (55.55%) raised young to the first fall. Of an estimated 54 eggs (two per pair), 18 (33.33%) produced full-grown young the first autumn."

Our program of feeding has become simplified with every season. We now start the cranes eating with earthworms, then switch to wet calves' liver, cut in thin strips and dipped in a high-protein broiler ration, which is fortified with antibiotics. The chicks are soon eating great quantities of liver. A deep container of broiler ration gives them a spot to probe with their beaks. They soon acquire the taste and feed themselves. When full-grown, they are switched to a commercial turkey breeder ration and whole oats. At no time is moldy food present, since this might result in the fungus disease, *Aspergillosus,* for which prevention seems to be the only "cure."

Even though some remarkable work has been done with rare birds by artificial insemination to fertilize the females, our cranes that we keep for breeders have never had problems of infertility. Hatched in captivity, fed the best high-protein feeds, and pinioned by clipping four feathers at the tip of one wing, they have a large acreage in which to roam, complete with natural food, marshes, and a running stream. Often, the wild cranes come in to visit. Here, from one pair of breeders, we gathered two clutches of two eggs each, and hatched four buff-colored cranes, gosling-sized. In each clutch, behavior was typical; the older chick persecuted the younger and all four of them had to be raised separately. Any attempt at reconciliation during the course of their growth resulted in a few minutes' peace and then—mayhem! Only when they were fully grown were we able to reconcile them to living peacefully together. These four young birds taught us much. They showed us that our simplified diet can produce perfect physical specimens, and for the first time enabled us to work out a system of feed control along with the freedom of wild birds.

When the young cranes were large enough that there was no risk to them of predation by horned owls, we gave them their freedom, feeding them daily at dawn and dusk. They soon established the habit of spending the night's dangerous hours with us, yet they developed magnificent powers of flight and spent most of their time far afield, feeding in the marshes, leg-deep in the blue lakes of penstemon, camas lily, and gentian. They were accepted by the wild sandhill cranes, with which they consorted daily. They were intelligent birds, easily conditioned to danger; and it is perfectly conceivable that we might raise young to any degree of wildness, even to the point of never having seen a man, or better yet, conditioned to regard man as a potential enemy.

It seems to be a conceit of man that he can change crane instincts through a generation or two in captivity. He might mask the instinct, but given expression it can well up and flow as purely as ever. The parents of these four cranes had been born in captivity, yet these four became wild and filled with beautiful, natural instincts. Even the instinct to migrate was there. One day in the fall, there seemed to be a restlessness about them. They followed me for a time in the fields, as they so loved to do, but I knew what was welling up deep inside them. They flew low over me where I worked, calling to me with words that were strange and unintelligible. I called to them, but for the first time they did not answer. Soon they were in the mighty vortex of flight, spiraling ever higher and higher; and soon the vortex itself began to drift southward and then was lost to view over the southern mountains.

Wild birds usually return, in their second spring, to the area where they were hatched. We have successfully populated lonely valleys with Canada geese where none had nested in twenty years, by bringing in eggs, hatching, rearing, and releasing the birds in the valley to be populated. These geese have migrated and returned to the valley as adults to breed. In a like manner, the greater sandhill might be reestablished in those portions of its range that are still suitable. Surplus crane eggs from captive breeders could be distributed and hatched at the area in which the stocking of the cranes was to be made. A sandhill crane egg, from captive stock, placed in a wild nest beside a wild egg, hatches out into a specimen just as wild and able to adjust to a dangerous world as its wild nest-mate.

There are people who maintain that if a wild species fails to adjust to a changing world then it deserves to die out. I am not one of them. Man has put the natural world about him to a terrible strain, and it is his moral responsibility to help species adjust to the changes in their world that he has made. I shall long remember a tourist who once stopped beside the road near me and gazed with some excitement at a pair of sandhill cranes feeding nearby. He had to share his happiness with me. "Mister," he said, "I'm from the Middle West, and I haven't seen a sandhill crane in twenty-five years."

Life among my sandhill cranes can be humorous—in an exasperating sort of way. To the cranes, I am more than a benefactor; I am the chosen leader of the gang, and it is often well-nigh impossible to escape their companionship. They often accompany me on long rides over the meadows, feeding unconcernedly until I am almost out of sight. Then, with worried calls, they fly after me, land in front of my horse, and are immediately nonchalant again. Faced with a busy day, I often tried to escape them and would be trying to corral some wild cattle, or stealing a ride on a nervous colt, when here would come my gang for a closer look, swooping down from the heavens, blasting my day's work into chaos. They are like a flock of mosquitoes; one is never safe from them unless one enters the house, and then they peer in at the doors in bafflement, often flying over the house, investigating all windows and the chimney to see that I don't escape. When I surrender, they are as unconcerned as ever and stroll along behind, feeding as they go, stabbing a dragonfly off a tansy stalk with pinpoint accuracy.

Their long bills are always probing. My wife finished planting a long row of strawberry plants only to find that they had pulled out every one behind her. Try to dig a can of earthworms to go fishing and they'll beat you to every worm. Dig a ditch and they'll superintend every moment. Hang up the wash, and they'll soon have the white garments muddy with their beaks. Let an airplane fly over, and they tip their heads back and clamor with indignation. To bend over to tie one's shoes (which they have untied), is to risk losing the buttons on one's back pocket. To my old setter dog they are the curse of many a summer day; they know her favorite resting spots and never, never let her sleep. Let a strange dog jump from a visitor's auto, however, and they are immediately airborne, fleeing to the fields like the wild birds they are.

To see the cranes dance, one has only to toss a small stick into the air. It is seized by the nearest crane, which tosses it in turn, and the bouncing, bowing, flapping dance is on. However aggravating their ways, one can't help liking the birds. I remember a very solemn, dignified, gray-haired cowboy of sixty-five who came to work for us. Whatever feelings the man had he kept completely to himself, and we were certain he thought us strange people to have all these cranes about. My fears vanished as I came around the corner of the barn one morning. There was the grizzled, old cowboy in a ring with the dancing cranes. Hat in hand, arms flapping, a wide grin on his face, he was bounding a good three feet in the air with every jump!

The Handsome Little Ringtail

NORMAN G. WOOLSEY

One Christmas Eve, the Pitt family that lives on the side of Camelback Mountain near Phoenix, Arizona, were gathered around their Christmas tree, opening gifts and awaiting Christmas guests. Suddenly some packages tumbled from a shelf in the darkened corner of their living room. Thinking that the boxes had been improperly stacked the Pitts replaced them. Seconds later the boxes fell again. Switching on an overhead light, the family got the surprise of their lives. An unscheduled furry guest with bright "night" eyes blinked at them in wonderment, then all two and a half pounds of it swished down the hall and into the basement.

The pleasant and ordinarily shy little visitor to the Pitt family was a wild ringtail, or *Bassariscus,* which they thought must have fallen into the house through a grating. The Pitts say that the ringtail must have liked the apples and other edibles it found, for even though they left the door open, it refused to leave. It remained hidden out of reach behind the furnace in the basement. It slept during the day, but came out at night to collect food, then returned to its cache in cozy comfort. The Pitts grew fond of it and considered it a permanent member of the family.

The ringtail, or ringtail-cat as it is sometimes called, is named for its long, bushy tail, which has seven black and white bars across it. In parts of the country it is also called cacomistle, coon-cat, and bassarisk. Its scientific name is *Bassariscus astutus,* and it is in a family by itself (Bassariscidae), which is between the raccoon and weasel families. Considered by many the most appealing of all our furry mammals, the ringtail has the face of a fox and the body of a buffy-gray marten. Its tail is the approximate length of the head and body; and the broad, black bands give the ringtail a conspicuous and fascinating appearance shared by no other North American animal.

Although the ringtail is a common resident over a great part of the southwestern United States and southward to Costa Rica, few persons have ever seen it. Normally it is exceedingly shy, keeps to dark crevices and caves, and preys on mice and wood rats. Miners and ranchers of the Southwest frequently capture young ringtails, and they quickly become useful pets that destroy rats and mice.

One summer, while working as a forest guard in the Mogollon Mountains of New Mexico, I had an opportunity to become quite well acquainted with this animal. I first became aware of the presence of this little night fellow when I saw its small, catlike, five-toed tracks around the cabin yard one morning. Although ringtails were quite common in the Lower Sonoran and Transition life zones, I was somewhat surprised to find them at elevation 7500 feet, in the yellow pine and aspen belts. The next few days I encouraged the animal's company by leaving scraps of meat and fruit in a coffee can at the doorstep. In the morning the can would be cleaned of its contents, but the interesting little mammal would leave before daylight.

Two weeks passed before I got my first look at the ringtail. I had left the door open and had purposely placed the coffee can, filled with scraps, on the threshold. About dusk I lit the lantern and sat facing the door from a darkened far corner of the cabin. At length I heard the coffee can rattle. As I glanced up I saw a delicately pointed face watching me curiously. Its eyes, accentuated by whitish circles around them, gave its foxlike face an appearance of being all eyes. Suddenly it flipped its barred tail and scampered away. It stopped just beyond the ring of lantern light and peeked back furtively at me.

I sat very quietly for perhaps five minutes, and soon it was back. This time it got hold of the can with its teeth and pulled it out of the door, where it dropped it with a clatter, spilling the bits of food. The noise didn't alarm the ringtail greatly, and presently it was back, crunching the food greedily. As the days passed it became braver, until at last it was entering the cabin and hunting bits of food under the table and searching the cupboard and shelves for other delicacies. With its now nightly presence in the cabin, I noticed the sudden disappearance of some mice that had been eating my food supplies.

Though the little ringtail never allowed me to pet it, it became so tame that it would leap upon my bunk in a playful manner and run across my feet. Then, with a cat's springy grace, it would jump to the window sill, then on the cabin wall, where it would cling without effort and switch its long tail back and forth in a manner that suggested it was completely happy in its new home.

In the latter part of July, the summer rains came and I was released from my position as fire guard. Before leaving the isolated mountain cabin, I cut a hole, two and a half inches in diameter, in the floor, large enough for my pet to come and go. On the inside of the door, before I left, I tacked a note:

"There's a pet ringtail that uses the cabin. Treat him to scraps and he'll repay by destroying rats."

What disposition was made of my pet I never knew until two years passed, when, mostly by chance, I was in the area and visited the old forest cabin. A college student had taken over as forest guard during that summer; and when I told him about a pet ringtail that used to frequent the place, he pointed to a box in the corner. There, dozing cozily on some old clothing, was a family of four ringtails. No doubt these were all progeny of my pet of former years, which through gradual trust of man and in response to his kindness, had grown to be as tame as any domestic pet.

The ringtail's young—usually two to four in number—are born in May or June. The den site almost always is in some crevice high up on the face of a bluff; but occasionally its dens have been found in hollow trees. The ringtail, with its semiretractible claws and the springy, curved, hind legs of a cat, is as much at home in the trees as in the bluffs. Its thick fur is golden brown on the back to light-gray on the underparts, and is used by some furriers. Economically, it is much more valuable in rodent control than as a furbearer, and its unique and appealing ways make it a highly desirable pet.

Owls are probably the most serious of the ringtail's natural enemies, the chief reason being that the ringtail hunts only at night. It never strays far from its natural habitat of bluffs and trees. Snakes, too, probably take young ringtails during the ringtail's denning season.

The presence of the ringtail in southwestern areas of the United

States always is a source of deep interest to the naturalist who is fortunate enough to see this shy and handsome furbearer as it streaks up and over the bluffs and cliffs in the bright moonlight. You can be sure that it strikes terror to rats and mice as there, under the desert stars, it enacts the time-old battle of the hunter and the hunted.

The Immortal Toughy

MYRTLE MORROW WILLIAMS

TOUGHY MALONE WAS A WAG. JUST A VIRGINIA mockingbird, but with such an abundance of what it takes that for four years, summers and winters, he drew us and our guests to the garden or the bow window with the pull of a circus parade. To watch Toughy and his antics; to see the product of his mischief, his slyness, and his plots to prove his superiority in his little world was a source of entertainment that never palled. We named him Toughy because he was a tough; and Malone because of his belligerency plus the fact that a bird with his individuality called for more than just a front name.

He attracted our attention the first winter we lived in Virginia; in fact, he furnished the inspiration that eventually made it possible for him to indulge his waggish instincts—perhaps to develop them. To wit, he made us so bird-conscious that we began putting out feed at once—come one, come all. And all kinds came. They became his subjects. It was upon these that he practiced his impish humors and among these that he demonstrated his ability as terrorist. But, I'll state here that, when raising a family, he did not stop at birds for victims. Anything on legs came under the jurisdiction of Toughy when the paternal urge stirred him. Nor was he practicing prankishness then. No, indeed! Being a father was deadly serious business!

That first winter when we noticed him, Toughy was a solemn-looking object and the only mocker that hung around. We thought him pathetic. So orphaned, dependent and apprehensive of life; sitting on the porch railing silhouetted against the snow. He would never be able to take it, we thought; never survive the season. He must be delicate, exotic. How wrong we were! That was before we knew Toughy and his unconquerable spirit. Anyway, that's when we built the bird-feeding platform for him.

He was a handsome figure, once aware of him; darker gray than others of his kind that we remembered seeing around in early and late spring. His body was bigger and brawnier and his legs longer. The white band on each of his wings was broader and whiter. And when he took off for a reconnaissance whirl, the white of his tail was a wide flash of snowy beauty, wider and whiter than most. We soon realized he had personality plus, for he sold us the idea that really he would have gone south with the rest of his folks only he'd taken such a terrible shine to us that he couldn't bear to leave. He had plenty of appeal and *oomph* and all the rest. One session with Mr. Toughy Malone and you were his for life.

At once he took to the feeding platform (something most birds shy away from for a while), thus demonstrating a bolder, freer attitude toward life than we had thought; and for days he stuffed in lonely splendor—raisins and cake crumbs, suet and apples. We gave him de luxe service. We placed the platform on a post among evergreen shrubbery, for safety from cats—near a spruce he could use for night coverage and around the corner from some holly trees, the berries of which might serve as a change in diet when his appetite grew fickle. Mr. Malone led the life of Mr. Reilly. Then, gossip got around and, of course, food smells, too. Other birds began to flirt with the idea of taking a chance on such tempting goodies and soon there were more and more customers. Toughy let them alone at first; he was bighearted and no bird-in-the-manger. . .besides, he wasn't paying the check. They ate in turns, wary-eyed and ready to fly at a moment's notice, but they ate. And they ate. And then, life went sour to Toughy. His table wasn't being kept in the manner to which he had become accustomed. . .particularly in the matter of apples.

Came the dawn of the hour when Toughy could stand no more. It was just midafternoon but only the shell of an apple was left! There was cracked corn and scratch feed that the other birds could use but he couldn't. His bill couldn't manage it. Besides, he'd been used to a snack of fruit just before going to bed, and now—there was no snack! But he kept his temper and used his head. We saw him sitting in a juniper at the corner of the garden watching and thinking; and, although looking so calm, he was undoubtedly coming closer to the boil every minute. Suddenly he flew straight at the platform—a ball-of-fire on the wing, but he didn't even alight. He barely brushed the branches of shrubbery. That was enough, however. Birds scattered in every direction and stayed scattered until hunger or greed lured them back. He let them alone for a bit then came at them again from another direction, from around the corner of the house where he had been hiding. And he kept this up periodically until their bedtime.

From then on he played this game. . .some days many times; hiding now one place, now another; waiting until a congregation was gathered and placidly eating. Then, like an army with banners, a gray and white streak hurtled through the air and birds flew in every direction as if a bomb were bursting. He didn't do this through spite but through mischief; we could tell by the impish lilt in his tail as he fetched up from a raiding expedition. He had had his revenge for the apple that first day. He'd wiped that out. Also, we had kept him better supplied with apples thereafter. But the spirit of the chase got into him and he liked to show off.

He didn't care how big the bird was, either, or its possibilities for fight. Wicked-billed woodpecker or large woodland dove or stocky cardinal—they were all the same to him. Not even a blue jay dared push him around. He would tangle with anything and truly was formidable looking as he swooped forward, hunched down, wings spread; drawing a baleful bead on the thing he was after. Just one bird stood up to Toughy Malone. He was a song sparrow—he had a sparrow for a mother, but we're positive his daddy was an eagle. He took Toughy's rarin' around as a joke and a bluff; flipped his tail and maybe side-stepped an inch, but was always still there on the platform when the smoke lifted. And Toughy could have gobbled him up and thought he was swallowing a bug, he was that tiny. We called him Kid Snitzle. Toughy tolerated him; but there came a time when something occurred that must have made all the birds, including Toughy, admire the Kid extravagantly.

One winter's day over a foot of unprecedentedly heavy snow covered the feeding platform. Until it could be cleared away, the birds hung around and did nothing, Toughy as unconstructive as the others. Due to the weight of the heavier birds, vainly wishing to get at the grain but doing nothing about it, and also due to the process of melting, the snow soon sagged in one spot, making a toboggan slide straight to the coveted food. Not a bird took advantage, however, not even Toughy. Go down there into that cavern? Stick their heads in a new-fangled trap and get caught? Not they! They were too smart!

But, they weren't smart enough. And the intrepid Kid was. With but little time wasted in surveying the situation, he took the plunge; practically rolled up his trousers and after a long breath, seated himself on his haunches and slid down the tobaggon. And it paid. Triumphant and cozy, down under, he gorged himself at his leisure and without competition. How he got out is the Kid's own secret; but after a while we saw his head emerge, then his body, and we guessed he did it the hard way—tooth and toenail. We may have imagined the leer of satiety on his face. At any rate, he won the respect of all present, and from then on the Kid strutted the platform unmolested.

Mr. Malone's mild, relaxed moments, when he cut out his clownish capers, came in the spring—courting and mating time. High on the top of a black gum was a branch, forked and leafless, and every afternoon Toughy could be seen swaying on this fork, comfy as if in a rocker and old slippers, singing his heart out. Endless trills, arias, cadenzas or what have you, poured from his throat. In between improvisations he mimicked every bird we knew and plenty we didn't. It was a concert aimed to melt the heart of any feathered maiden. Whether he married for keeps and caroled thus to a steady wife of his bosom or whether each year he went courting anew, we didn't know. Mrs. Malone (or the Mrs. Malones) kept demurely in the background as befitted the helpmate of a type like Toughy, and she (or they) had no particular characteristics by which we could tell. I will admit, however, that in view of what happened four years later, there are doubts in our minds as to the emotional constancy of Toughy. However, he may have been a widower by then. Who can say?

When Toughy became a father he was even more of a changed man. Parenthood seemed to bring out the Mr. Hyde in him, and he more than lived up to the name we had given him. Tough and hard-boiled, he was full of fire and brimstone for all comers on the garden side of the house. That was his bailiwick. He threatened persons; he pecked the dogs; he pecked the cats— one of them, at least. He swarmed over that one and chased her clear to the house, pecking steadily at the base of her tail. He did the same thing to dogs. The other cat had more of Toughy's caliber; either he hid under chairs or a hedge or he turned over on his back with four paws extended, daring his tormentor to come nearer. And Toughy did go nearer . . .nearer and nearer. Snarling every inch of the way, with dancing little side steps, then a hop into the air, he came so close to his four-legged baiter we held our breath. He knew how near was safe, however.

We never saw the Malone nest nor their children until they were up and doing. But we often saw evidence of the care with which they were surrounded; the wide, wing-spread hoverings of the parents when a cat or any danger appeared like the umbrella of planes we threw over our advancing armies during the last war. We witnessed also a comical display of the divergent views on discipline for the young that Mr. and Mrs. Malone held. Mrs. M. apparently went in for new ideas; Father M. was definitely old-fashioned. It was one afternoon on the occasion of a trip to the feeding platform by the parents and one youngster. The lad knew how to eat; the great sputtering lummox was well developed and no nestling, but the brat in him was uppermost that day. He stood on a board that partially protected the platform; looked down on his parents; stamped his feet with spleen and yelled for service. The give and take of conversation between his elders was probably this:

"Let him express himself," says Mrs. Malone, placidly nibbling cookies and raisins. "He'll come out of it if you leave him alone."

"Express himself? He-eck!" raged her jittery spouse. "He's got to learn to shift for himself! I'll teach him!" And with a rush at the insubordinate young mocker he suddenly remembered his wife was watching, deflected his course, and pretended to be going for suet.

But Papa Malone couldn't hold on to this Spartan self-discipline. He tried to ignore the racket; then his nerves frayed, and with a mouthful of food he dashed over and crammed it down the youngster's throat. Young Malone didn't impress his mother, however. Her system won out. He finally recognized the truism that a man helps himself more if he helps himself; the youngster came down off his perch and the battle ended. I can imagine Mrs. M. making a noise like a wife on the way home and saying:

"You see? I told you so."

And so, each year for four years, we entertained and were entertained by Toughy. Then, as all good things eventually come to an end, one March his saga was completed. I reveal it with reluctance for it's not a worthy ending. He didn't pass out heroically . . . gobbled up by a cat while defending his young, nor did he freeze or starve to death. Women were his undoing!

One winter he packed off his family to a warmer climate and loafed in our garden—alone, as usual. Then came a Sunday afternoon early in March. The weather was mild and warm with hints of spring that tickled a young man's fancy. Toughy was not young now, by bird standards, but apparently he wanted to be. I had thought all winter that he looked more solitary than usual; melancholy and, at times, even droopy. His attacks at the crowds on the platform lacked the verve and dash of earlier days. This Sunday I had watched him pecking at his apple outside the big library window and was disturbed by his listless manner.

Suddenly, as if from nowhere, with indescribable twitters of excitement and jaunty bustling, a flock of birds appeared. They were young mockers, slim and so freshly feathered that their pale gray and white colors seemed vivid. They hovered over the feeding station . . . now on it, now flirting and fluttering in the air. And they chirped and cheeped for all the world like a bunch of giggling schoolgirls. I counted seven, when I could count them, but they were so full of animation it was difficult to follow their movements. Seven is good enough, however; the appearance of a septet of young southern belles would make a difference in any man's life. I lost sight of Toughy as this galaxy of beauty, bubbling gaiety and charm took over. I was too occupied with watching the streamlined girl orchestra.

They flew to the skeleton awning frame that hangs over the terrace; chased one another playfully—or maybe it was Toughy they were after; romped and then all together flew to an oak tree. For a few minutes that old oak blossomed with gayness and the giddy essence of youth. Then came a burst of melody, an aria of incredible sweetness; from one throat only, maybe Toughy's . . . maybe his farewell to us who had cared for him, his swan song . . . and then all the mockingbirds were gone. And we never saw Toughy again. Some overpowering impulse must have possessed him, born of winter loneliness and depression; and he thought; What the heck, you're only young once—and went off with the bevy of beauties.

There is another mocker that spends the winters in our garden now; a smaller, less lively bird. We don't know whether he is Toughy's ghost (if Toughy is dead) or a scion of the Malone family, who, while sitting at his papa's knee, absorbed and vowed to carry on the spirit and traditions of the Malone dynasty. So far, the Malone mischief hasn't shown up in him. But he's young yet. We'll give him time.

One summer night, after Toughy had gone, with the moon a round silvery lantern and the air fragrant with honeysuckle, a mocker throbbed his song of ecstacy in the old gum tree. It sounded like Toughy at one of his matinee performances—Toughy in good voice and full of love in the springtime. And maybe it was. Maybe it was Toughy sounding off through one of his young ones. We like to think so, anyway.

The Horned Toad — Desert Oddity

LORUS J. and MARGERY J. MILNE

OF ALL THE WILD NATIVE ANIMALS FAMILIAR TO THE American public, probably none rank higher than the bear, fox, wolf, and eagle. In every newspaper they appear in one guise or another, often as characters in cartoons. Similarly the old nickel with its bison turns up in each handful of change. Yet nationally recognized as these animals are, not one of them achieves the local esteem of a certain small lizard in Texas. You can't carry a live eagle or bison around in your pocket, but many a western child has wailed over the loss of his pet "horny toad."

The horned "toad" (a lizard) living so deep in the heart of Texans, is brown-flecked and sand-colored. Its back is rough, as though someone had rubbed its dry scales the wrong way. An angular head bears a crest of tapered spines only a little less sharp than the needles of the prickly pear. Over the arid plains this mouse-sized creature scampers—a symbol of adaptability—finding food and shelter in deserts man has just begun to know.

The horned toad is one of the very few lizards that makes no great attempt to run away. If you pick it up (and many people want to), the creature's little black eyes seem lidless as they stare at you. The body stiffens from head to tail, and only the throat pulsates. The animal is busy pumping air, and soon its small body is a flattened balloon, fairly firm to the touch, rounded in all its contours. Between fore and hind legs, a scale-fringed border curves to the back where the roughness of the darker top surface meets the smooth pale underside. The short, spine-studded tail sticks out straight, tapering to a point like a kitten's. Four sturdy legs cling to your fingers with clear, hooked claws. But unless you turn the trusting reptile on its back, it offers little resistance to being handled. Even the back and horns may be stroked without the lizard doing more than closing its eyes. Scratching the belly surface leads the creature to alert itself, and puff more air inside.

Left to itself, the horned toad deflates its body. It can run like a chipmunk, but most of its time is spent in standing still. With forelegs stretched to raise head and shoulders well above the ground, it peers intently for insects within reach. If an insect comes into view, the lizard watches it awhile, then creeps toward it. As the horned toad stalks the bug, it curls its tail jerkily from side to side like a cat, its excitement evidenced only in this one amusing gesture. Otherwise the horned toad seems all too slow and careful. Within a step of the insect, the lizard stops, twists its head into the best possible position, and makes a sudden dart at its prey. Like a flash the horned toad's mouth opens and a soft sticky tongue darts out to flick the bug into the ample throat. Then the reptile steps back a pace and, with head held up, parts its lips a trifle and shows its tongue again, with all the satisfaction of a man who has just finished a particularly enjoyable dinner.

Horned toads seem especially fond of ants, and often settle beside an ant trail to pick up the workers coming along it in either direction. Given an opportunity, however, the lizard will attack even grasshoppers as long as its own body. In managing such a big insect, the chief requirement for its success seems to be to start at the head end. The little reptile studies the situation before making the first bite. If it is successful, the horned toad throws head and shoulders into a perfect frenzy, twisting and switching the jaws from side to side, pressing the prey against the ground, and at the same time backing up rapidly to keep its struggling victim from getting crosswise in its mouth. Soon nothing remains to be swallowed but the wing tips and hind feet of the 'hopper. Two minutes later the lizard may be looking for new prey. Opportunity knocks all too seldom in the desert, and insects are this reptile's sole source of both food and drink.

Through a strip of our country parallel to the Mexican border, the roadrunner, a bird of the Southwest, is a constant menace to the horned toad population. Otherwise this creature seems remarkably free from enemies and may owe its placid disposition to its relative freedom from danger.

Each horned toad matches the ground on which it normally lives. Over the yellow sands of Texas, the eight brown marks on a tan back blend with pebbles and fallen leaves so that only a practiced eye will see the lizard as it crouches motionless. Where the earth is full of limestone particles, as on the Pecos plains, horned toads are paler, almost ashy in their coloration, so that again they are very inconspicuous. And as one journeys through New Mexico and northward to the Okanagan Valley of British Columbia, or westward to the Pacific coast, the desert areas have other kinds of horned toads. Some have shorter horns; some, great regal crowns; but all bear on their backs patterns and hues that match the land they inhabit. Where lava beds lie in the midst of piñon pine or ponderosa, these lizards may have two distinct forms within a mile or less. One has an almost uniformly glossy brown-black upper surface, which blends with cinder in the *malpais,* that part of the country overlain by dark lava. The other is mottled greenish yellow and rich reddish brown, flecked with gray and black, that makes it vanish among fallen needles and flakes of pine cone. Yet both are the same kind of horned toad; only their pigments differ. Turn them over and one sees that each has a pale gray belly surface freckled with black and brown and orange.

Horned toads hibernate in winter, burying themselves to a depth of a foot or so, keeping below the point to which true frost will reach. When the spring sun warms the ground again, the lizards soon become active. By mid-June mating is underway, and in July the Texas reptiles lay soft-shelled, creamy eggs. Each egg weighs about one eighteenth as much as the parent does after she has laid them all on the sand. The astonishing feature is the number of eggs in a clutch—twenty to thirty of them—with a combined weight much greater than that of the mother. She has not only stocked each egg with food and covered it with a tough, leathery shell; but for her brood she has also extracted from the desert more than her own weight in water to add to the eggs as the "white." In the arid plains of Texas this is quite a feat!

Among the horned toads, the Texas kind is almost unique in laying eggs. Most of the others add no shell, but retain the young within the mother's body until late August when they are past their embryonic helplessness. Then for some two hours, the parent labors at six-minute intervals to bring forth each toadlet. Only thirty seconds or so is required for a birth. There on the desert sand or forest floor will lie a miniature horned toad, legs hugged to its sides, tail curled under against its belly surface. Around it is a capsule of clear liquid, enclosed in a thin, cellophanelike sac. With eyes and nostrils still closed tightly, the youngster begins to wriggle in its aquarium; and before two minutes have elapsed, it has punctured the membrane at the front end. The fluid drains away, giving off an unmistakable odor, like the albumin of a hen's egg. The pale tan toadlet stretches its head through the broken sac and begins to breathe hot desert air. A few more squirmings and the membrance slides off the hind legs and tail. The infant lizard is free. Its jet-black eyes open, and away it scampers after its parent. At twenty minutes of age the youngster's weight bears the same relationship to its mother's as did the Texan horned toad's egg. And this active baby is already rushing up to tiny ants, snapping them into its eager jaws.

From time to time each horned toad molts its skin. The old epidermis comes away in great patches like peeling sunburn, embossed with the scale pattern of the back or head or belly, cloudy but translucent. As the lizard uncovers the bright colors of its pigmented surface, something happens to its disposition. At this time most horned toads become pugnacious and, if molested, may spring a special surprise. From each eye the creature can squirt a jet of harmless blood into the face of its attacker! The quantity is small, but force directs the stream almost horizontally for five feet or more. The creature's blood vessels include mechanisms that make this possible. This is the horned toad's secret defense—a most amazing performance without duplicate in the animal kingdom.

Smoky, the Catbird

CHARLOTTE ORR GANTZ

SMOKY WAS RESPONSIBLE FOR A COMPLETE UPSET IN OUR view on birds— and a thorough job he did of it. Until his advent, we supposed that tame birds were something attainable only by raising fledglings, an undertaking that would scare me almost as much as trying to raise a baby without benefit of a doctor. Anyway, I thought you had to have infinite patience and a very special gift with animals, which I didn't pretend to have. I should never have had the nerve to offer my friendship to Smoky if he had not taken the initiative in adopting us.

One Sunday early in August, Bob (my husband) and I were standing under the silver maple in our yard when we suddenly became conscious of being stared at. Looking up, we discovered a young catbird just above our heads. We said, "Hello," but he merely looked at us solemnly without moving.

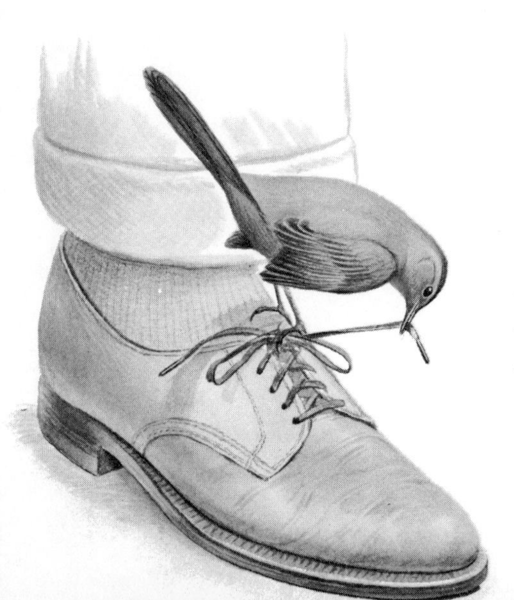

Presently, I went over to the garden to gather tomatoes. To my surprise the catbird followed and alighted on a tomato stake a few feet away. No bird had ever before shown such confidence in me, and I was flattered. Bob ran in for the camera, and Smoky and I gazed at each other in silence under the blazing Virginia sun. The picture taken, I hurried for the shade, the tomatoes in my arms; and again the catbird flew after me, this time trying to alight on the tomatoes themselves, but becoming wary and swerving just before he got there.

I put a small, very ripe tomato on the ground, and he flew right to it but couldn't break the skin. As I bent to break it in two, he backed off and opened his beak wide in a highly comical fashion—half defiant, half pathetic, as if to remind us he was only recently from the nest where food was put down his throat.

He fell upon the opened tomato ravenously. We watched while he finished it, then we gave him a second one and went inside, assuming that, like other wild things, he would prefer to eat by himself. Not at all! As soon as we left, Smoky flew up to the silver maple but the moment I returned he came right down again and went happily to work at his feast.

"If you want a nursemaid," I said, "just let me get some work to do." Smoky flew up into the tree while I collected my pen and stationery, but he came down again when I had settled myself on the bench. Half of the second tomato went the way of the first, and I wrote most of a letter. Then Bob put the remaining half of the tomato on the bench beside me. Smoky watched, then approached very cautiously, mouth wide open and feathers fluffed as if threatening me with the worst, should I move. I paid no attention but went on writing; and after a few minutes he hauled down his feathers, closed his beak, and got to work. He worried the tomato until it turned upside down. Righting it for him. I held it steady.

The tomato finished, Smoky fluttered down to my shoe and began tugging at the lacings. Then he tried my bare leg, but could get no foothold. Getting bolder, he lit on my arm, then fluttered to the paper on my lap and walked over it carefully as if studying what I had written.

Bob and I watched, thoroughly entranced, until Smoky decided he'd had enough of us and flew to a tree some distance down the lawn. This was a steadier flight than any made before he'd been fed and we congratulated ourselves on having provided food at the right time.

Our lawn became his base for operations, and he was known as my bird. He always returned to the silver maple at night. Of his past, we gleaned a little from questions around the neighborhood. He had been hatched two lawns down and had unquestionably been turned out of the nest at too early an age. For some weeks, the people there scattered food for him, but they never had tried to get near him. When strong enough, he moved to other fields and apparently foraged for himself until he selected us as his foster parents.

We took our new responsibilities very seriously. I worried because Smoky confined himself to tomatoes and wild cherries and this seemed too liquid and acid a diet. Bob, on the other hand, was concerned over his refusal to drink water. Smoky never went near the birdbath and couldn't be coaxed into drinking, even when we put water into a scooped-out tomato.

Our worries were unnecessary, for Smoky seemed to thrive. However, I worried as all good parents do—even foster ones—and tried to get him to take some bread and milk. To my amusement, he turned down the nicely moistened bread crumbs, but drank the milk with considerable satisfaction. Later I offered him dry bread crumbs and found he had no objection to them at all. He liked the crust particularly. Whenever crumbs appeared, Smoky held his beak wide open and before long he had both Bob and me trained to put crumbs into his mouth. He obviously much preferred being fed this way even though he was far too big for such babyish ways.

When he came into our lives he was able to fly, although the downiness of his head plainly showed his youth. His wing and tail feathers were not too well developed, and the tail feathers had a way of coming out. Just in time, of course, new ones came in—much bigger and stronger ones—and by the middle of September, Smoky had a proper catbird tail.

From eight to nine each morning was my hour for gardening. In this pursuit, Smoky was my unfailing companion, never missing a morning. I would pull a weed or draw my fork through the earth and then wait while Smoky disposed of the insect life. Ordinary grubs were satisfactory, and he ate ants when nothing better showed up. Occasionally I would find something that he failed to see and my efforts at imitating a mother bird's anxious feeding calls were probably extremely ludicrous. I chirped; I coaxed; I all but fluttered my arms. Smoky understood perfectly what this odd performance meant, but he had a willful streak and wouldn't always mind.

When he had had enough he would wander off for a short time—frequently upon my back, which made a fairly flat surface to wander about on as I worked down on my hands and knees. If I walked about the garden, he perched on my head or a shoulder and learned to stay on as I walked.

As he grew older Smoky's diet changed. Beetles, which involved a real chase, interested him more than the dull grubs, although he liked the big Japanese beetle larvae. Crickets also pleased him. He no longer ate his tomato with quite the same enthusiasm, but small amounts of fruit and vegetables he still welcomed.

One of our problems was Smoky's insistence on his preeminent right to the outdoor fireplace. This had been one of his favorite spots ever since we put one of the original tomatoes beside it. My approach to the fireplace, hence, was a signal for Smoky to come, too. When I started a fire my willful bird insisted on flying right into it. I used to sneak out when he wasn't around to get my litter burned—all to no avail. The sign of smoke would call him and after he evaded my outstretched hands one day and landed on some glowing coals, I gave up trying to burn anything in the outside fireplace.

The reactions of other birds to our companionship with Smoky were interesting. Generally, our joint weeding operations were done to the accompaniment of anxious chirpings and warning calls from other birds which, however, seemed not to bother my catbird at all. A neighbor told us that one day when Smoky was perched on her shoulder a cardinal had become so agitated that he flew past her face repeatedly, so close that she thought he was going to attack her. It was curious that a bird of another species should go to such limits to effect a "rescue."

Smoky himself was for weeks oblivious to the excited calls of other birds. In September, however, he began to notice other catbirds, two of whom took to frequenting the garden, evidently because of his presence here. One day, when he had just begun to eat some grapes which I was holding for him, a catbird called insistently from the rooftop. After a moment's struggle between his desire for the grape and his new interest, Smoky was off after the other bird. Sometimes a teasing catbird would call and then fly off. Smoky, ready to follow, would call and call without receiving any answer. I would then go out to comfort my slighted bird.

Finally, these pleasant weeks came to an end. The first break came one morning early in September, when he failed to show up for our daily weeding. I worked alone, feeling heartsick for fear a cat had caught him. Throughout the morning I hunted and called for him without success. Finally, in mid-afternoon, Smoky appeared on the fence looking as cool as a cucumber, as if nothing had happened. He refused to come near me, however, and throughout the week, remained aloof. He left the silver maple for a home in a different backyard, though he came to us for a few minutes each day.

Then we noticed another change in his behavior. His visits became more frequent; and he announced his coming imperiously, clinging to the porch screen and demanding attention. As soon as I set foot outside he would fairly catapult himself into my hand and eat whatever I held—but only if I *held* it. If I put it down he was no longer interested. Hitherto he had preferred to eat on the ground; but now his main interest was in feeding from our hands, not in getting food.

Apparently, like many youngsters, he had been eager to try his wings, to get out from under the parental roof. Having found that he was free to go, he came back to us with more show of attachment than ever before.

After the education that Smoky gave us, I no longer wonder that in the old fairy tales small birds were often transformed into enchanted princes. But the world being what it is, I suppose Smoky will remain a catbird.

Shag

LYNN TRIMM

WE WERE LUCKY, WE WERE ASSURED SOME YEARS AGO, TO find an apartment near Kansas State College. It had about as much space and airy comfort as a medieval dungeon. The windows were foot-high slits at ceiling level, the walls of damp plaster and the floors of clammy concrete. To add to the unhappy illusion, every time it rained we had a subterranean river flowing through the hall. To this cozy nest my husband Wayne and I brought our six-months-old fledgling, Steve. It was here that I was exposed to claustrophobia and might have developed an impressive case had it not been for the congenial companionships that resulted from entertaining wild animal guests in our backyard.

The yard was, in itself, unprepossessing. It was an expanse of unmowed buffalo grass that grew over and through an ancient strawberry bed. A half-built garage made of cinder blocks dominated the yard. A couple of disconsolate clothesline poles leaned with the prevailing winds. Two big, unpruned cottonwoods stood sentinel above battered trash and garbage cans at the far end of the lot. An unlikely place for friendships to begin and flourish, perhaps, but in our case they did not.

To prevent indoor pallor in our son, we built a wire-enclosed play yard for him. Every day when my husband had left for college, and after my household tasks were in hand, the baby and I came above ground for as many hours as we could spend in the sunlight and fresh air. Stevie spent his time solemnly pulling blades of buffalo grass to poke through the fence or digging for just the right pebble to toss at the near corner of the garage. I joined him in his grass-pulling enterprise long enough to weed the strawberry bed and in his rock-moving projects sufficiently to prop up the sad clothesline poles, then relaxed to enjoy the sunshine and to get acquainted with our animal guests as they arrived. These came to us as a result of graduate studies in zoology by my husband, Wayne, at Kansas State College. He often brought live animals home to sketch and photograph them. Of them all, Shag, the baby coyote, was our favorite.

She was brought to us when she was less than a month old. Her siblings had been killed and a bounty collected on them. The farmer's son who had kept Shag briefly was afraid she might grow up to be a chicken killer.

Shag was a typical coyote in appearance. She had long, yellowish brown fur and a pointed muzzle. She had an obvious distrust of her domestic cousins, the dogs—especially big ones. When unknown canines appeared in the yard Shag barked ferociously and bared her teeth until the strangers moved on. With a pair of bird dogs in the yard to the right, she worked out a nonaggression pact. Shag became actually friendly only with the Dalmatian puppy (of approximately Shag's own size and age) that lived in the yard to the left; and this only after a long preliminary period of wariness on Shag's part.

We installed Shag in a doghouse shelter close to the unfinished garage. We fastened a leash on her collar, which we had trouble finding in a small enough size. The leash was sufficiently long so

that Shag could visit Stevie through the play yard fence. Following an interlude of mutual indifference, the two began to show off to one another to the extent of their limited abilities.

Shag stayed out-of-doors except in rainy weather, when we brought her indoors as we would have done with a puppy. She learned quickly and after several reprimands (a rolled newspaper tapped across her nose, plus some disparaging remarks sufficed) she was dependably housebroken. On those occasions when thunder and lightning accompanied the rain, Shag became a pitiable object. With the first mutterings of thunder, she grew restless, getting as close to one of us as she could and following that person from room to room as if for reassurance. When the storm became really violent, she abandoned any pretense of bravery and cowered in a corner behind our bed. It was interesting to me to note that the corner she selected was the very one recommended to us by neighbors, who knew about such things, as being the safest shelter in a tornado.

Shag felt at home with all of us, but her affection was lavished on Wayne. Indoors or out, she spent as much time as possible curled in his lap. She reached this haven with a flying leap and settled down only after licking his chin with apparent satisfaction. She never offered such homage to me, knowing, perhaps, that squatter's rights on my lap were reserved for the baby. Shag was willing to take our word about the reliability of visiting humans and never challenged their presence in her domain. At least one human, however, questioned Shag's occupancy of our backyard. He was the tax collector in charge of dog licenses who paid us a visit one afternoon.

"Nice pup you have there," he remarked, patting Shag with one hand while whipping out a pad of blank licenses with the other.

"Is it necessary to license coyotes?" I asked.

He backed off rather suddenly. We reached prompt agreement that Shag, if kept on a leash, need not have a license, and then he departed at a comically fast pace.

Officially, Kansas holds coyotes in low esteem, since the state pays a bounty for every coyote proved killed. Even so, many farmers and ranchers of the area respect this animal and often look to it to provide a peculiar type of sport, locally called "coyote chasing." Briefly, this pits the cunning of the coyote against the speed of the greyhounds. Carrying the hounds in a crate aboard a stripped-down truck, the hunter drives over the prairie until a coyote is sighted.

Then the hounds are released and the chase is on, followed by the careening "coyote wagon." Often the coyote, seeming to know that the hounds depend more on sight than on scent for their trailing, simply tops a rise, locates a hollow on the far slope and curls up in it to watch safely as they race by. Craft and familiarity with the terrain more often than not allow the coyote to escape entirely. He is honored for his intelligence and left to be chased on another day.

Research on the diet of the midwestern coyote has indicated that in normal years this animal lives largely on rodents, particularly rabbits and mice. In Kansas rabbits are considered to be pests rather than game, and no opprobrium attaches to depleting their numbers. Since rabbits and mice increase and decrease in cycles, it is apparent that in those years when their natural prey is scarce coyotes may turn to the farmer's chickens and other livestock for food. The habit, once adopted, may continue even after the natural food supply is again plentiful.

Our little coyote didn't seem to miss her natural fare. When we first had her, we fed her twice a day on prepared dog food and milk. As she grew, her feedings were cut to one a day. At maturity, Shag weighed close to twenty pounds.

We did wonder, though, if she would ever become a killer, as the farmer's boy feared she might. Wayne took her on a leash to the poultry farm where he was doing a series of experiments with pheasants. Here Shag went through the motions of stalking the chickens, though she never attempted to kill one, rather making a game of it. The pheasants were more aware of her than she was of them, skittering to the far edge of their pen as she approached. One of the few things that Shag ever killed was a mole which she dug out of the ground at the farm. She snarled as she killed it, the only such sound we ever heard her make. Apparently the killer instinct was not strong in Shag. She had no need to find prey, since she was well fed and seldom hungry.

We worried that our coyote might howl at night, an activity typical of wild coyote behavior. She never did, even though we could often hear her relatives in the nearby hills. Instead Shag slept quietly, her head on her front paws and her bushy tail spread around and over her like a furry robe.

Shag was insatiably curious. Any quick movement brought her to investigate it. Grasshoppers intrigued her and she spent many hours in pursuit of them, an enterprise which puzzled our young son, Steve, enormously.

Part of her curiosity found an outlet when Wayne took Shag out for exercise. In town she wore the leash, though she answered to her name, to a whistle, or to spoken commands. Once in the country, Wayne removed the leash and Shag ran free. She loved running and carried her tail high as she did so. On such excursions our coyote chased collared lizards from sunny rocks; dug for skinks beneath limestone ridges; and, on one memorable afternoon, flushed an unexpected migrant Harris's sparrow from a hedgerow. Shag romped happily till Wayne whistled her to him, when they literally ran home together.

While we knew Shag would tolerate, and eventually welcome, human guests in our backyard, we could never predict her reaction to our other pets, acquired after her arrival. The agility and climbing ability of Houdini, our raccoon, aroused Shag to imitation. She tried hard to climb the cinder-block wall of the garage, whether to sit beside Houdini in his window perch or to drive him from it, we never knew. For Tabu, our baby skunk and the only real rival for our affections in the animal world, Shag had only lofty contempt. She had no innate fear of the skunk, perhaps because it was descented. Shag simply tried to pretend that Tabu wasn't there.

Not everything about Shag was pure joy. The very curiosity that endeared her to us made her a nuisance when Wayne attempted to photograph live specimens. The collared lizards, like small dinosaurs, and the sleek Sonoran skinks made no impression on Shag while in their sandy-bottomed wire cage. But let Wayne put any one of them on a contrasting surface in the sunlight of our backyard, and the color and movement brought Shag's inquisitive nose immediately into camera focus. Wayne had to banish his self-appointed coyote assistant in order to work undisturbed.

This was Shag, the personality that helped to make our backyard the interesting and friendly place it became. Drawn by curiosity, a good many of the people who came to see Shag remained to become her friends and ours. There were school children, college students, housewives, tradespeople, and professional folk who visited once, and came again. Our companionships had a cogenial bond of common interest. And suddenly Kansas, in spite of our forlorn living conditions, became a happy spot.

When we left, we could not take Shag to our new home. We gave her to Dr. H. T. Gier, knowing that she would be well and wisely treated, for Dr. Gier and his young sons have had experience with coyotes and are fond of them.

We receive reports on her progress, and as I read them I am reminded that wherever we go there will be a backyard of sorts. And with such a spot for entertaining, we'll always have a lot of friends.

Comical Downy— Clown of the Woods

PEGGY MOWERY

LIVING ON AN ABANDONED FARM NEAR WARWICK, NEW York, it is my father's habit, and mine, to make regular nature-observing hikes over every fascinating acre of the woods, fields, and pastures of our old place. Within a few years we have gotten well acquainted with our wild neighbors, from deer mice and wood-chucks to foxes and white-tailed deer; but we give particular attention to the birds. Of the many interesting kinds to which we play host, downy woodpeckers are the most cheerful and cocky of all.

Last winter we had several of them regularly visit the suet we hung out for them. Each was a clown to watch and went through a performance that never varied from day to day. Arriving at the suet post utterly famished, a downy pecks off big mouthfuls until he notices you standing close by. Instantly he pretends complete indifference to the food—sidling up and down and around, acting as if he hadn't even seen the suet, hadn't the faintest idea of taking a bite—for all the world like a small boy caught in the cooky jar.

One day in the spring we found a young downy woodpecker huddled miserably against the root of a tree. Of all the wild orphan fledglings that Dad and I have raised, not one turned out more rollicking and lively than this fellow. We had raised a bluebird, a chipping sparrow, and an evening grosbeak. The bluebird, Happy, was forever trilling; Twitter, the chipping sparrow, made much small talk; and Beauty, the grosbeak, was shy and lovely. But Downy —well, he was a bird clown. Almost everything he did was comical.

There were no parent woodpeckers around that cold spring afternoon, and we couldn't locate the nest-hole in the tall maples to return the baby to. So finally we bundled him into our fieldsack and started home.

Within an hour or two after we arrived at the house, Downy was quite friendly and at ease perched on my finger. As we watched him stow away an enormous meal of bread and milk and display typical woodpecker curiosity at his new surroundings, the puzzle as to why he had been abandoned grew deeper and deeper. He had no broken bones, no digestive ailment; and, except for being weak, the fledgling was perfectly healthy.

But after he was warmed and fed, we noticed that he fluffed out his baby feathers more than was natural. That was the tip-off. The bird was so badly covered with mites that the parents had abandoned it, their whole brood, and even the nest. After the mites had fatally weakened the rest of the brood, the parent birds had concentrated on the remaining one until the baby bird got up out of the nest and fell to the ground, calling to the adults that would never come.

I believe that adult birds keep a mite infestation under control by taking dust baths and then flying back to the nest still dusty. Apparently, the downy woodpecker nest was too deep in a tree limb for the dust cure to be effective.

We had treated mite infestations on other fledglings, so we went to work on this one. With a cloth dampened in five per cent DDT solution we wiped the bird off lightly, using a stroking motion on the back, breast, wings, and head, taking care not to get any DDT in the bird's eyes or mouth. This treatment relieved young Downy so quickly that he went to sleep still perched on my finger. He was never bothered again by mites because of the lasting residual effects of DDT.

His new nest was a medium-sized carton lined with absorbent

paper towels, which were thrown away when soiled, and several lengths of tree limbs about three inches in diameter for perches, propped firmly at an angle against the sides of the box. Then the top was covered to keep it cool and dark inside.

For the next several weeks young Downy was the life of the household. If the bird heard somebody going past the box, he would whistle his loud, friendly, *"Peek! peek!"* and drill a lively tattoo on a perching limb to signal for a ride on my finger and a handout. He loved scrambled eggs best, then slivers of soft-cooked beef and wheat bread soaked in milk.

But the most interesting thing about Downy, when he drank water, was to watch his agile tongue flicker in and out, incredibly fast. A woodpecker's tongue is hollow, has two barbs on the end, and can be extended more than two inches. The length and barbs are for reaching a grub after pecking a hole in the bark of a tree or shrub; the hollow tube is for literally sucking it up. We gave our Downy water with an ordinary eyedropper and he quickly learned to thrust his tongue up inside the glass tube for a drink. The bird's marksmanship was amazing—in all the times he aimed for the end of the eyedropper, he never missed once!

Downy feathered out in a few weeks and was big enough to go outside and spend his time in the trees around the yard all day. At twilight we'd step out on the porch with the feeding saucer and strike a teaspoon against the dish a few times. Almost immediately Downy flew down, because from his very first feeding on that cold spring night he had been conditioned to the fact that the sound of a teaspoon against a saucer meant food.

In his cocky, unafraid way Downy investigated every piece of wicker furniture on our front porch and learned to rock the hanging flower basket to and fro with a flying, halfspeed landing. When he tired of gymnastics, he turned to tapping the bright metal ashtrays smartly with his beak. Usually when somebody came to see about the commotion on the front porch, Downy affected an "I-had-nothing-to-do-with-it" air and sidled around the table top, completely indifferent to that fascinating ashtray.

In line with our policy of never caging a bird or other animal pet, Downy was given the freedom of the woods around our house. During the lazy summer days he buddied up with other woodpeckers there; but whenever we hiked through those woods he flew down to the shoulder of the lead man of the safari. The bird spent most of his time in the woods and preferred to roost outdoors, but he came in for an hour or two every day for the evening feeding.

Toward the end of fall we visited an ornithologist friend in Pennsylvania. We took Downy along in his dark-box so our friend could observe his feeding and drinking habits. A real gadabout at heart, Downy liked to go driving and had become a noisy, sociable passenger perched on the edge of his box whenever we went out in the car.

Our friend's home is built on a high bluff overlooking the Delaware River. Rising from the river are wild, thickly-wooded mountains, divided by beautiful, blue-misty hollows. The country is so remote that it supports bear, deer, bald eagles, and many of the smaller fur-bearing animals. From our lookout terrace we watched eagles soaring in slow majestic circles against the backdrop of the green mountains just across the river.

After Downy had clowned through his feeding and drinking—and he was a show-off when he had an audience—he flew to a willow not far from the terrace. We all settled back for some earnest visiting. Suddenly our host's tilted chair came down with a thump and he mutely pointed at the willow tree where Downy was hopping jauntily around the trunk in plain sight.

One of the circling eagles had seen the woodpecker, too, and was maneuvering for a dive. We whistled and called for Downy, but he paid no attention, tapping busily on the tree trunk, as bold and confident as though perched on the suet post back home. Every now and then he cocked an eye nonchalantly at the eagle and then went back to drilling. Suddenly the eagle folded its wings and dove toward the woodpecker, and at the last second—with those talons reaching for him—Downy nimbly hopped around the opposite side of the tree trunk from his attacker and continued drilling.

The eagle banked heavily and flew away, screaming with rage. Downy sidled back into plain sight on the tree. For half an hour this deadly game of hide-and-seek went on: Downy pretending complete indifference to the hovering eagle, tantalizing it into diving for him, and then hopping around the tree to safety in the nick of time. Although I felt sure that Downy could take care of himself, I was relieved when the eagle soared away high over the river.

Winter is a quieter time on the farm. We look forward to the change in seasons, with the shift in bird species and changes in wild animal ways. This winter promises not to be so quiet for us. It's really going to liven things up to have Downy come bouncing in on the back porch at twilight, whistling his loud, friendly *"Peek! peek!"* and drilling at the door to get in. We expect to enjoy his bumptious ways until next spring, when we hope he'll raise a bunch of equally lively youngsters in one of the maples of our front yard. Then Downy will either gradually lose his tameness or, heaven forbid, we will have a six-piece band of woodpeckers drumming on the metal ashtrays on the porch!

White-foot

HARRIET BURKHART

A BIRD-BANDER NEVER KNOWS WHAT HE WILL FIND IN HIS live traps. Often the occupant of the trap is not a bird at all, but some other small animal, particularly if the trap is left set overnight for those early morning hours when trapping is usually good.

Once, at midnight, near my home in western Pennsylvania, I found a baby rabbit, drowsy after feeding well in the trap. Often I have to go out before breakfast on chilly winter mornings to release a shivering little white-footed mouse, his feet pink with the cold, but busily nibbling away at the bait of seeds and bread crumbs. I am always finding their hoards of neatly shelled nuts and seeds, which may be made up of beechnuts from the nearby woods—said to be their favorite food when available and sometimes found in quantities of two to three quarts; flat green kernels taken from the large winged "keys" of the Norway maples near my house; or sunflower seeds pilfered from my bird feeders. These stores are thriftily tucked away against the winter in odd places, such as the toes of boots or the springs of upholstered furniture. I have found them underneath the paper linings in my old cherry chests of drawers, between the layers in a box of steel wool, and even under a paper of pins on top of the sewing machine.

There are few nooks or crannies that the active white-foots do *not* investigate; and their insatiable curiosity is sometimes disastrous—as in the case of the two little fellows that managed to trap themselves in an empty gallon jug, left open in my photographic darkroom last winter, while my house was closed.

In the days before I had my pet Siamese cats, when only sleeping dogs stretched before the fireside blaze, these engaging little mice often sat trustfully on the mantelpiece. Apparently they felt completely at ease, for they sometimes licked their pink paws, then washed their small faces and groomed their bright coats—fawn color above and immaculate white below. Often, as the family sat quietly in the firelight, soft but audible thuds would come from the dark stairway. It was some little time before we connected these tiny but distinct sounds, each followed by a slight pause, with the white-footed mice and realized that one of them was coming downstairs by a series of leaps from step to step.

I have found their nests in almost every conceivable location about my house and grounds, as white-foots will make their homes almost anywhere that is warm and dry. (I have read that these ubiquitous mice have actually been found in winter living right in a hive with honey bees!) Last November as I was putting tools away and setting my garden house to rights for the winter, I happened to knock the cover off a bucket of gravel under the potting shelf. To my surprise a startled white-footed mouse popped out and vanished behind a stack of flower pots. On top of the gravel in the pail was one of the most beautiful nests I have ever seen, a real work of art. It was made almost entirely of fibers taken from the supply of old burlap I keep for various garden purposes, and some of the ravelings had been shredded almost as fine as down. The roughly circular structure was so closely woven and felted together that I could pick up the whole thing in my hands, intact. I inserted an exploratory finger into the neat round entrance hole and ran it around inside the snug circular chamber, which was perhaps a little over two inches in diameter. It was still warm from the owner's sleek, plump body. As I stopped to replace the nest, I discovered that little white-foot had been sleeping atop his dinner. There on the gravel floor of the "basement" of his winter residence was a generous supply of unshelled sunflower seeds.

As I started to clear a space in which to set up my camera and tripod, I found that a pail of ground limestone contained another mouse nest of a different sort. It looked like a squirrel's nest, for it was a loose collection of dried leaves and grasses and rabbit fur, together with a little torn brown paper and pieces of soft binding twine from baled hay. It almost filled the quart-size waxed food container that I had been using as a scoop for the limestone. As both nests were apparently winter quarters, I tried to leave them as nearly as possible just as I had found them.

White-footed mice have often been tenants of my birdhouses, too, always effectually plugging their entrances with soft, bulky material. The chief component of these nests is usually burlap ravelings, perhaps because there is always a dependable source of supply at hand. They sometimes carry this favorite nest material an amazingly long distance from the outbuildings—even into the woods, a long haul for a creature as small as a white-footed mouse. Along with the burlap, they use dried leaves and grasses and bark fibers.

Indoors, these mice appear to like seldom-opened drawers for their nests, and they seem to like cupboards best of all for nest sites. They will use bedding, clothing, or anything stored there to make a large, untidy wad of soft fluff.

Although in the wild they prefer a hollow tree to all other nest sites, they may also, like some of the squirrels, select as a foundation an abandoned bird's nest in the undergrowth—very often that of a catbird. The entrance is usually on the lower side, and several mice may occasionally share a nest.

The white-footed mouse has also been known to occupy the same cavity with the gentle flying squirrel. It has always seemed to me that these two animals, though not closely related, resemble each other in their beauty and agile grace, as well as in their large, lustrous dark eyes, long whiskers, and handsome fur. Also, both animals are abroad at night—which habit of becoming active in the dusk of early evening has earned the name of "vesper mouse" for the white-foot in some parts of our country. White-footed mice seem much more like little squirrels than mice in many ways. They have cheek pouches like chipmunks, and they are quite at home in trees, too. In winter they may run out to the very tips of beech or maple branches to nibble the buds. They never hibernate, even in the Far North.

White-footed mice have a strong attachment for home and have been known to return when released from as far as two miles away. The little white-foot mother is a devoted homebody, for she spends almost every moment of her time during the breeding season in caring for one or another of the litters of youngsters that follow each other in quick succession. The white-footed mouse, like all mice, is a prolific breeder, with a gestation period of only twenty-one days.

She usually produces several litters of from one to nine each, with three or four as the average. The young are only about an inch and a half long and are born naked and blind. During this period or at other times in cold weather, the mother places a perfectly proportioned plug in the entrance hole to her nest if she has to leave it. The young white-footed mice soon grow fur, gray above and white below. After they open their eyes for the first time, when they are about two weeks old, they mature quickly. The mother weans them at three weeks; they are full-grown at ten to twelve weeks; but they may mate even before this, at only eight weeks of age. One authority says that the female is capable of breeding when thirty-nine days old; the male is sexually mature about ten days later.

I have been told that when the baby white-footed mice are very young and still small enough to be moved, in this manner, if danger threatens, the mother may flee to a place of safety with her nursing babies securely attached to her teats. There she will hurriedly construct a new nest. When they are older and too large to be transported in this convenient fashion, the inteprid little mother may make trip after trip back to the nest in the face of grave danger, to carry her brood away, one at a time, by the scuff of the neck, just as a mother cat carries her kittens.

The mother usually builds a new nest for each brood because the old nest is apt to be contaminated, although the previous offspring may remain in it for a while. Probably Mrs. White-foot is kept too busy by her arduous maternal duties to be a very good housekeeper, although she is so meticulous about her personal toilet that she is forever grooming her own immaculate fur.

I am accustomed to the sounds that white-footed mice make at night in my house in the country—the familiar scampering and scurrying overhead in the attic, the gnawing in the partitions, and the rustling of paper in my wastebaskets. But they have been known to make other, more purposeful sounds. George G. Goodwin of the American Museum of Natural History says that they sometimes produce a drumming sound by tapping their front feet rapidly on some object such as a dry hollow reed or a leaf. It seems as though this might, like the drumming of some of the woodpeckers, be intended as a communication of some sort.

For years I have hoped that I might sometime hear one of these little animals "sing," having read several accounts of amazing vocal performances on their part. The most plausible explanation of these rare musical individuals, according to Robert Snedigar, formerly of the American Museum of Natural History, is the known ability of many animals to hear sounds high above the range audible to the human ear. He thinks it likely that most species of mice have a normal song or twittering above the range of our hearing. In exceptional cases the pitch is lowered enough to become audible to humans—and the mouse sings!

On one occasion I stood listening halfway up the ladder leading to the hayloft, where white-foots abound, sure I must be hearing them sing at last. But the thin, high-pitched song was issuing from the throat of a bird, a brown creeper that had come in through an open window and could not find its way out again. Instead of fluttering frantically about in foolish panic, the small brown bird was busily spiraling in its customary manner around one bale of hay after another, exactly as if they were tree trunks, all the while uttering its strange, almost supersonic notes.

All accounts describe white-footed mice as very gentle and confiding. They usually will not bite, even when first captured; and they make excellent pets in only a few days' time. One February night, in California, I discovered a live California white-footed mouse in one of my portable bird-banding traps. The mouse, it seemed to me, was *enormous*—almost twice the size of the little white-foots that scamper about at night in my house in Pennsylvania. My captive "California mouse," as I called it, started at once to nibble at the bait of crumbs, under bright lights and with several people crowding around it. After it had eaten its fill and had accepted a drink of water, it curled up in a corner of the box trap with its tail over its eyes and proceeded to go to sleep, even though night is ordinarily day to this creature.

Its striking physical characters—big, dark, lustrous eyes; long quivering nose; luxuriant whiskers; and, especially, its large, thin ears, its prodigiously long white-tipped tail, and its large size—made identification easy. It proved to be exactly what I had been calling it: the California mouse (*Peromyscus californicus*), also called the parasitic white-footed mouse, because of its habit of occupying abandoned woodrat nests on the ground and making them over with beautifully domed tops and small side entrances. This largest member of the whole white-foot tribe north of the Rio Grande is found in the chaparral in areas where liveoaks grow.

When I took a few pictures the next afternoon—at first cautiously through the wire mesh of the trap and later with the door open wide—the captive mouse showed no inclination to leave. Perhaps this was because it was frightened or because the species is not active in the daytime. After an hour or more it ventured out through the open door of the trap. At last, discovering suddenly that it was free, this giant white-foot scurried back into the sagebrush under the laurel sumacs at the edge of the lawn, where it had entered the trap the night before.

A day or two later I live-trapped another white-footed mouse, but this one was appreciably smaller. It was more sharply bicolored, too, and had a shorter tail that was not tipped with white. Its coat showed more fulvous, especially along its sides, than that of the more grayish California mouse—a coloration which established it beyond any doubt as a full-grown individual of a different species, since young white-footed mice are quite uniformly gray above. This new find proved to be a brush mouse (*Peromyscus boylei*), a close relative of the California mouse that thrives under similar conditions.

I could not help but marvel at the amazing diversity in the far-flung white-footed genus, which on this continent, from Panama to the Arctic Circle, includes 178 recognized species and subspecies. The white-footed mouse is one of the commonest small rodents in North America, and thus constitutes the staff of life for almost all of the predators—hawks, owls, foxes, snakes, and many others. Its range is so wide that it occurs in almost any environment that will support higher life. It lives in forests, where it is also called the wood mouse. It is found on plains and the drier deserts—even below sea level in Death Valley, the lowest point in the United States—or in the rocky barren mountains to the limit of grasses and shrubs. It can survive in regions of searing heat or of intense cold, of snow or heavy rains. By going underground, it thrives in open country where protective cover is lacking. This mouse will dig its own burrows if necessary, but in Florida it is known as the gopher mouse because it commonly occupies gopher holes. But wherever they are found, white-footed, or deer, mice run true to the same general type, although their habits may differ according to their homes.

The Constant Carolinas

RUTH THOMAS

OUR OLD PAIR OF CAROLINA WRENS WE HAD LOST IN A bitter January spell. It was weather that might come to central Arkansas only once in a decade. For a week snow had covered the ground, and one morning the temperature was two degrees below zero.

The Carolina wrens of the woods, it seemed, were content to stay in their wild territories. For the rest of the winter, and all that spring and summer we had heard the loud antiphonal singing, each male proclaiming his sovereignty. In the autum, the woods' pairs were restless and came visiting. I saw them in my garden and the old brush heaps, they fluttered at the porch eaves, explored shed and garage and barn, but in the end returned to their woodland thickets. We hoped a young bachelor Carolina wren would claim our hilltop and sing up a mate. We never thought to have a lone maiden.

On a cold, sunny morning in January she arrived. I first saw the little cinnamon-brown bird at the woodpile, hopping from one log to another, peering and pecking at the rough bark and tinkling low friendly notes. Later in the day the wren went into one of my banding traps and I placed the government's metal band, 40-143599, on the right leg. Because Wren-99 was surprisingly small in my hands, I was almost certain it was a female.

Many times in the next weeks I saw the wren with the new bright band. From the windows I watched her eat my suet and peanut butter and chopped nutmeats. I met her again at the woodpile and almost everywhere that I roamed with our Scotties. Sometimes she was talking in pretty rattles. Proof of sex was that she never sang (a male could not have held in songs for as much as half a day), and so we came to call her our "lone maiden wren."

The Carolina wrens of the woods were singing every day. Back and forth, in the voices so great for their size, they hurled joy and pride and defiance—one, it might be, with the rousing *"Sweetheart, sweetheart, sweetheart, sweet!"* and the other with the beautiful *"Dear-erest, dear-erest, dear-erest, dear!"* And with all the might of her tiny body, our lone maiden replied in a long, raspy, rolling screech, *"Prrrrrrrrrr!"* Technically, this peculiar utterance may be a trill, but that word suggests a happy musical quality here quite lacking.

For years I had known that a female Carolina wren replied to her mate not only in summer but *in autumn and winter.* Foraging near one another in the wild honeysuckle hedge, they carried on an affectionate, conversational rattling; but if the female strayed to the rose tangle while her lord lingered in the hedge, he soon missed her and began a series of songs, whereupon she screeched and they were quickly reunited. Through the nesting season, the pair had a closer working partnership, with nest or fledglings the focus of their lives, and then I rarely heard the screech.

"Prrrrrrrrrr," I also knew, was the speech of wren wives to one another. Let a woods' pair wander to the fringe of our resident pair's domain and, while the two males dared and defied with songs, the two females screeched in loudest voices. A lone wren's screech was new to me. Did our maiden, from the midst of her acres of homeland, cry to the far singers, *"Here I live, come find me, come find me?"* Day after day, the songs rang out and the maiden screeched, but she would not leave the hilltop. All autumn she must have wandered; now she would have a mate come to her.

On March fifth, a lone Carolina wren came singing out of the north woods. Our lone maiden, stretching tiptoe atop my garden gate, screeched and screeched and screeched.

At last we had a pair of Carolinas. "The *Singingest* Wren," we called the male. Our maiden's prattle, we thought, was sweeter than his reiterated carols. Happily they wandered down to the plum thickets at the foot of the hill; up again to my garden, the tool shed, the woodpile, the feeding shelves; and then across the ridge to the long low barn. The Bewick's wren that thought he owned the barn would scold (like a victrola record going around in one groove, on and on), but he dared not chase the bigger wrens. And so they tinkled and rattled, flitted from one end of the old building to the other, and looked at the rafters and the shadowy corners and all the places where wrens might build a nest. Within a week, I had live-trapped Singingest Wren and had slipped a band, numbered 40–180314, on his right leg.

For nearly three years these two Carolina wrens were faithful mates. There was no doubt of their constancy to each other and to the hilltop home. Early in their history I had again caught the male and had given him, in addition to the metal band, a red celluloid band that I might recognize him at sight. He wore it all his long life —into his seventh year! His gentle mate so often entrapped herself, permitting me to check the number, 143599, that I knew her to be the former lone maiden.

No birds that ever lived with us were so tireless and so successful at nesting. True, in their first summer they twice lost eggs to an enemy, and it was only from the final nest that five young ones were fledged. But in the next two summers they raised six families of four to six babies each, in all thirty-two youngsters, which, including the first year family of five, totaled thirty-seven! Of course, the wrens hustled over a long season. They began nest-making in the stir and promise of March, and through August's scorching days they worked, with no apparent diminution of zeal and energy, to feed the last children.

Liking change, they moved to raise each family. Favorite locations were the tool shed near our house and the barn two hundred yards to the west. Usually the Carolina wrens claimed one of these buildings and the Bewick's wrens the other, but twice the two pairs nested in the barn only thirty feet apart. Neither pair interfered with the other's nesting, although the two males disliked and mistrusted one another. If the arrogant Carolina chose to peek into his neighbor's nest, the tiny owner could do no more than teeter and twitch and sputter rage. But if the male Bewick's was caught snooping near Carolina's home, he was driven off with pounces and pecks and the angriest notes. The two females, as far as I knew, took no notice of one another.

Singingest Wren and his mate built sometimes in my birdhouses and at other times in odd nooks. One of the nests that I watched closely, from its start to the day the youngsters flew, was crowded into a narrow space between a box of salt and a brush on a shelf above the feed bin at the barn. We had milk goats then; and morning and evening I worked, measuring out grain, within a few inches of the wren in her cavelike nest. I was careful not to stare, and so calm and trusting was the little female that had lived with us since maiden days that she never flew out in fright.

When making a nest, both Carolina wrens worked with intense concentration. Like brown shuttles flying back and forth, they picked up and carried to the chosen site whatever loose rubbish was near. Straw, green moss, dry grasses, oak catkins, bits of old leaves—anything would do; the nest above the grain bin was built almost wholly of the lespedeza hay so conveniently at hand. How the wrens fashioned the snug cave in their mass of material, I never knew. Usually it was lined with goats' soft hair, rarely with feathers; and, if not as pretty as the Bewick's wrens' nest, it was nevertheless just as soft and warm.

"Time enough if it isn't wasted," might have been the Carolinas' philosophy. Their rule was to coax the fledglings, which left the nest at twelve to fifteen days of age, to the thickets at the foot of the hill, and then, on the third or fourth morning, to lead the youngsters again to the ridge, stow them in hedge or brush heap, and begin the next nest. Singingest Wren was never so extravagant of songs as at the start of a cycle. When for most of a forenoon I heard *"Sweetheart, sweetheart, sweetheart, sweet!"* from the area of the shed or barn, I had only to go out and spend a few minutes of watching to discover the new nest.

For an hour or two, the wrens might work like furies at carrying trash, then give the rest of the day to feeding their hungry family. In little more than a week the nest was finished and the eggs laid; Wife began to incubate and Wren took sole charge of the fast-growing children. By the time he was needed to feed the newly hatched youngsters, the young wrens of the previous brood were able to fend for themselves. In fact, the precocious sons might be singing in weak, wobbly voices. If they loitered too long around the home place, their father ordered them off with his "pounce, peck, scat" technique.

I particularly remember the last nesting during their third summer, for Wren's crossness and his mate's patience with seven young Bewick's wrens that played almost at the Carolina threshold—going in and out of the shrubs, sliding and wallowing in the dusty places and forever talking *"Eek, eek, eek!"* With the heat, the summer's hard work, and the time near for molting, both Carolina wrens might have been forgiven a touch of temper; but it was only the male who pecked those Bewick's children till they squealed and fled. Yet they never learned; within the hour I again heard smacks and squeals.

The Carolina youngsters fluttered out of the nest and were escorted down the hill to the woods. During the next month, the parents only now and then came home; and Wren, ordinarily lavish with his songs, was for once stingy and saving. Both wrens were pale and ragged with molt, subdued in spirit. One day the female went into a trap; I was glad to have another check of her band, 143599, but I was appalled by her lightness; she was like nothing in my hand. "Tireless," we say of these active little birds, but this cannot be true. The labor required to raise three families in a summer must sap their life forces.

In October, Singingest Wren and his mate returned from the woods to stay. And so changed they were, so beautiful in new plumage, that I would not have known them for old friends except for their leg bands. They looked plumper; their color was a deep reddish-brown, rich and lustrous; and their breasts were a warm cinnamon hue. All their ways were livelier.

Winter was our Carolina wrens' happiest season. Perhaps mine, too. The cold mornings, Singingest Wren's great songs, his breath making puffs of vapor. He knew many songs—my favorite, *"Sweetheart"*; the smooth, sliding *"Dear-erest"*; the shorter and more spirited *"Whee-udel," "Jew-peter,"* and *"Joe Hurley"*; and far more than I can find syllables for.

And the drowsy noons, the sun on the south hillside like spring! The Carolina wrens in the honeysuckle hedge—I could hear their affectionate chatter. Not often were they so far apart that Wren had to summon with song, his mate to reply with a screech.

Mild days, the Carolinas spent many hours at the foot of the hill;

but long before dark they returned to a brush heap near the barn, there to wait the moment for going to bed. It was the time that I cared for my goats, and I dawdled, watching the wrens. The male bobbed and turned from side to side, with each jerky bob giving a hard *"Chur!"* That was the note for a minor alarm, but in the evenings it seemed to be simply masculine assertiveness. While he *churred,* his mate might hop nearby, or just rest sleepily, and tinkle to her mate.

The sleeping place, all their winters together, was a house in which the Bewick's wrens had nested, at the east end of the barn. The neighbors' nest was not, according to Carolina ways, the proper kind for young ones; but is must have been warm and right for the bed of two grown-up wrens. In the evening, the female was the first to fly up to the nest. Wren would give a few last *churs* and then, with quickness and phantom quietness, slip into the nest beside her.

On a bleak, sleety day in February—it was the fourteenth—Singingest Wren began to sing early in the morning, repeating one series as many as fifty times, and he sang nearly all day long. Not for a first nest in spring had he ever sung with scarce time out to eat! *Have you lost your wits, little man?* Next day it was the same; and then I realized, with a catch at my heart and some chagrin, that I hadn't known that he had lost his wife.

Could there be any other reason for a little bird to sing from morning to night in cold February weather? I followed Singingest Wren east and west and up and down the hill, listening for his mate's rattled answer. He sang till he had all the wrens of the woods singing, and I could hear the wren wives screeching to one another; but on our hill there was no female wren to reply.

I looked everywhere that our wrens ever had foraged. Impossible, I said, to find a tiny brown bird body in winter's fallen leaves—still I searched the woodpile, the brush heaps, all the thickety places. At one end of the barn I found scattered red feathers. A cardinal had roosted there, and at last the screech owl had eaten him. Perhaps an owl had eaten my wren!

On the morning of February twenty-fourth I walked to the foot of the hill; and there, in the plum thicket, the male Carolina wren sang and sang. He was perched high on a bare twig, and I could see the red band on one leg. Grief I felt for my lost wren, but a greater pity for the living bird.

I turned back up the hill, along the path that I walked every day. But now at the top I thought to look again in the brush heap, and leaving the path, chanced to glance down. I had almost stepped on the little body of the "lone maiden wren," rumpled and sprawled in the leaves. I turned the smooth band in my fingers and read the familiar number, 143599. There was no sign of fatal hurt, no clue to the cause of her death.

I buried her deep under a shrub in my garden, while near the barn the male wren sang loudly, *"Sweetheart, sweetheart, sweetheart sweet!"*

The Black "Cat" of the Forest

ROBERT G. SNYDER

ONE OF THE LEAST-KNOWN CARNIVOROUS ANIMALS OF the northern woods of America is the fisher, or pekan. The fact that this large member of the weasel tribe is nowhere abundant, and is rarely seen alive in the thick, green timber where it chooses to live, probably accounts for the lack of detailed information about it. I have been fortunate enough to meet the fisher three times in one of its few strongholds in the continental United States—the Adirondack Mountains of New York.

My first meeting with the black "cat," as it is often called in the North Woods, occurred several years ago on a golden morning in late September. My wife and I were walking along an old woods road a few miles north of the Fulton chain of lakes. The frost was

still heavy along the shaded ground, though it was mid-morning, and the foliage was brightening with the brilliant hues of early autumn in the mountains. We had hopes of seeing a few of the deer that daily frequented this section of the road which traverses a low balsam flat.

A movement in the roadside bushes caused us to halt, and a large, minklike animal loped out into the open before us. It discovered us immediately, but showed little fear, acting almost as if it had never seen a human being before. It stared at us, constantly testing the air with its black, rather pointed nose. Then it completely ignored us and began casting about in little circles with its nose to the ground, as if it were attempting to pick up a lost trail, and soon worked its way into the thick woods and out of our sight.

At that time, I had not met anyone in that section who had actually seen a fisher in the woods, and I would have been at a loss to identify our unexpected visitor had I not once seen one in a private museum. Since then, fishers have become more plentiful and, if the New York State Conservation Department affords them enough protection, they will continue to be an interesting part of the animal life of the Adirondacks.

The fisher looks a great deal like an overgrown mink. The one we saw that September morning appeared to be about three feet long from its nose to the tip of its long tail. Its tail is much more bushy than that of the mink, thick at the base and tapering somewhat toward the tip. Its fur is mostly a rich, dark brown, and is very luxuriant, excepting for the largest males, which tend to have a coarser coat. Unlike the mink and otter, which are both close relatives, the fisher spends very little time around water; and it is very puzzling to see how it got the name "fisher" because it definitely is not a fisherman. It seeks its prey in the thick forest of the higher swamps and ridges and fears no other dweller of the woods, regardless of size.

One of the top dishes on the fisher's bill of fare is the well-armored porcupine. I have heard many rumors as to just how a fisher can overcome this living pincushion without inflicting severe pain upon itself. To me, at least, it is no longer a mystery, because the second time I crossed trails with a fisher I had the rare privilege of witnessing its method of subduing the prickly porcupine.

Again my wife was with me, for we love to ramble through the woods and are ever searching out intimate glimpses of wild creatures at work and at play. A few years later, this meeting occurred within a mile of our first one and at the dead end of another little-traveled woods road that had once been used extensively by lumbermen. We were on an all-day hike, intent upon exploring a little valley several miles farther back in the woods, one that we had never visited before.

It was early morning when we reached the end of the rough, sandy road; and it was there that we saw the porcupine that was to figure in the episode. It was sleeping soundly in an old box that had been discarded at that point by someone who cares little for unlittered natural scenery. Perhaps we should have slipped quietly past the porcupine while it slept, but we couldn't resist nosing around and exclaiming over the quaintness of its chosen place for taking a snooze. It awoke in a rather grumpy mood, and we soon left it.

Dusk was closing in upon the woods when we returned to that spot after our day's excursion. I was in the lead and suddenly noted activity of some kind ahead of us. We cautiously worked our way a little closer and saw a large fisher bounding about in a small area close beside the box in which we had previously seen the porcupine. But the porcupine was no longer in the box, nor was it sleepy—though later examination proved it to be very groggy. It was strictly on the defensive and not at all unruffled like a normal porcupine should be. The fisher not only had the porky confused, but had it completely unnerved.

The fisher's stratagem was simply a war of nerves, one more proof that many animals are not nearly so unintelligent as we humans may consider them to be. The fisher would dash up to within a few inches of the porcupine's head; and the porcupine would keep its head tucked low but slowly turn so as to put its lethal, quill-studded tail in position for a defensive blow. The fisher would then lightly bound directly over its intended victim, out of reach of the slashing tail, and force the porcupine to revolve around some more. This maneuvering went on for perhaps four or five minutes. Then some slight movement on our part, or a breath of wind, caught the fisher's attention; it looked in our direction, testing the air, and then it bounded into the darkening woods.

We went up to the porcupine and found it in a stupor. The slightest movement on our part would cause it to turn dully about. It was so dazed that it didn't move in any way that would better its own position from a possible attack from us; it just weakly shifted its position without any justification. Its eyes had a dull, listless appearance, not at all like the brightness that had been in them in the morning. It was easy to see how the fisher could have brought it to a complete state of collapse within a short time and would have been able to turn the animal over. The fisher could then have finished the job by slashing through the porcupine's weakly-protected underside. How long the fisher had been working on its victim we, of course, do not know, but probably for quite some time. By continually presenting itself at the front of the porcupine, no matter which way it turned, the fisher had prevented it from reaching the protection of a log or stump where the porcupine might have remained secure for hours with its front protected and its tail ever ready to ward off attacks from the rear and sides. Perhaps the fisher came back and finished its work after we left, for by now the porcupine seemed to lack the strength of inclination to seek a better place of refuge.

My third glimpse of a fisher was very brief. I was eating lunch in an open glade, enjoying the sights, sounds, and smells of the forest around me. I hardly heard it before it entered the glade, and it was traveling so swiftly that two effortless, graceful bounds took it across the opening and into the woods on the other side. I doubt if I have ever seen a deer or rabbit move so fast, yet it gave the impression that it was just loafing and not trying at all. When glimpsed momentarily like that, the animal appears almost jet black, so dark is the brown of its fur; doubtless, such quick glimpses are responsible for its nickname of "black cat."

I do not know why it was traveling so fast. Perhaps it was merely heading for the next county, for fishers are great roamers and may travel as much as twenty or thirty miles in a day. I did not see anything that it could have been chasing, though I now see why it is claimed that the fisher can run down snowshoe rabbits, and that it can catch squirrels and even martens in trees, for it is an agile climber.

In addition to porcupines, rabbits, and squirrels, the fisher is fond of mice, birds, and raccoons. In fact, there are probably very few creatures living in the forest that it will not attack and devour. It has even been said that it will pull down and kill deer, though such deer as it might kill would most likely be weaklings or starving animals that would not survive anyway. One thing is certain, the fisher is one of the most unusual and interesting creatures inhabiting the semiwilderness areas still left in the northern part of our country. I am looking forward eagerly to meeting one of them again.

The Ptarmigan of Glacier National Park

J. GORDON EDWARDS

IN THE LUSH ALPINE MEADOWS OF THE NORTHERN Rockies, cool breezes from the snowfields flutter the showy petals of acres of brilliantly colored flowers. The sharp, birdlike chirp of the Columbian ground squirrel and the long shrill whistle of the marmot precede hikers through the meadows, warning all wild creatures that an intruder is approaching. The cony retreats into the protection of its talus slope, but its brief nasal bleats are often heard as one passes those impregnable masses of jumbled rock fragments. Flocks of pipits wheel and turn in almost perfect flying synchrony, and high overhead an occasional hawk or eagle wheels in its persistent search for prey. Clark's nutcrackers hurl strident invectives from the scattered clusters of stunted alpine fir trees or indulge in their plaintive conversational notes. The showy little rosy finches throng over the snowfields and feast on immobilized insects that have been blown up from the valleys and numbed by the cold.

In this environment there are dozens of birds and mammals of great interest, but none are more eagerly looked for by visitors to Glacier National Park than the famous ptarmigan, or alpine grouse. These birds are common in the frigid northern part of our continent, but come into the United States only in places where high mountains create conditions suitable for their existence.

There are three species of ptarmigan in North America, but only the white-tailed ptarmigan, *Lagopus leucurus,* nests in the United States.

It is natural that such interesting and scarce birds should attract wide attention and great interest on the part of scientists. Ornithologists have striven to learn the most intimate details of the feeding, mating, and nesting behavior of these grouse, and numerous observations about them have been published. Hoping to contribute something of value concerning the biology of the ptarmigan, the ranger-naturalists of Glacier National Park have searched for nests containing eggs for many years, but usually without success. Park-Naturalist Lloyd Parratt joined the search for ten summers before he finally discovered such a nest in June 1955.

Although it was only one hundred feet from a heavily traveled trail near the Logan Pass parking area, the nest Parratt discovered would probably have escaped detection were it not for the diligent searching and sharp eyes of Parratt and his son, Mark. When I was shown the nest on June thirtieth, I was warned to tread cautiously lest I step on it before seeing it. After I was halted and told that the female was sitting on the nest on the bare ground less than ten feet in front of me, it was still almost a full minute before I could see it. It was located on a very small, barren ridge surrounded by snowfields, at an elevation of 6690 feet above sea level. In a shallow depression in the rocky soil, a few bits of dried vegetation had been loosely interlaced to form a flimsy saucer five or six inches in diameter, lined with half a dozen downy feathers. Lloyd had taken pictures of three eggs in this nest on June twenty-third, at which time there were apparently no feathers present. In the interim, also, one more egg had been added to the clutch; and there seemed to be room for only five eggs in the nest, at most.

As is characteristic with females of this species, the mother chose to remain motionless on the nest as we drew nearer and surrounded her, and even when I slowly reached out and touched her on the head her only response was a subdued clucking. At that time we didn't want to frighten the bird away from her nest, so we quietly departed, vowing to keep close watch over her in an attempt to see how the nesting activities compared with those of other species and subspecies of ptarmigan.

I once saw six baby chicks with a mother bird at Iceberg Lake but have several times observed only four or five in a brood. Based upon these observations and published references, it seems safe to state that the normal number of eggs per nest in Glacier National Park is four to six.

I have often flushed ptarmigan from the bare, rocky slopes more than a thousand vertical feet above timberline, but they are far more common near the moist alpine meadows or beside the high snowfields and glaciers. In summer they feed on flower pollen and on seeds and their pods. T. M. Trippe stated that they also eat insects and the leaves of pines and firs; and Major Bendire has seen them eating the flowers and leaves of marsh marigold, *Caltha leptosepala,* and leaf buds and catkins of dwarf birch. Dr. A. K. Fisher examined stomach contents of two ptarmigan chicks from Mt. Rainier and found they had eaten beetles and flowers of blueberry and heather, *Cassiope mertensiana.* Mrs. Bailey found fruiting spikes of *Polygonum viviparum* in the crop of a specimen from New Mexico; and the gizzard of the same bird contained "mainly seeds of *Polygonum* and a few other seeds, a few small grasshoppers, and other small insects." In winter these birds form flocks and usually remain in their high, frigid environment. At that time they feed mostly on the buds and twigs of willow and other small shrubs. During severe winters or when the snow is extremely deep, they descend into the mountain valleys where they find better shelter and more food.

On Friday afternoon, July 1, 1955, a violent snowstorm swept over Logan Pass, depositing five inches of snow and drifting to more than a foot deep in places. I hiked to the vicinity of the nest but couldn't find it, even though I thought I had marked its exact location with reference to a small shrub. There was no sign of the female, but I saw a male flying about in the storm and alighting to pick seeds from plants still sticking through the fresh snow.

The blizzard continued all night and the following morning, and on July second, the Going-to-the-Sun Highway was completely closed by fresh snow almost two feet deep, which formed very deep drifts in some places. By mid-morning of July third, the road had been cleared and I returned to Logan Pass for information duty. At that time the covering of fresh snow extended to the floor of McDonald Valley (4000 feet above sea level) and was knee deep above the 6000 foot elevation. This snow covered over the four- to six-foot-deep snow-pack remaining from the previous winter, and persisted for about a week. On July third, I spent considerable time searching for the nest, but could find no trace of it, even though I dug through the snow in several places where I thought it might be. I assumed that the nest not only had been abandoned but also must have been destroyed and the eggs removed.

On July fourth, Dr. C. O. Harris and his wife Carla accompanied me in another search for the nest. Imagine our surprise when we saw the female bird nestled in a deep cavity in the snow, still sitting on her nest! I had missed the nest by six feet while digging for it the day before, and felt fortunate that I had not stepped on the mother where she had been sitting quietly beneath a foot of the fresh snow. Apparently as the snow melted away or was blown from the ridge by strong winds the female had eventually been able to clear away enough of it from above her to expose her to the outside world again. I realize that it is not unusual for grouse, including ptarmigan, to burrow into the snowbanks for protection during severe winter weather; but I have not seen any previous reference made to nesting behavior under these conditions.

We all admired the ptarmigan's perseverance and anticipated the hatching of her brood, but disaster struck just two days later. On July sixth, as I waded through snow toward the nest, following the trail made on our last visit, I noticed mountain lion tracks ahead that had followed our route. Carnivores will often follow a human trail or scent for miles, sometimes finding bits of food along the way. Knowing this, I had been careful to avoid spending much time near the nest on previous visits, and had continued my tracks beyond the nest in a great circle leading back to the parking area. That precaution proved insufficient in this case, for the cougar discovered the nesting bird. The story of what had happened was clearly evident by the tracks in the snow. The mother ptarmigan had finally lost her composure and had flushed from the nest with the lion in hot pursuit. The great cat had taken two prodigious bounds through the snow after her, but the lack of blood or feathers on the snow proved that the bird had escaped. The puma had then returned to the nest and crunched the eggs in its mouth, dropping portions of shell over an area about a yard square around the nest. It then retraced its steps to the main trail and continued toward Hidden Lake.

Four weeks later Lloyd found another ptarmigan nest near the parking area at Logan Pass, and from that one the birds had hatched successfully. I took pictures showing the typical construction of the nest and the remains of four eggs which had hatched. A few days later I saw a mother ptarmigan with four chicks nearby, but they were easily alarmed and were so fully developed that I could not approach them for pictures.

I saw ptarmigan every day during the summer, while leading my hikes from Logan Pass to Hidden Lake Viewpoint. I was thrilled one day to find six adult males feeding on a single grassy ledge beside the trail. We approached to within a few feet of them before they walked leisurely away.

While these birds are in their brown, beige, and white mottled or barred summer plumage it is difficult to get them to stay on snowy surfaces for any length of time. They seem self-confident and unafraid *while on soil or rocks,* but they shun snowfields and run almost frantically when crossing snowbanks. In winter both sexes become pure white, except for black bill and eyes; and their behavior at that time is the opposite. H. M. Albright has observed that the summer behavior is then reversed and the birds seem unalarmed when approached on snowfields, but if chased onto bare soil or rocks they run rapidly back onto the snow. They actually seem to sense it when they are on the most concealing background. I feel certain that the mother I approached while she was sitting on her nest surrounded by fresh snow must have been undergoing a tremendous conflict between the instinct to brood the eggs and her desire to move to a camouflaging background to escape detection.

The summer had been most productive and interesting for me, but it held yet another delight in store. One day about noon as I was returning from Hidden Lake I suddenly came upon a male and female ptarmigan together on a mossy ledge beside a large snowbank. They showed little alarm, and I approached to within three feet of them and took pictures illustrating the sexual differences in summer plumage. The birds posed for me first on the bare earth, then, briefly, on the snow. I used up all of my movie film and began taking a series of kodachrome transparencies. Soon a crowd of hikers had accumulated and the number of them crowding about the birds evidently became too annoying. At last, with an appearance of reluctance, the grouse uttered their characteristic cackle and fluttered noisily away, alternating their rapid wingbeats with gliding, or sailing. Certainly volumes could be devoted to discussions of these hardy, attractive, courageous, "foolish," and interesting birds.

The Bushy-Tailed Pack Rat —Furry Trader

NORMAN C. NEGUS

THE CABIN WAS VERY QUIET AT FIRST, SO SILENT THAT the heavy breathing of one of my sleeping companions was quite audible. Suddenly I was aware of a steady tapping in the night from somewhere over my head. I listened, wondering what might be its source; then abruptly it ceased, and some animal thumped over the loose boards that lay across the rafters. The noise was so loud that I thought of a bear or a nest of porcupines. The first running and tapping seemed to start a chain reaction. From every corner of the cabin came a variety of sounds—loud scuffling and scratching, gnawing and thumping, and the occasional thud of some object moving suddenly.

By this time my friends were wide awake. At the moment I found my flashlight, something clattered among our silverware and mess kits on the table. I flashed on my light and for a few seconds I saw nothing. Then, as I shifted the beam across the table, it played on a furry form about the size of a squirrel. The animal sat there as if transfixed, its large eyes staring, its long whiskers twitching nervously. I knew then that our mysterious visitor was one of the famed pack rats of the West.

This clean, bright-eyed creature bore little resemblance to the house rat that so many people think of when they hear the term "rat" used. In fact, no American animal has been more maligned by this comparison than the pack, or wood, rat, for no two animals could be so different and still look so much alike. The pack rat is somewhat larger; the fur on its back is a beautiful reddish brown, blending to pinkish buff on the sides and snow white on the belly. Its long bushy tail, which it flicked derisively, gave it a squirrel-like appearance. After a minute or two it thumped loudly on the table with a hind leg, sprang to the floor, and was gone.

Wherever man's habitations penetrate the mountainous regions of the West, pack rats are found. Often in the ghost towns of the Rockies they remain as residents long after the surrounding hills have been gleaned of their mineral wealth and the towns abandoned. Even the dank, dark, deserted mine shafts are considered suitable homesites by the bushy-tailed pack rat, so-called because of its habit of packing home an incredible number of useless objects.

The most casual observer cannot help but notice signs of pack rats. Often their presence is betrayed by large disorderly piles of sticks and leaves and every sort of miscellaneous object they can move. These large debris piles may form a protective maze over the entrance to their nests in rock crevices and cracks, or they may simply cover the nest itself. From this odd habit of collecting materials, pack rats have gained the reputation as traders and as robbers of camps and cabins. Despite their collecting habits, they are remarkably clean and sanitary. Their nests are neat structures, usually cup-shaped, with thick walls made of shredded cotton or other material that is available. The stuffing of old mattresses is a favorite for this purpose, and is one of the first things pack rats will pilfer when they invade cabins.

Most objects will appeal to a pack rat's collecting fancy. A great variety of articles have been found in their debris piles, including coins, watches, rings, cartridges, knives, and spoons. Dr. Walter P. Taylor, a well-known scientist, compiled a huge list of articles from a single pack rat nest in the state of Washington, which included several bars of soap, ten chocolate bars, and fifteen lumps of sugar. It is not without good reason that the experienced mountaineer turns to neighboring pack rat nests when searching for lost articles around camp.

Old-timers staunchly claim that when a pack rat steals an article it invariably leaves something else in its place. As a result they are often called by the common name of "trade rat," rather than "pack rat" or "wood rat." Such purposeful trading is undoubtedly not the case. It is more likely that a pack rat finds an object more attractive than the one it is carrying, and drops what it has in order to abscond with the more alluring loot.

Legends galore have resulted from their supposed trading habits, some of which are based on facts. Tales of gold nuggets and valuable watches carried off are common stories among mountain men. One old fellow is reported to have removed his false teeth for the night and placed them on a table in his cabin. He awoke in the morning to find they had been stolen, and in their place was left, ironically enough, a toothpick!

Pack rats have been known to make hundreds of return trips to remove quantitites of materials that particularly appeal to them. A large male that I kept in the laboratory escaped one day from his cage, and despite thorough searching I failed to discover his hiding place. After a few days, however, I noticed that a large box in which I kept rat food pellets was being emptied rapidly of its contents. Within two or three days not a pellet remained. Suspecting my pack rat of the deed, I replenished the food supply in the box and set a live-trap nearby, baited with some of the pellets. Eventually I caught the rascal, but not before I realized what a great many return trips he had made. Originally the box contained several hundred pellets. When I discovered that he had carried only one pellet at a time, I had some idea of the hundreds of trips he must have made back and forth between the food box and his hidden cache somewhere beneath the floorboards of the building.

Since pack rats do not hibernate, their collecting habits stand them in good stead. In addition to the collection of odd articles, they store large piles of leaves and other food materials around their nests as a reserve supply during the winter.

Pack rats are primarily vegetarians, but are not adverse to eating all kinds of meat. One need scarcely worry about what type of bait to use in trapping them, for anything that is edible would probably be successful. Dr. Walter Dalquest has described a captive pack rat at the University of Washington in Seattle which escaped and ate a number of lizards. Arthur F. Halloran reported a pack rat trapped while carrying a young cottontail rabbit in its mouth. Such data indicates that pack rats may be quite omnivorous animals when the opportunity presents itself.

Commonly, aspen leaves are stored by the bushy-tailed species in the mountains; sagebrush and cacti are collected by the desert-inhabiting species. There are several records of mushroom caches found around pack rat nests, but whether they are used as a food supply is questionable.

Though occasionally pack rats come out during the day to feed or collect nest material, they usually venture forth at night after most human activities have ceased. They are highly nervous and are easily frightened by sudden movements and noises, scurrying to their nests at the slightest provocation. Their perpetual curiosity soon overcomes their fear, and they resume their activities.

When cornered, a pack rat assumes its favorite defensive position. Rearing up on its hind legs, it backs warily against a wall or boulder and uses its forelegs like a boxer to ward off its enemy. Often with amazing swiftness it strikes out at its tormentor with its short forelegs, and if the opportunity presents itself it sinks its powerful incisors into some vulnerable spot. Sometimes it turns half on its side with only one foreleg raised in defense.

An adult pack rat seldom emits any vocal sound during its busy lifetime. Occasionally, when attacked or when fighting with others, it will squeal in a high-pitched note; but more often the characteristic rabbitlike thumping with a hind foot is a sure indication that a pack rat is excited or alarmed. It is the source of much noise in old cabins where loose boards reverberate to the drumming of furry feet.

Perhaps the greatest enemies of these rodents are the nocturnal carnivorous animals such as owls, foxes, and coyotes. It is improbable that hawks have much opportunity to capture them in the daytime. A food habits analysis of coyote stomachs from all over the country revealed that four per cent contained pack rat remains. The large owls are probably their most formidable enemies.

Being rather solitary animals, pack rats are not closely associated with other mammals. Around old buildings in the mountains red squirrels and white-footed mice often have nests established nearby without apparent conflict with pack rats. I have found pack rats living in close association with the little rabbitlike conies in the talus slides of the mountain slopes in the West, but I do not know if there is competition between them.

Though pack rats' feet do not appear to be particularly adapted for climbing, they are capable of scurrying up trees almost with the speed and agility of frisky red squirrels. Unaware of this, I innocently assumed that I could easily recapture a large adult that escaped from me one day and started up a tall yellow pine tree. With difficulty I pursued the elusive fellow to the very top of the tree where I thought surely I had cornered it at last. But at this point it merely leaped from the branch above me to one several feet below and scampered down to the ground.

In captivity pack rats make interesting pets. Their inquisitive nature keeps them constantly active, investigating anything that is new to them. In cages they maintain orderly nests, designating a definite corner for excretion and a particular place for food storage. However, they never seem to lose their innate nervousness even after long periods in captivity, and hence rarely make calm and ideal pets.

Apparently it is unwise to keep a male and female in the same cage. When it is not the mating season they will fight bitterly with each other, and even during mating periods there is often antagonism between the two sexes. Males are very choosy about mates and will remain peacefully in a cage only with certain females.

The first mating takes place in early spring. After a gestation period of about six weeks an average litter of three or four young are born. At birth they appear quite like other rodents, being pink and almost hairless, and having both their eyes and ears closed. Within two or three weeks their eyes open and they acquire a juvenile fur that resembles the fur of the adults, but is grayer and thinner. At the age of two months they are gradually weaned. In some of the smooth-tailed species a second litter is born at this time. The bushy-tailed pack rats usually have only one litter a year.

Often when the female is frightened from her nest the young cling tightly to her nipples and bounce along over the ground as she runs to some safe retreat. When they are weaned the young become independent of their mother. Through the fall and winter they continue to mature, and in the spring they are ready to raise families of their own. A pack rat's average life span probably does not exceed two or three years in its natural environment, but under ideal conditions in captivity it may live much longer.

The bushy-tailed pack rats of the western mountainous regions have several close relatives that inhabit diverse environments in North America. In the arid southwestern deserts, smooth-tailed species live among the cacti and sagebrush, building huge nests, often five feet high. In the eastern states the Allegheny wood rat makes its home in limestone cliffs.

In some regions pack rats are so numerous that they are nuisances. Around Pocatello, Idaho, rodent control methods have been used to decrease their numbers in certain areas. Nevertheless, when you kindle a lonely campfire in the evening near the base of a huge gray talus slide, or in a deserted cabin high in the mountains, or even among the cacti and sagebrush of the deserts, you should find these little furry traders delightful and interesting companions at your fireside.

Out of the Soft, Black Night

WILLIAM BYRON MOWERY

IT WAS A BEAUTIFUL MIDSUMMER NIGHT, SOFT, SULTRY, and velvety black, with an occasional flare of heat lightning on the horizon but not a breath of air stirring. You could smell the rich, moist earth of the rocky, wooded hollow. Here and there, on stump and rotting log, we saw the eerie, ghostly glow of foxfire, in pale yellow, reddish and amethyst. Except for the high-pitched squeak of a flying squirrel now and then, the dark woods of the upstate New York hill country seemed wholly deserted and asleep.

But it only seemed so. A woods on a summer night is teeming with life, far more than in the day; a silent, pulsing life of myriad strange winged creatures, big and little. Their lives are brief and feverishly busy. Into only one night or two they must crowd the whole span of emerging, feeding, mating, egg-laying, dying. Though this night life of the woods is there for anybody to go and see who wants to, it's something that most people never have glimpsed or even thought existed—a queer, nocturnal world like nothing else on earth.

I was particularly on the lookout that

trip for a certain species of Pandorus hawk-moth. Using only our small hand flashes, we went quietly up along the brook that came down the hollow. In a patch of hydrophila or waterplant I showed little Helen, my friend Chris's nine-year-old daughter, a colony of sleeping butterflies, silver fritillaries, hundreds of them. Big Chris, who lives on a small farm way back in these headwater hills, was carrying his little girl in a slingseat he'd made for that purpose. You see, Helen had been all crippled up by infantile paralysis.

By the glow of our flashes we began seeing white tigers, rosy maples, and other small tame moths. Out beyond the periphery of our lights I could see, vaguely and dimly, the flip of bigger wings; glimpses of spectral white; vanishing blurs of ruby and brown; and the tiny, brilliant gleam of moth eyes, the most jewel-like things in nature. The August night was right, the woods were right, and I knew we were in for a fine hunt.

On a small open flat a few hundred yards up the hollow we made our first stand. I merely set my searchlight on the ground, pointed it straight up and adjusted the focusing for a diffused floodlight instead of a beam. Then we crouched down, sat quiet, and waited.

Hardly ten seconds had passed when in fluttered one of the beauties among the woods moths, the so-called Io, a medium-sized species, its forewings a light, bright yellow, its aft-wings yellow and wine. The Io is a common species, comparatively; there were literally hundreds of them there in Chris's hollow, close by his house; but neither he nor Helen had ever seen one or imagined such a creature lived. You should have seen Helen's fascinated stare as the Io lit on the moss near her, its wings atremble, and her joy when I caught the moth and told her she could take it home to mount and keep.

Out of the soft, black night other woods moths came drifting in, light-drawn, till in half an hour we had several dozen of them fluttering around us or sitting on the sphagnum moss. Most moths don't have any common names, so I'll just have to tell you that we were practically snowed under by Catocalas, Ios, silver-and-purple Apanteses, and many others. All of these were sort of old-hat with me, but with Chris and particularly little Helen each pretty, strange-hued arrival was something new and spectacular—creatures from a world that lay right at their back door but which they'd never known a whisper about.

I caught several of the finer specimens for Helen to take home.

You can be sure I kept a sharp eye out for the Pandorus I wanted, but none showed up. However, I did have one piece of utterly unexpected good luck there at that stand. For four summers I'd been hunting high and low for a certain very rare, bullet-swift, extremely wild "hummingbird moth." Ordinarily you look for this species in the open fields, and catching one in your net is like shagging a winged bullet. But just as I was snapping off our big light to move on, in came a fine specimen of this prize species and lit on a sprig of club-moss right in front of my nose. With no trouble, without even using the net, I popped her into my best-padded live bottle, and by morning she was laying her eggs.

Here maybe I should explain that a "live bottle" is any sort of small, wide-mouth jar—mayonnaise jars do fine—with a couple of air holes punched in the top. To avoid breakage, wrap them in some kind of padding. A "killing bottle" is an airtight jar with a wad of absorbent material in the bottom, this material charged with a little chloroform, cyanide, or tetrachloride. For large moths I've always preferred chloroform. An ordinary butterfly net, a light, and a six-volt battery are all the rest of the equipment necessary. A five-cell flashlight will do for the beginner, but the stronger light is really needed to "shoot down" the bigger and wilder moths.

As we started on up the hollow I smelled walnut on the heavy night air. Then I remembered, from my daytime field trips, that in the next open flat above us there was a walnut tree, with the low-crowned, roundish shape that trees assume when they grow solitarily. Speaking mostly to little Helen, I said:

"If we sneak up quietly, and if we're lucky, you're going to see a real sight. I want you to take a good look at it and then tell me what you think it is."

Keeping our flashlights pointed down at the ground, we slipped up to within forty feet of the tree and stopped. I adjusted my big beam to a broad, diffused light and swung it slowly onto the walnut. I'd been afraid that the season was a few weeks too late for the spectacle I wanted Helen to see, but no, there it was!

At the walnut in the open glade about a dozen little Tom Thumb creatures were executing a slow, weird-looking dance up and down and around and around the tree. Against the dark green walnut foliage their white bodies, about the size of your thumb, were strikingly conspicuous. They had big graceful wings of apple green; and their eyes were brilliant, flashing rubies.

Helen was so bug-eyed and speechless that I had to poke her with a finger and repeat: "Tell me what it is."

She got out just the one word: *"Fairies!"*

That was the honest, naïve, instinctive reaction of a child. But it's also the reaction of most adults the first time they see this walnut-tree tableau of the woods on a summer night. I've seen this sight myself half a hundred times and still it always reminds me cogently of fairies. Of the Little *White* Folk. I always have to blink my eyes a time or two before I realize that it's only a troupe of Luna moths, gravid females, laying their eggs on the outer foliage of the tree.

There's always a small core of fact or reality to fantasies, like the grain of sand that a pearl forms around. And there's no doubt in my mind—and other observers have said the same thing—that the big, wild, showy moths were the originating factor of our fairy lore. Europe has several races of Luna moth—the Irish, Apennine, Alpine, Carpathian; and these became the Little White People, who go in troupes, aren't too wild, and never do any mischief.

The Little *Brown* People—the pixies, brownies, elves, gremlins—are entirely different. According to the traditional lore about the Wee People, the brownies don't go in troupes but individually; they're so shy and wild that all you usually see of them is the flip of a vanishing wing; and there are many different kinds of brownies, whereas the Little White People are all one kind.

All of these folklore descriptions match up, amazingly, with the actual traits of the big brown moths, such as the Polyphemus, Samia, Rothschild, etc. These moths never gather in egg-laying groups, but are solitary; they're very wild, and are swift and erratic in flight; and the different species vary a great deal in size, habits, and other characteristics. No doubt whatever about it, the Wee Brown People originated from the big brown moths of the summer-night woods.

I wanted to show Helen some of these big browns, and as we went on up the hollow I specialized on them. Believe me, capturing those boys can take some doing. With your light adjusted to a narrow, blinding beam, you pick up one of them out in the dark woods and try to keep the beam trained on him as he zooms and dives, zigs and zags, to get away. If you're good you can "shoot down" about one in a dozen that you flush and get your beam on.

In that section of the hollow there were plenty of spicebush thickets along the brook and scrub sassafras up against the hillsides. It was a perfect night for moth ovipositing (egg-laying) and I knew there were lots of the big browns all around us, working those aromatic bushes and trees. But mostly all I could catch of them was a vanishing blur, a zip and a flop of brown. I gunned around for half an hour before I finally managed to shoot down and capture a Polyphemus, a very large, fawn-and-brown moth with a single eye, like an isinglass window, in each of its four wings.

It was long after Helen's bedtime, but she was as wide awake as a barn owl and thoroughly entranced with the strange world she was seeing for the first time. As for Chris, her daddy, he wasn't making any more remarks about moth-hunting being a pantywaist and slightly balmy business. In fact, it got so that half the time I was toting Helen and he was cat-footing it around in the woods trying to stalk and shoot down a big brown. One surprising thing was the way those two people caught onto moth identification. When we started up that hollow they didn't know one moth from another, didn't really know the name of a single one. But by now they were calling out, like old China hands at the game: "Looky, there's an Io!" Or "I've got a Catocala!" Or "Daddy, there goes a Polyphemus—shoot him!"

Although you have the richest and most pleasant hunting in the months of June, July, August, and September, you can begin mothing in mid-April and continue till the first hard freeze. In fact, after you've had some experience and worked up some know-how about it, mothing is a year-round pleasure. When I go out in wintertime for a snootful of fresh air I always take along a couple of live bottles and bring back some moth pupae or cocoons. You find these hanging in silken shrouds on bushes, under stones and logs and loose bark, in the ground, or just about anywhere you look. A few days in your warm house and they emerge, and you have a perfect specimen for your collection or for mounting in plastic as an *objet d'art.*

I'll tell you one more incident about that night up Chris's hollow. We had many thrills, many glimpses of winged prettiness; but this incident was the beat of them all, by a mile and a toad hop. I'd seen this same thing before, a few times. Mostly it happens more by accident than through planning or good stalking. But however it happens, there's nothing outdoors by day or night, summer or winter, that can touch it for sheer, outlandish, out-of-this-world, breathtaking beauty.

We were up near the head of the hollow, standing halfway up against the south hillside. I had the searchlight focused to a sharp, small beam, and was playing this beam up at some tall hickories across on the north slope. Away up at the top of a hickory, at a steep slant and about three hundred feet distant, I picked up a large moth. The white of its body, tiny at that distance, and the ruby glint of its eyes, told me it was a Luna. She was up there ovipositing, high in the hickory top.

When my light caught her, she fluttered this way and that for a few moments trying to escape. But I managed to hold her in the beam, and pretty soon she gave up, turned and faced the light, fixed her wings, and without further protest came gliding down that bright shaft of light toward us. With her long green wings outstretched, her white body gleaming, her eyes like ruby stars, no Wee White Person was ever prettier, no diminutive angel could stun you more with its loveliness. . . .

It was two o'clock in the morning when we got back to the house. Helen was so dead asleep that Chris just put her in bed, clothes and all. While the coffee warmed up, Chris and I talked about the night's doing. Moth-hunting had taken hold of him, from merely the one trip. On top of that he realized that Helen had fallen for it hard; that it was something at which his crippled girl could spend long and pleasurable hours. So I explained a few of the rudiments to him. Also, I left them one of my manuals, some bottles and other gear, and hoped these would be put to good use.

That, by all means, is how a person ought to learn moth-hunting. Right out in the fields and woods. Not out of books. To be sure, a person needs a moth manual, which you can get at any good-sized book store, to identify your catches. But put the field work—the chasing and catching, the delightful, unforgettable hours in the summer-night woods—put that first.

Old Mame

MIRIAM POPE CIMINO

For eight years we had had no house pets because our work had taken us each day several miles away to my husband's studio. During this time, however, we had been enjoying a wild pet—a big gray squirrel, "Old Mame"—that took up with us in a wholehearted manner and managed her affairs beautifully while we were away.

Our fat and sassy Old Mame could be both doglike and catlike, as well as human, in her actions, yet completely wild-squirrel when chasing her various relations or enemies from her claimed territory and caring for herself through any kind of weather or squirrel troubles.

No dog could show a livelier welcome when we stepped from the car with our arms full of grocery bags. The trip from our car to the kitchen door took a special kind of walking with Old Mame leaping enthusiastically against our legs and weaving circles, loops, and rectangles around us. She always beat us to the door; and after a few impatient rushes to see what was keeping us, she crouched eagerly there—waiting. When the door crack became wide enough, she bounded in, and doglike, let her swinging tail help her say that she was mighty glad we were home and about time, *and hurry with something good!*

For a while, graham crackers, the bigger the better, were her favorite treats. Then it was small, hard, whole wheat crackers, which were more exciting than peanuts to her. With such a greedy cracker-eater and cracker-burier around, we were forced to look for something cheaper than fig newtons, cocktail wafers, and cheese-bits for the too-frequent handouts. We found that the large old-fashioned soda crackers were the best in holding down the many cracker items on our grocery bill. Also we decided that they—the unsalted kind—were probably better for her as a steady diet. We usually had a supply of peanuts and other nuts handy; in fact, Mame got more chestnuts than we did on holiday occasions. Instead of our being able to stuff them into the turkey she stuffed them lightly into the top of the ground or snow and dashed back to beg for more and more.

Old Mame showed a catlike contentment stretched flat on her stomach on the summer grass, or in the same position on a limb of the willow tree by the kitchen door; or when pretending a lazy indifference to human beings. She could be really human in her diabolically clever way of handling the front door knocker or the old-fashioned latch on the kitchen door, or in showing off before company.

When we first noticed Old Mame, she was only another wild squirrel taking advantage of the food we put out for birds in the winter. Snow comes often and lies deep in the Berkshire Hills of northwest Connecticut. We had grown accustomed to hearing the radio weatherman finish a rosy recitation about good weather expected locally with, "but a possibility of a light snowfall over the higher elevations." This usually meant a real humdinger with our not getting plowed out for several days. His "and perhaps a few snowflakes over the higher elevations" meant an ordinary snowstorm. We were told when arriving here thirty years ago that it's a snowstorm if you can track a cat through it.

It had been our custom to keep a circle of ground spaded free from snow around the old willow near the kitchen for a bird feeding ground. Incidentally, it made a very interesting place to watch from our breakfast table in the kitchen. Although we kept the usual winter suet swinging from tree branches, and it was much appreciated by certain birds, many of them enjoyed scratching, chicken style, against the frozen grass for their food.

Gradually we became aware that one raiding squirrel was more daring than the others in feeding with the birds, and it annoyed us by picking all the sunflower seeds from the mixed birdfeed. Nor would this squirrel dash away in fright when we came near to toss out more food. In fact, she kept eating quite close to our feet, like the tame little chickadees. So we began to give her leftover toast, then peanuts and other tidbits not given the birds. By the second year she was eating from our hands, and then we learned that our squirrel friend was "she" and not "he." In the meantime, my artist husband had made a sketch of "Mr. Bush" as we first called "him," which we used on our Christmas cards that year.

The transition from Mr. Bush to Old Mame came about rather unexpectedly. A repairman was lying on the kitchen floor examining the bottom of our refrigerator when he looked up to see a gray squirrel hanging flat, like a flying squirrel, on the screen door. "There's a squirrel on your door!" he shouted in surprise, and added after I had explained about our pet, "Looks like she's ready to have some young ones." And so she did, very shortly afterward.

When this batch of young ones followed her to our yard the first time, we were quite delighted at the unusual sight. Such cute little things, about half her size, and copying everything she did, such as sitting up on the flower pots on the terrace outside the kitchen. But Old Mame was furious with them for following her, and she made frantic rushes at them, all the time growling alarmingly. Since then, many of her children have followed her here. They get pretty good pickings, but not the special fare we set before our star boarder. After all, there are a lot of squirrels on Sugar Hill.

Our intimate acquaintance with Old Mame was quite educational for us. For instance, I had never known that squirrels made noises beyond the familiar chattering sound. Now I know that they do. Any other squirrel encroaching on Old Mame's property rights was met with an angry growl, which increased in ferocity if the intruder needed more frightening. If mad enough, she sort of talked, in deep guttural words. It was very plain what she was saying: "You get away, while the getting is good!"

We learned that gray squirrels are not so guilty about robbing birds' nests as some people say. We never knew it to happen here where there are many birds' nests each year. We learned that gray squirrels do not hibernate each winter as certain other small animals do. We learned that a squirrel can be quite bold about going upstairs, given the chance, but terrified about coming down. On the one occasion that we allowed Old Mame to go upstairs, she grew wilder and wilder until we finally opened a window for her to swing out of, onto the shutter, which enabled her to climb down the side of the house. We learned that they can be as nosy as party-line listeners, finding the right spot in certain trees around the house to peep into the rooms we happen to be in.

Let us get a gathering in the back garden and there, always, was Old Mame. Watching at a discreet distance as guests arrived, she stood upright, with her paws neatly folded over her white apron, like a little old neighbor woman getting an eyeful. There is not a canapé tidbit she refused, even if she had to bury it in disgust the next moment. And regardless of the number of people at our garden party she selected my husband as the giver. He was the one who allowed her to run up his legs and sit begging for something to eat.

One more thing we learned—that it *is* possible for a wild creature to *like* being near you without benefit of handouts. There were times when, completely sated, and tired of burying things, she was content to sit quietly near us where we were seated on our garden chairs.

Our most interesting experience with Old Mame happened one summer. Our guest house had not been used since the previous summer, but my husband's sister and her husband were using it. They came over for breakfast, after their first night there, looking rather haggard. They explained that they had been kept awake by strange noises in the chimney off and on during the night, and that our brother-in-law had finally got up and had pounded heavily against the pipe that went up through their bedroom. They thought, and so had we, that the sounds were made by roosting chimney swifts.

Early that afternoon, while we sat quietly on the shaded lawn to escape the heat, we saw a strange sight. Old Mame came staggering wearily across the lawn, carrying something heavy. She went a short distance, then put it down to rest before going on again. From the limpness of the object she carried, my husband at first thought it was a dead squirrel. But as she came closer we saw that it was a live young squirrel. She had it wrapped around her neck like a furpiece. One of her resting spells was next to a dry stone wall, and the young one rose from the grass where she had laid it and crawled into a crack in the wall.

Old Mame tried with human patience for a long time to get it out. But she could get herself only partly into the crack. While we sat motionless and watched, she made gentle, pleading sounds and kept poking in a paw and waiting. Finally she came straight to my husband and looked up at him before leading him to the wall, from which, with his manipulation of stones, the young one was finally extracted. Taking it by the neck she went wearily off up the hill toward some old apple trees. We respected her privacy, and did not follow her, but kept quiet and watched.

When she returned she first climbed an elm tree by the guest house, then swung over to the roof and went down the chimney. While we watched, she made two more trips to carry her youngsters out of the chimney. But on these trips, although she did stop to rest, she did not go near the wall. She rested herself, with the last young one, on the grass quite near our feet. And we were almost too amazed to whisper.

"If we'd only known," my sister-in-law kept worrying afterward. "We had no idea it was Old Mame and her babies in there." We never did pry into where she took them. She had let us share the secret of their removal from the chimney, which was quite enough.

One winter, we spent two and a half months in Florida and worried a bit about Old Mame. Then a most disturbing letter came from my daughter. She had gone into our house and had found a scene of destruction. Broken dishes, glassware, lamps, torn curtains, upstairs and down, and a very dead squirrel on the hearthrug in the living room. We guessed what had happened. A squirrel—and neither of us could say the words, "Old Mame"—must have got in somehow through the cellar and had tried in vain to get out of the place.

Then, on the morning after we had returned from Florida, there she was, sitting on the kitchen roof outside my window. It *had* to be Old Mame, I said. I dashed downstairs and gathered a box of graham crackers on my way to the kitchen door. Sure enough, it *was* Old Mame! I opened the door and let her in. My husband came down to greet her with, "What are you doing in here, you old wet rat?"

Old Mame has shown no signs of aging since she came into our lives. She has had her battle wounds, but none of them too serious. Her mate, the male squirrel, has appeared a few times and knocked her about. It must have been he, the father of her children, or she would not have taken so much from him. One day, she came to us with a cauliflower ear and much thinner tail. She looked quite unlike herself when I opened the kitchen door. But what other squirrel would be roosting on the door latch and chattering indignation over my delay?

Christopher and Jenny

MYRTLE MORROW WILLIAMS

MOST PEOPLE THINK THAT BIRDS ARE JUST BIRDS AND haven't a trait in common with persons. But I think I know better. Anyway, I know pretty much about house wrens now, from tail to bill, and know they have virtues that human beings think are exclusively their own—namely, appreciation for tradition, shown by their love for the old homestead; a sense of beauty, expressed by tidiness; tenacity of purpose; responsibility to offspring. I know one more attribute we all possess in common, too, only generally it's not listed as a virtue. But that's a moot question. Wives would call it strictly a husbandly vice—and vice versa. Anyway, it's *temper,* and this summer I witnessed a perfect demonstration of how a male reacts when crossed in matters domestic.

For three summers I had watched two wrens, Jenny and Christopher, come back to a house nailed to the trunk of an old oak tree. I was sure it was the same pair by the familiarity with which they set up housekeeping. No chattering about drains and draughts or whether sleeping quarters were suitable; no pecking at an inadequate paint job; no squawks at the tree's proximity to the house. They came and settled in, knowing from past experience just how large the nursery was, in which corner to build the nest so rain and wind could not despoil it, knowing they had good neighbors. One day the male's song would be heard and shortly thereafter they were moving in—figuratively, with bed slats over their shoulders.

One year, as an experiment, that oak tree house was moved to a spot above a window on the terrace to give me a ringside seat at the Wren Revue and to test my theory that it was the same couple. And I'm sure it was. They appeared. First, they examined the oak and flew about awhile; then, directly as a child's nose leads him to the kitchen when cookies are baking, they proceeded to their old unpainted homestead that had been placed above the window. They ignored completely another wren house placed beside the back porch.

It wasn't long before Jenny got to work with stripped, pliable twigs from the evergreens while Christopher, his throat swelling with songs about the marvels he had seen on his trip south the past winter, flitted about, giving the neighborhood a treat. All one afternoon I watched tiny Jenny move her furniture in, marveling at her single-mindedness, amazed at the skill with which she darted through the small door while carrying twigs sideways so they paralleled her body. If a twig were too long or balked at the doorway, or perhaps had an imperfection, she dropped it on the stone terrace and flew off for another. No fallen twigs were retrieved. No secondhand material went into *her* carpentering. All day Jenny worked and, apparently, all day Christopher played. It's the only way I can explain what happened.

Next afternoon I took my sewing to the terrace where I had sat the previous day, not ten feet away from the window below the wren home. I hoped to find Christopher working this day; hoped (using a homely comparison) to at least find him steadying the ladder while Jenny pounded the nails. But there was complete absence of activity. Silence hung over the villa. No busy little brown body flew in and out and round about. No burst of song nor ecstatic trills came from the trees or the garden. It made me strangely uneasy. I wondered if something dire had happened in my absence through the morning.

Sorrowfully, I decided it had been a mistake to move the house; that feathered things have no urge for change and newness. Then, suddenly, I heard angry bird words down in the garden—high female twitters and angrier other ones. A bird flew across the terrace and darted straight to the wren house, sat on the roof, threw out his chest, and swelled up belligerently. It was Christopher, and I hardly recognized him. His tail was perked up like that of an airplane about to land; he seemed paler brown, almost gray. With rage,

I suppose. And, tagging him, close behind him like a misunderstood wife, flew Jenny, suffused with jitters. She lit on the awning alongside the wren home and fluttered and quivered with indignation and argument. But Christopher wanted no part of her. He hurled insults; hopped down and into the house; appeared in the door again, looking as though he were about to lift his hand against a woman; and disappeared inside in a flash. Soon twigs came hurtling through the doorway. There was a pause—then, as if he were too beside himself to continue the destruction, he darted out and away, Jenny following with protestations or apologies or what have you.

They went off to the woods, I suppose, so the neighbors couldn't hear any more, and I didn't see or hear them again that day. I never learned, of course, what started the brawl. But I figured like this. Christopher, getting through with his dallying round the neighborhood, came back to check up on how the little woman had arranged the furniture. And he didn't like it. Perhaps the head of the bed would have let the morning sun into his eyes—or perhaps down south he'd had more elegant quarters. Or maybe he was peevish because his house had been moved, or a bad bug for luncheon had upset his digestion. Or again, perhaps it was all an act, just to show his authority. At any rate, they made it up somehow for, though next day the terrace was strewn with the twigs Jenny had so painstakingly gathered and placed in her little house, she held no grudge. He forgave her, and she was a dutiful wife. She let him get away with it. She must have got in a few words for herself, however, for this time they *both* worked at building and Christopher proved himself a match for her zeal.

In due time there were murmurs and whispers within the house which signified that Christopher again was the head of a family. Activity then was unceasing. One guessed at the stage of development in the young by the size of the insects brought for their consumption. First, little gnats, flies, and bugs; then, bigger and better moths and flying or crawling things. One could guess by the voices inside, also. At first, faint peeps and squeaks gradually swelling to a chorus of chatter whenever either parent appeared in the doorway with succulent groceries. Those inside always knew when mess time was approaching. They had prophetic souls. I could see little mouths stretched wide even before a parent's shadow fell across the doorway. Between meals, all was silent.

I often wondered about the number of occupants of that small house and guessed at three. Four at the very outside. I wondered also how Jenny and Christopher knew which one had been fed last—which one rated the next bite of ragout-of-bug of moth-en-casserole. But I'm sure they had some way of checking because often they perched outside the door to turn the head to each side and listen earnestly before thrusting head inside and cramming the borne morsel down a small throat. I believed that some special note in the chorus of voices must determine who was next.

Such evidence of solicitous parenthood might be used as a pattern for humans. And their neatness could be pointed to as Exhibit A in Side Talks With Young Mothers, too. They were great for sanitation. In the matter of disposing of excrement from their young, they were neither careless nor procrastinating. They didn't dally around and let the work pile up or give the nest a good cleaning out once a day, nor did they send out an S.O.S. for the Bird Didy Wash. Their care was personal and continuous. And they were efficiency experts as to waste motion. Each trip they made to home port was a round trip. Groceries were brought on the in-going one and on the outward one they carried away a white substance—the excrement or what was left after their small charges had extracted sustenance from their food. Furthermore, they carried that white substance away and out of sight, whether from their sense of neatness only, or to deposit it as a lure for some fated insect, or both, I have yet to find out. But, their dooryard was always spotless.

The weeks went by but still the young tenants of Wren Villa did not appear. I grew impatient. Were they going to stick in that crowded tenement the rest of their lives, and mine, too? Had Jenny and Christopher brought young parasites into the world? I had seen nestlings of robins, catbirds, and song sparrows on the ground—pitifully scrawny, sparsely feathered objects; thumping around in their efforts to fly and achieving nothing more than awkward, hard bumps. Were my little wrens lacking in initiative, or pluck? Were they morons? But, no! Wren parents were wise. Therein lay their sense of responsibility to their offspring. They would wait for the finished product before allowing it off the assembly line. Apparently, before turning it loose in a competitive world, each wren child got a full high school education plus a college degree.

Came the Big Day. The Zero Hour. The Hegira. Jenny and Christopher sat in the oak tree, fifty feet away from the terrace. Their calls were cajoling; chirping notes unlike the songs they flung out as they busily hustled for food for their young. And they brought no food to the little house. No action, no groceries, was plainly their slogan. They didn't go near Wren Villa except for vague flutterings to the edge of the terrace and back to the oak tree. Still, no signs from the children. I burned with embarrassment.

Finally, a little head poked adventurously out of the door of the villa, but drew back. There were twitters, perhaps giggles, of delicious apprehension. Half of a small body protruded and withdrew again. A few repeats; then, with one swift swoop, Number One Wren darted forth—a beautifully developed and feathered bird; a perfect model, complete in every detail. Straight as a bee and proudly, as though knowing his way about, he flew to the old oak and his parents. Leaves and branches hid him from view, but I could hear his triumphant chirpings. I waited for the next, and he came out shortly after. Number Two Wren. A perfect model also. But he was a rugged individualist. He had to show off. With a sweeping detour, a wide, graceful arc, he headed for the lilac bushes; soared up again; banked and returned to make an elegant three-point landing on an oak branch. I was sure Jenny and Christopher fairly burst with pride.

One more to come I had figured—two more, perhaps—for there were rustlings in the old homestead and I was sure I heard conversation there. That would make four and certainly no more could that wee house have held. Sure enough, two more flew out—one after the other at intervals. Both good models, too, although Number Four came a cropper and lit on a bush at the edge of the terrace. Probably a little weak in the struts. Perhaps, from time to time, when the bugs were passed, he'd been elbowed out of the way by that individualist, Number Two Wren. But Jenny was on the job and hovered encouragingly until he took to the air again. I drew a long breath of relief. Jenny and Christopher had got their brood off all right. All beautiful, capable birds—diplomas in their hands. I called out congratulations. Suddenly, there was activity in the villa. Could there be another? Could there be five?

A head appeared in the door, and Number Five made a successful flight to the oak tree. Good Heavens! It began to look like a clown act I once saw in the circus in which clowns poured out of a tiny coupe—one after another until twenty or so emerged. For now came Number Six Wren, shortly after Number Five! But he was the Timid Soul. He only made the awning; from the awning he hopped back to the roof of Wren Villa. Then Jenny showed real concern—and her sense of neatness. With due coaxing and flutters and hovering, she got him up on his wings to join the others, then she went back and removed the white substance he had dropped on the roof in his excitement.

And then I felt sad. Happy for Jenny and Christopher because they had pulled it off so successfully, but sad for myself and the empty little house whose tenants had provided me with so much entertainment. But, the house was not empty *yet!* The tiniest of tiny heads appeared at the door and Number Seven Wren peeped out forlornly with a wistful eye. Jenny dropped her work and darted to him; hopped on the roof and leaned over; sat on the tiny perch below the door; flew around and back with words of assurance. And, after much backing and filling and grinding of gears, Tiny Tim finally made it.

I waited to see if there were more because by this time I would believe anything. But soon Christopher and Jenny flew proudly across the garden, surrounded by their seven children; and I knew the show was over. The curtain had gone down on Wren Revue. I must wait until next season to see the act repeated.

Aloysius the Independent

WILLIAM D. BERRY

It was about four-thirty in the morning when the porcupine went under our bed. We were at Camp Bear Paw, a Girl Scout summer camp in the northern Sierra Nevadas of California. I didn't find out about it until several hours later when Liz, my wife, greeted me with a description of a colossus among porcupines that had ambled beneath us on his way to some undisclosed destination. I wish she had awakened me. It would have saved a lot of trouble later on, for Aloysius [pronounced Al-oh-is'ius] and I were destined to cross trails only once again. At that time she didn't think it was important. After all, the porcupine hadn't been bothering us, and after four summers at camp my wife had accepted the big rodents as a part of the forest.

Rucker Lake, at 5600 feet above sea level, is the culmination of a forest of cedar, black oak, and ponderosa pine that climbs the long western slope of the mountains. Oaks reach up sixty feet toward the sun, and the giant ponderosas rise a hundred feet above them. The pines are monumental boundary markers of their own range, for on the slopes above they give way to somber ranks of firs. These living towers are the retreats of many porcupines, animals that are unspectacular in appearance and possess neither beauty nor cleverness. However, in our minds, porcupines are the outstanding inhabitants of that area, probably because we lived so close to them. The black-tailed deer, the bucks trotting stiff-necked over a ridge, carefully balancing new velvet antlers, made an instant and lasting impression. So did the great, black pileated woodpecker with his ringing cry. But these were creatures glimpsed and gone; the porcupines, refusing to be disturbed, gave us a chance to know something of their world.

The porcupine, protected by his coat of needle-sharp quills, ambles unconcernedly about his business. When smaller rodents flee the slightest hint of danger, he merely stops and sniffs. Only a visible enemy can alter his course, and his right-of-way is seldom challenged.

The porcupine is comparatively self-sufficient from the very beginning. On May twenty-fourth we found a tiny porcupine that had died at birth, still attached to its placenta. Its thick, dark coat already concealed minute but effective quills. Solitary youngsters appear to be the rule, for when camp opened on July thirteenth someone discovered another baby under one of the tent platforms; and later in the summer one more was taken from its hiding place in a little hollow under a fallen tree. Deceptively cuddly balls of woolly black fur, these infants were far from helpless, for they displayed a bristling array of short spines under the soft fur, and their teeth were already sharp. In a sense the little porcupine is never really a baby. He accompanies his mother for the duration of the summer, learning the trails and retreats of his forest, but he is always on the verge of independence.

By fall his coat is acquiring a grizzled look, as the first of the long yellowish guard hairs so characteristic of the adult porcupine appear, but he will not attain the dimensions of maturity until he has passed his first birthday. Yearling porcupines, safely through their first winter, have established their solitary domains. Their lives fall into the routine accorded to the powerful or the protected, and they assume the self-centered indifference of those that take their right-of-way for granted.

Occasionally their routine is interrupted. A young coyote, unskilled and adventurous, may brave the warning display of quills and be sent on his way with a mouthful of needles. Or the deep midwinter snows may drive a more cautious mountain lion or the cunning fisher to bring a porcupine's life to a violent end. The spring thaws always disclose a certain number of porcupine skeletons, buried in bundles of still sharp, but useless, quills. Some of the porcupines survive these encounters year after year and in time seem to become an indestructible and permanent part of the forest.

Such a porcupine was old Aloysius. We don't know who named him, but to the little Girl Scouts camping under the pines he embodied the forest at night, and to name him was the first step in understanding him. "Aloysius" denoted someone of importance, but at the same time someone who was not to be taken too seriously when he suddenly appeared at some unknown hour of the night. An indefinable shape in the gloom, he gained solidity from the dry leaves crunching under his weight, the rustling of his hollow quills and coarse hair, and the determination of his approach. The trails he followed had the permanence of his will; they recognized no obstructions like cots and campers. Completely oblivious to any small girl who had unknowingly chosen to sleep with her toes in his path, he would brush the legs of her cot in passing, and she might even hear his grunting complaints as he mulled over some problem. Then his portly shape receded, fading in the dim light; and soon the hitching, scraping sound of his return up the pillarlike trunk of a ponderosa pine heralded the approaching dawn. Later, in the normal perspective of daylight, he might be located and pointed out to the awe and admiration of the entire camp—a shaggy, yellow mass sprawled far above. Even at a distance his bulk was impressive, and the yellow stain of his long hair gave him an air of antiquity.

Aloysius did recognize the attractiveness of one part of the camp, a small storage cabin called the Chalet. The camp counselors occasionally left oranges or other delicacies there, and besides, its dark interior appealed to him. Unless the doors were securely fastened, the old porcupine would swing them open with his strong, hooked forepaws and make himself at home. Early risers often caught a glimpse of his bristling backside disappearing into a "subapartment" he maintained under the foundations.

All summer I heard of Aloysius and his exploits; he was becoming a local legend, as the grandfather of all porcupines. That same summer I was commissioned to do the paintings for the National Audubon Society's series of cards on North American mammals, and when "porcupine" turned up on the list my model was already decided upon. The entire camp was put on the alert for Aloysius' next appearance, with instructions to detain the old porcupine by any means possible. Aloysius, the independent, was going to sit for his portrait, whether he liked it or not.

In the ensuing weeks we learned a lot about the many porcupines around camp. Most of them lived in the trees, and their home trees were easily identified by the piles of droppings around their trunks.

Sometimes the big rodent itself could be located, but as the animals usually slept sitting up, hunched into shapeless balls of yellow hair, they were almost indistinguishable from the clumps of dead or dying needles scattered through the branches. A few porcupines were ground-dwellers; we found one den in a rocky crevice that looked as if it had been used for generations. All of the porcupines spent a good deal of time on the ground at night, wandering from one food tree to another. It was there we usually surprised them, and their reactions were varied. Often they merely ambled out of our way and paused to reconnoiter, sometimes standing on their hind legs and sniffing to catch our scent. If we followed, they might break into a clumsy gallop, heading for a nearby tree. They crashed through the undergrowth with no attempt at secrecy, and once at a height just above our reach they would invariably stop again and wait for us to leave.

Clumsy as a climbing porcupine may appear at first glance, he is very much at home in trees. There is great strength in his hooked claws, and his tubercle-studded soles are sure of their grip. If he can get one forepaw hooked over a sturdy limb he can pull his entire weight up onto that support, and his tubby body is surprisingly flexible. Ancestors of our present-day porcupines once climbed through our prehistoric forests. Today, the bowed legs of their descendants are fitted to the cylindrical structure of trunks and branches. The animal's method of scaling the sheer column of a giant pine is unique. Long claws hooked securely into the bark, its body close to the trunk, it pulls itself up one step at a time. The stumpy tail braces it against slipping, for on its undersurface the hair grows into a cuplike, matted mass of short stiff bristles that grip the side of the tree. What the porcupine lacks in speed it makes up for in tenacity.

Trees are both haven and food supply for the porcupines. Around Rucker Lake the bark of ponderosa pines and white firs seemed to be their basic diet, with black oak leaves added as a summer luxury. Although strict vegetarians, they undoubtedly varied this fare with a wide variety of forest products; for captive porcupines liked carrots, lettuce, many kinds of fruit, and even bread. Ax handles, salty with absorbed perspiration, they whittled down with their chisel-like incisors, and plywood left out during the winter was gnawed full of great holes, apparently because the glue that held it together was tasty. The surprising thing was that, despite the local abundance of porcupines, the forest suffered no discernible damage from their appetites. In other locations girdled and dying timber had branded the porcupine a scourge; but here, at least, they scattered their depredations and left the trees, as a whole, unchanged.

We saw porcupines young and old, affectionate porcupines, angry porcupines, and just plain indifferent porcupines; but it began to appear that Aloysius owed his present exalted position to some innate ability for avoiding interference. Although he left innumerable proofs of his existence, it appeared that if I were to meet him, I must hack away the stony foundations of the Chalet or travel through the treetops. I got a stiff neck doing my only sketch, a distant view of Aloysius' bulbous silhouette as it appeared from directly below. Waiting for him to descend from a known perch proved to be the most futile and frustrating of all. It is said that a porcupine will remain for weeks in the top of a single tree, but none of us had the perseverance to stay at its base to find out. Camp closed for the season, and we left it to the care of Aloysius and the approaching winter. Had it not been for an unexpected change in our plans, we would probably never have seen him again.

The following spring my wife and I planned a pack trip into the Santa Lucia Mountains of central California, but human plans are subject to diversion. Instead we found ourselves once again under the familiar pines of Bear Paw. We were sitting around the table in the cookshack with several friends, finishing our evening coffee and enjoying the familiar quiet of the mountains. A little deer mouse, running silently out from behind the jars of flour, sugar, and matches, was surprised to find outsiders usurping his claim, and streaked behind the stove. Then someone detected the familiar scratching sound of something coming down a tree. There was no time for careful planning; we jumped and organized and shouted directions as we ran.

We couldn't see the porcupine at first, because he was screened by the lower tree branches. Finally, his fat, yellow-fringed tail descended into our light, a wedge-shaped tail that culminated in a great yellow-haired body. It was Aloysius!

We rushed in, the girls in our party wielding brooms (versatile instruments in feminine hands), while two of us noisily maneuvered a big galvanized can into a position below Aloysius. The big porcupine suddenly realized he had backed into trouble; his long hair stood out in a golden fringe, baring countless black-tipped quills that covered his back and tail in an impenetrable mass. He started up the tree, but a barricade of brooms suddenly blocked his way, pushing against his unprotected muzzle. He reversed, slid for the ground, bumped the rim of the can, and his tail automatically slapped in defense. It was easy to see how the legend of the shooting quills had started, for the tail made a blurred arc and struck with a force that would have filled any surface but metal with a host of stinging spines. Then Aloysius had backed into the can, and we slammed on the lid and proclaimed ourselves hunters of rare skill and determination. To give him more comfortable quarters, we then dumped him out of the can into a cage.

The next morning I went down to get my first good look at the fabled Aloysius by daylight, and to see how much damage he had done to the cage.

He was gone! The boards we had pounded in so securely had been swept aside, and the porcupine had ambled to his freedom. I haven't seen him since, but I am sure he is back in his pine, sprawled at ease on a limb high above a forest that is his by undisputed right of way. I suppose it's just as well we never got a good look at him that day, for a strong light may dispel a legend. The porcupine I finally painted was a composite of all those that I studied in the process of trying to trap the patriarch. I combined the best features of many, and I should have foreseen the result.

It was a portrait of Aloysius.

My Favorite Bird

FRANK F. GANDER

UNTIL RECENTLY, WHENEVER SOMEONE ASKED ME WHICH bird I liked most, I was at a loss for an answer. There were many birds of which I was very fond, but not one that stood out above all others. Now this is changed, and only in the last few years have I had an answer. The species which has so endeared itself to me is one with which I was not previously acquainted, the Brewer's sparrow.

I had seen stuffed specimens of Brewer's sparrows in museums—pale and washed-out—and had been totally unimpressed by them. How different is the living bird! Pale it may be, but vibrant with life and personality. There is something eternally babyish about this little bird, perhaps because it is so small. It is about the size of a chipping sparrow, but there is more than just its tiny form to give this impression. It has an innocent, trusting face, like that of a newly-hatched chick, and it is friendly and confiding. I have never known any other bird to tame so rapidly.

Brown towhees, rufous-crowned sparrows, green-backed goldfinches, house finches, house wrens, and three kinds of hummingbirds are so accustomed to seeing me work around my garden in southern California that they pay but slight attention to my presence. Roadrunners, California thrashers, California quail, Bell's sparrows, lark sparrows, and black phoebes are almost as casual about our meetings. But none of these has shown an active interest in me, personally, as have the Brewer's sparrows.

Before they left my yard for their summer home, these tiny birds would come flying to meet me and circle around me as I walked along the garden path, or, as spring drew near, they would perch in a manzanita not three feet away and sing their delightfully varied little song. I have known tame canaries to sing to humans in this way, but I had never met it before in a wild bird. An animal behaviorist would probably be able to account for this entirely by instinct; but, whatever its cause, it was a delightful experience to have one of these little birds come flying to me, alight, and, looking right into my eyes, sing as if it were pleased by my presence. This has happened too many times to have been a coincidence of time and place.

From the first appearance of these birds in my garden, they were less timid than most birds. It was a December day when the first two Brewer's sparrows arrived and joined the white-crowned and golden-crowned sparrows, lark sparrows, and brown towhees at the feeding stations that I maintain on two large granite boulders in my garden. This garden is a naturalistic planting of native plants of California and other drought-tolerant species on a bolder-strewn hillside and is adjacent to wild chaparral. A path winds over the hillside, and the area is a haven for birds. Although many species visit me here, none have so quickly come to trust me as did the Brewer's sparrows.

By their third day in the area, these first two would fly to meet me; then fly ahead and alight upon a rock. They would fly again as I came near, but would be back again, often coming within a foot of my hand as I scattered the baby-chick scratchfeed over the top of the rock.

With this example before them, the white-crowned and golden-crowned sparrows and the brown towhees soon became much tamer. Even the lark sparrows grew less timid. Soon I could stand on the path, not more than five feet from the rock feeding station, and have these five species feeding there. Even groups of twenty or thirty people could stand nearby without frightening the birds, but cameras and field glasses made them nervous.

On the morning of April eighteenth, only a handful of my wintering birds were left to greet me—one Brewer's sparrow, two white-crowns, and three goldens. The rest had started their spring migration. These few were about for possibly ten days longer; and then they, too, were gone. Somewhere on their nesting grounds in summer in the sagebrush flats of the Great Basin there were some little birds that I missed greatly. They had gone; but their influence continued, for my year-round birds were markedly tamer. I hoped that these residents, in turn, would impart some of this tameness to the birds that came to summer with us.

For their winsome ways and for their part in taming the other birds of my garden, I grew very fond of the Brewer's sparrows. I hoped that bird-watchers in the nesting territory might come to know them and enjoy them as I had during the short four months they were with me.

Red Squirrels Are Good Company

HARRISON F. LEWIS

THE MOTHER RED SQUIRREL HAD EASY ACCESS TO ALL but one of the birds' feeding stations at our country home in Nova Scotia. Food was as readily available to her as to the chickadees, woodpeckers, or jays, and she was made equally welcome at these places.

The only feeder presumably not accessible to her was a horizontal one that I had made from a short spruce stick. It was suspended, about five feet above the ground, from the lower strand of a pulley clothesline of aluminum wire. The spruce-stick feeder hung about fifteen feet away from my back porch and was intended to provide a reserve food supply that could be reached by birds alone. But our red squirrel had a growing family to feed and she wanted access to *all* the good food in her territory. She may have been spurred on by the fact that birds visited the clothesline feeder before her eyes and she could not follow them. Time and again she ran nimbly up the wall of our house, clambered over the pulley and tried to walk along the wire toward the suspended feeder. It was useless! She would make uncertain progress for two or three feet, then begin to lose her balance. For a few seconds she would struggle, jerking her tail wildly to right herself. But always she became rapidly more unstable, until she had to admit defeat and drop to the ground! That clothesline barrier between her and the feeder seemed insurmountable.

This was a squirrel, however, that would not give up. Her motto, it seemed, was that sound old one, "Try was never beat." Eventually it rewarded her, as it has rewarded many others. One day, to our astonishment, there she was, seated comfortably on the swinging feeder, while she calmly ate the food that had so long tantalized her! How did she get there? We watched, and soon discovered that she ran up the supporting pulley; grasped the *lower* strand of wire with all four feet; and swung, back downward, beneath it, where she couldn't lose her balance. Then she ran rapidly, hand over hand, or paw over paw, to a position a few inches above the feeder. From there she dropped down on the spruce-stick feeder. Easy enough, once she had worked out a method!

One of her children, grown as big as his mother, and confident in his newly acquired abilities, undertook it, too. He couldn't run up the wall of the house, but he overcame that difficulty by climbing some temporary staging to the roof above the porch. Once on the roof, he saw the clothesline only a few inches below its outer edge, and was able to step gingerly down to it. Following his mother's example, he swung his body beneath it and moved toward the feeder, paw over paw. His advance was awkward and slow, but at last he hung above that attractive feeder. But he was hanging, back toward the ground, from the *upper* wire, with the lower wire of the trolley between him and the feeder. The feeder was suspended from that lower strand, which sagged downward because of the feeder's weight! To reach the feeder, he needed to drop at least three feet through the air, and, worst of all, that taut lower line was directly interposed between him and his goal!

The young hopeful worked back and forth along the upper line, seeking a good position for a drop. While creeping along the upper wire, with his back toward the ground, he could not look downward. And so he stopped from time to time to look below him. Always that lower wire was in his way! At last he jumped for the feeder, struck the lower strand of wire, and bounced to the ground. When he struck, he showed no pain or disappointment, but instantly busied himself in searching for food at the spot where he had landed, as though to give us to understand that *this* was his objective from the first!

In our part of southwestern Nova Scotia, though there is practically no hunting of red squirrels by men or dogs, our experience shows that the lives of these little creatures are short. One red squirrel at a time maintains a territorial claim to our house, adjacent feeding stations, and a surrounding tract. It permits no squirrel intruders, except its mate, which shares its territory and food in winter.

If the territory-holder is a female, her youngsters have similar privileges for a short period in spring. No individual squirrel, however, retains control of the area for much more than a year. Not long after one has disappeared, a new landholder, apparently a young animal, comes into the territory and takes over.

Though we have had one or more red squirrels in our yard under close observation much of the time, we have yet to see one of them cause any harm to birds or their eggs. Squirrels and small birds, especially juncos, may feed only a foot or two apart. It seems that a tendency to attack birds and rob their nests is a trait exhibited only by certain individual squirrels.

Red squirrels differ much in their ways and in what we may call their natures or personalities. Belligerency and peacefulness, friendliness and unconquerable suspicion, neatness and gross untidiness—all these characteristics we have observed as the squirrels and the years have passed by.

The most delightful of all the red squirrels we have known was a male that we called Buster. He charmed us for a year or so, and we still like to think of him. He soon lost his natural suspicion of humans and would take food readily from our hands or from those of our guests who might be complete strangers to him. Most of the squirrels that live about our home learn, eventually, to feed from our hands. Usually they remain suspicious and show frequent nervous fits and starts. They will stand as far away from us as possible and stretch their necks forward to the utmost when taking a tidbit. But not so with Buster. If he was nearby when our back door was opened, he dashed up happily and unhesitatingly to be fed. If he found the door ajar, he would slip into the house and wander from room to room. Though we did not encourage him to come into the house, it was amusing to see him staring about at walls and furniture, as though saying to himself, *My! what a place! I have always wondered what kind of nest these big creatures had!* When permitted to run about the house freely, he would run up and down the window drapes and investigate nooks and corners.

Some squirrels, during all the time that they spend with us, do not enter the cellar; others visit it regularly and spend much time there. The route they take is presumably through some underground tunnel, and we have yet to discover it. They munch a few apples and tear up newspaper on the shelves, but they do no serious harm.

In January of 1954, the greater part of a squirrel courtship was apparently carried on in our cellar. When outside the house, the two squirrels might sit demurely side by side; but day after day we could hear, through the floor under our feet, a deal of wild scurrying and chasing in the cellar. At times we could hear one of the animals utter a soft, quickly wavering, continuous chatter, resembling somewhat the gurgling sound made by water flowing from an inverted bottle.

North of our house, the sheltering woods are only twenty yards away. When the ground is bare of snow, a red squirrel will readily cross the gap. But if ten inches of snow covered the ground, the squirrel tunneled its way toward our yard. The tunnel extended from the border of the woods toward a feeding station beside the house, but it ended midway between. Along its course, at intervals of about six feet, there were openings to the surface—"squirrel-holes," corresponding to the "manholes" in a conduit.

With due regard for its own safety, the squirrel would enter the woodland end of the tunnel, but apparently its nervous curiosity made it reluctant to remain under for long without surveying its surroundings. At each "squirrelhole," it would pop up, head and shoulders above the snow, and take a good look round. Sometimes, after it had dropped back out of sight, it would reappear at the nearest opening toward its starting point, rather than at the next one toward its destination! When, after this backward and forward tracking, it reached the end of the tunnel, it would cover the rest of the distance to the house by a quick dash across the surface of the snow. Apparently it preferred the risk of a short distance above the snow to the labor of tunneling under it.

In the spring of 1955, the female squirrel which then shared our home area provided us with some new experiences. She found an opening under a bottom clapboard of our house, giving her access to the interior of the outer wall. Eventually, by this route, she reached the attic; and in the wall beside our dining room she made her nest and brought forth her young. We did not realize what was going on until the young, still in the nest, began to squeak loudly enough for us to hear them. While we were not exactly pleased at this development, we could not, at that stage, stop up the entrance. As a matter of fact, this unplanned sharing of our house with a squirrel family caused us neither harm nor damage of any kind. When the youngsters were half grown, they left the nest, and, spurred on by their natural curiosity, explored every cranny of their sheltered surroundings, as young squirrels should. In due course their wanderings took them to our attic, where they scampered about, but harmed nothing. It was more than a little fun to go up there and glimpse several slender, half-furred squirrel tails disappearing down into the open walls of the unfinished sides of the attic. Then, in a minute or two, if one remained quiet, eager, bright-eyed little squirrel faces appeared above the floor, looking about to reconnoiter the situation!

The young left the house as soon as they were well grown. Their mother, for a time, led them to the feeding shelf on the back porch. Once we were assured that the whole family was outside of the house, we blocked the opening under the clapboard. A future squirrel tenant inside our house might not be so well behaved!

Great was our surprise when, on a September day, the red squirrel that was then occupying our home area limped to our back door with five or six porcupine quills protruding from its body. Two were in a foreleg; the others were in its hips and sides. The animal held the injured leg off the ground and hobbled clumsily about. Where the quills protruded from its body and leg, the flesh was badly swollen, and the poor little creature appeared to be in great misery. We supposed that it could not live long. On the following day, when it did not reappear, we assumed that it had perished.

But another surprise was in store for us. Four days after we had first seen the injured squirrel, it reappeared at our feeding station! Only three quills protruded from its body. Although it was still very lame, it seemed to be suffering less. Five days later only two quills were visible, and on the following day, or ten days after we first saw the injured squirrel, it was completely free of quills and seemed to be in normal health and good spirits. The points of penetration of the quills were visible as scars for some time thereafter, but eventually they become indistinguishable.

More than a year later, when the porcupine-injured squirrel had been succeeded by another, we observed a somewhat similar experience. This time, the squirrel frequenting our feeding stations appeared one day with a porcupine quill in the end of its nose. This probably caused it much pain, but insertion of one quill did not appear to result in the severe general distress that was so obvious with the first squirrel. This one continued to come regularly to the feeding station, where it took food as best it could. After a few days, the quill had disappeared from its nose.

Prior to these experiences, we had not realized that a red squirrel ever ventured close enough to a porcupine to be wounded by its quills. We still have no idea how it comes about.

In what way do the squirrels become rid of the quills? It has been suggested that part of the quill is absorbed by the squirrel's body and that the rest then drops off or is pulled off by the wounded animal. Even if absorption proceeds only so far as to remove or render pliable the tiny barbs on the quill, loss of the quill should readily follow. While that is one possibility, the impression that we received from our observations was that marked suppuration around each quill was the effective process which rid the squirrel of the quill. If a quill became surrounded by sufficient matter, it presumably would lose contact with tissues and pass out unhindered from the wound. Its exit would be assisted by any friction of the quill with surrounding objects; perhaps by the squirrel's deliberate efforts to remove it.

The red squirrels that share our home area with us provide a great deal of pleasure, and any annoyance they have caused us has been trivial and fleeting. Can we expect the wild creatures about us to furnish only recognized benefits? In our relations with them, as in relations among people, there should be tolerance, patience, and a reasonable spirit of give and take. We enjoy our squirrels and would not be without them. They are good company.

A Thrasher Talks His Way to Fame

MARIE V. BEALS

LET YOUR NEIGHBORS KNOW THAT YOU ARE A REAL bird-lover and, sooner or later, you will hear about every bird in distress for miles around. No telling how many new and interesting experiences await you just around the corner, nor what small "discoveries" you may make to add to the growing accumulation of bird facts useful to science.

It was on a bright July day that a telephone call brought two tiny brown thrashers into my life. "What shall I do with these two baby birds I have found on the ground?" asked the voice at the other end of the wire. "Why, just bring them over to me," I replied.

That was the beginning of my intimate friendship with Tom and Jerry, so christened by my husband, and the beginning of an association that brought many happy hours to the Beals family—and to the lives of Tom and Jerry Thrasher, too, I believe.

Although I had been a bird-watcher since I was a child, I had never approved of captive, caged birds as pets. My joy had been in making my Long Island, New York, garden so attractive to birds that they came and shared it with me of their own free will.

The tiny fledgings were almost lifeless when I received them. Their eyes were still unopened, but they had strength enough to beg for food. I put them in a berry box lined with woolen cloth. I fed them every fifteen minutes for several days. Small bits of moistened whole wheat bread, pieces of earthworm, wireworm, mealworm, millipede, blueberry, cherry, and a very small quantity of hamburger made up the menu; and Vitamin D in the form of a drop of cod-liver oil was the "pick-me-up" with which they began each day. I put the food well down in their throats so that their throat muscles, with which they swallow, could function.

When their eyes began to open and their feathers to grow, I moved them to a canary cage. Jerry slept on the perch. Tom's right leg was afflicted, so he slept on the floor. Jerry had an affliction, too; his bill was crossed. When he was old enough to pick up food for himself, I kept the tip of the two mandibles clipped, shortening them about an eighth of an inch every three months.

When their tails were full grown, each bird was given his own cage made of half-inch wire mesh, 3′ x 2′ x 2′. Notches were cut in the perches in Tom's cage to support his weak leg. In clear weather the thrashers spent several hours each day in an outdoor wire enclosure. Here they passed the time sunbathing and hunting for food—tossing aside dead leaves on the ground to find insects and earthworms or catching insects on the wing. Their sunbathing was a sight to behold —with bills wide open and a wild stare in their eyes, they sat on the perch lifting their feathers and turning and twisting, so that full rays of sunshine touched all parts of their bodies.

Part of my daily routine with Tom and Jerry was "indoor exploration." The signal for this adventure was for me to open the cage doors. The two birds hurried out and began to fly through the house as if some wild spirit had suddenly taken possession of them. Under chairs and tables they went, over the sofa and across the desk. They cut corners and darted from here to there with a speed that made a mere human dizzy, but never once during their daily dozen did they collide with anything.

Nothing escaped their notice. Was a wrapped package private property? I should say not! They soon had the string pulled off, the wrapping punched and torn, so that bits of paper floated through the air. When the doorbell rang, they reached the door first; when the telephone rang, they flew to the table where it stood.

They were endlessly inquisitive about me. They flew to my head when I entered the room, pulled out hairpins, tugged at my hair, pecked at my nose, investigated my ears and poked their bills into them. Their favorite game was to have me drag a piece of paper, tied to a string, across the floor. They would chase it the way kittens do, snatch it in their bills, and toss it into the air.

When they were six weeks old they gave their first call—a loud "smack!" A couple of weeks later, they sang for the first time. The singing continued all winter, a low medley of sounds that became louder as spring approached; by May both were in full song.

During spring migration, when brown thrashers began to appear in my garden, I released Tom (May seventh). He stayed in the garden all day, mingling with others of his kind. I saw him last around six o'clock that afternoon when he sat in a shrub near the kitchen window, calling and scolding. The next morning all the thrashers were gone—and with them, Tom.

On May twelfth, I released Jerry. He, too, stayed in the garden all day, answering my call and alighting on my hand for mealworms. After a thunderstorm the next day, he disappeared. For two days I called for him with no result. On the afternoon of the second day, I found him in one of the shrubs, looking chipper as you please. In his bill he held a red cherry—one that I had placed in his dish in the garden. He dropped the cherry, flew to my head, and clung there as I entered the house. He chattered happily, pulled at my hair, and came tumbling down with it. I opened a window to see what he would do. He flew to the sill and began to sing, but in a few minutes he was back on my head. Then and there, I decided to keep him.

Now had come the opportunity to try out a theory which I had long entertained: that is, that members of the mockingbird family (to which thrashers belong) have the ability to mimic human conversation just as they have the ability to mimic the songs of the bird world.

One day when Jerry was on the sunporch, I called to him from an adjoining room.

"What are you doing? What are you doing?" I asked over and over.

Suddenly, my own phrases came back to me.

"What are you doing? What are you doing?" Jerry answered. He liked the words. He kept repeating them all day.

The next day, I tried him on the word "paper."

"Paper, paper," Jerry said over and over. Very soon he was calling his own name, "Jerry." Then my name. "Beals! Beals!" he shouted. Usually he repeated a word twice, sometimes three and four times. "Goody, goody, goody," he said, and "Peter, Peter, Peter, Peter."

His vocabulary soon consisted of ninety individual words and an extensive repertory of phrases or sentences.

Strawberry, blueberry, cherry, cheese, peanut, mealworm, radio, birdie, naughty, hurry, quick were common words with him. Sometimes he said "Sleepy" and "Oh, dear!"; or "All right," "Stay there," "This way," "Pretty Jerry," "It's raining," "Peek-a-boo," and "A and P." When he called my brother, Santo, it was, "Santo-to-to!"

He imitated the songs of the redwing, Baltimore oriole, northern yellow-throat and many others, and pronounced such names as chewink, bobwhite, phoebe, killdeer, whippoorwill and pewee. He loved the word "busy" and repeated it many times during the day, with inflection and interrogation: "Busy, busy, busy?"

Jerry sang and talked every day in the year except during the molting period from the end of July until the end of August. May, June, and July were the months when he "displayed." He perched on the chandelier or on a shelf in the bathroom and even on the floor, tilted his spreading tail high into the air, held his wings upright, and lowered his head until his bill touched the floor. In this attitude, he strutted along, mumbling curious sounds and fluttering his wings. Then he flew off and sang very loudly, exclaiming "Marie's right here," "Watch out," "Pretty Jerry," "Hello, Jerry."

I consulted a number of ornithologists about the talking habits of thrashers, among them Dr. Frank M. Chapman and Dr. Robert Cushman Murphy of the American Museum of Natural History, and Dr. Lee S. Crandall of the New York Zoological Society, but found no one who had heard of a conversational thrasher. Could it be that Jerry had taught us all something new about thrashers?

For seven years, Jerry and I were chums. He did not resent the other members of the family, but he did not respond to their approaches as he did to mine. He repeated only the words and sentences spoken by me, and he used my intonations and inflections. In the morning, he flew upstairs to my room to greet me. If I pretended to be asleep, he perched on the footboard of the bed and said softly, "Lazy bones," "How do you do?" "Wake up!" If I were awake, he perched on my hands and touched my fingers repeatedly with his bill, uttering low gurgling sounds and fluttering his wings. Then, suddenly, he straightened up and pointed his bill toward the ceiling. I have often wondered if wild thrashers greet each other in this fashion in the early morning?

The finger-caress which he gave me in the morning was the same greeting he gave me when I returned to the house after an absence of a few hours and put my hand on or in his cage. No other member of the family was so honored. As I typed this story, Jerry squatted on the table and said to me, "How do you do?" and touched my fingers with his bill. But I believe I know why he hung around the typewriter. He was waiting for me to leave—so that he could pull the ribbon out!

Jerry was both my friend and teacher. He taught me much about bird reactions and bird ways; he gave me many hours of pleasure; and he brought a cheerfulness into our family life that we all appreciated. But what a care, you say? True, Jerry kept me busy finding food for him, but I was repaid for all my trouble, because Jerry never forgot to say: "Thank you. Thank you."

A Black-Tailed Deer Comes of Age

IRVING PETITE

ONE JUNE DAY, A BLACK-TAILED FAWN RAN INTO THE yard of our home in the wooded Tiger Mountains east of Seattle, Washington. Most young deer of the Pacific Northwest—whether they are white-tailed, black-tailed, or mule deer—are born in late May or in June. Perhaps dogs had chased this one and had frightened his mother away. Whatever the tragedy that had separated them, she never came for him. We called the fawn "Man," because of his forthright, independent way that had apparently been his from birth, and which he never lost.

Far from being voiceless, as we had supposed deer were, we found Man to be as vocal as a human child. He "mewed" like a kitten, and whenever he wanted food or companionship he bleated loudly and demandingly. This habit continued until he was in his third or fourth month. Then his voice changed, but even at fifteen months he uttered a nasal *"nmph"* or *"omph,"* audible throughout the house when he was at an outside door.

At first Man drank milk from a bottle, but by the third day he was nudging kittens from their bowl of milk and drinking from it on the back stoop. A Washington State law, enforced by the Game Department, does not allow deer to be penned or shut up, so Man did his eating outside, except when he leaped through an open window into our house or wedged in past the opened kitchen door. He shared cat food and dog food of all varieties—canned, cubed, or kibbled, with or without "liver added." Sliced bacon also pleased him, and he ate it raw. Like any infant, his lips were often dark with sand and dirt. Coal, washed down a nearby slope from a deserted mine dump in

the woods above, likewise satisfied some mineral deficiency of his, or a curiosity in his appetite.

Like Ferdinand the bull, Man loved flowers, and he ate them whole. Around our house and garden, he specialized in sweet-smelling cabbage roses and spicy-fragrant hawthorn blooms. Chrysanthemums he liked, particularly those grown out of season in hot-houses. He enjoyed all small flowers, such as violets, and the flowering racemes of trees like broadleaved maples, which were still lying on the ground in June. As they matured, he also ate the yellow blooms of Oregon grape and the pink, cuplike flowers of red huckleberry. In our dooryard, he ate crocus blooms, and the trilliums that we had transplanted there from the woods. He did not care for daffodils.

Flowers that did not appeal to Man included wild snapdragons, foxgloves, dogwood blooms, bleeding heart, and the oxeye daisies that grew up with the grass seed we had purchased from Iowa. But he did relish dandelions and their seed crowns, wild white daisies, thistles (he carefully avoided the thorns), "miners' lettuce," and dozens of others. As his first summer lengthened, he browsed on the leaves of apple and cherry trees, he pruned the plum trees, ate whole raspberry plants—the leaves, blooms, and berries. Our yard and the surrounding 160 acres were *his*. We never once chased him from any place; he was such a svelte, graceful animal and such a wonder to behold as he pressed down the raspberry canes to browse them or to nibble at low-hanging crabapple boughs. And, like a domestic goat, he stood on a tree stump and stretched high to get the leaves of a willow tree in his front teeth.

Paste from the labels on cans lured him, too; and when a door was open and he tap-danced into our house, the slick paper covers of books disappeared down his throat. Man liked both pocket books and the classics—James M. Cain, the College Standard Dictionary, Keats and Shelley, the journals of Lewis and Clark. He liked to lick metals and machinery: doorknobs; the car, after a washing; the axe blade and the wedges; the teeth of the crosscut saw as it sang through logs. Often we had to stop sawing while Man ate fresh sawdust or the chips the axe had flung from an undercut.

Unlike most domestic animals we had raised, we discovered that Man had a single-hearted, intense, *loyalty* to humans. Every day, unless he was jolted off-course by dogs, he traveled over his same paths on our property to graze; every morning and night for over a year he returned to our house, and he missed only three evening calls in all that time. The three "misses" occurred when the weather was unusually stormy or when he was badly frightened by roving dogs.

Even in his freedom, Man adopted humans completely and followed us at work or play. Identifying us by his keen sense of smell and by our voices, he ignored other people. Bedded alongside a woods road, he let others walk past within a few feet of him; but when I returned home and walked the road, he came leaping out to greet me. Then he would lick the legs and knees of my overalls or lick salt from my forearms, as his expression of joy at my homecoming.

Next to the salt in human perspiration, Man had a taste for the leaves, twigs, and berries of a buckthorn, *Rhamnus purshiana,* commonly called Cascara Sagrada. This medicinal shrub, from which digestive remedies are manufactured, grows only in the Pacific Northwest. Man had common, even slightly vulgar, tastes, too. Sometimes he took a long drink of used dishwater, which had a dash of Purex in it; and when we went swimming, he ate our soap. Cigarettes and cigars he relished (and even the cellophane packages), without preference for any brand. In Man's first autumn, he ate fallen leaves; sometimes it seemed that their colors attracted him, or perhaps it was their crispness. In the winter, he munched dead thimbleberry leaves, cedar foliage, and blackberry vines. Then he would come up to the house for a handout of apples or banana skins.

Wherever Man appeared on his rounds—whether he was grazing,

resting, standing near our house, or overseeing our field work—his ears were his constant guide. Even the semidomesticated doe of W. H. Hudson's *A Hind in Richmond Park* had "wild" ears. Hudson observed her lying with one ear cocked forward to catch the sounds of the near path, the other ear at a different angle, to catch woods sounds.

This can be observed by anyone who has ever seen a deer at close range, but particularly in wild ones whose ears are nervous "parabolic antennae," constantly tilted, shifted, and always cocked.

The first time Man heard the creek gurgling, his ears flicked with the delicious sensation its sound brought him, and he made small, running, jog-steps along the ledge of the canyon to look down at it in the ravine. Later, the creek practically became his home. He stood in it to drink, as it came, icy cold, from the mountains. He waded along its banks and ate dead leaves or the blackberry foliage that overhung it. A thicket of thorny-stemmed wild plums on a terrace above the creek became his favorite bedding ground. He lay concealed there, sometimes lashed by rain or wind; but when snow came and the plum leaves were fallen he went into the dense cedar thickets to sleep.

Man's world was mostly a safe and happy one. When dogs chased him, he would go off across the fields with a springing run, bouncing off the ground with all four feet and coming down on all four hoofs at once. Within minutes we would hear the dogs yelping on a cold trail and might catch a glimpse of Man wading the creek or kneeling to get under logs, far in advance of the dogs. Once, when he was quite young, the dogs nipped his ears a bit; but by the time he was fourteen or fifteen months old he had only to stop when the dogs were chasing him, and they would turn and skulk homeward. The dogs no longer wanted to get near his hoofs or within reach of his formidable spike horns, which had been forming since his eleventh month. At that time, when Man's horns were mere nubbins beneath the slowly-stretching skin, there began the only disturbing theme, to us, in Man's life. A five-year-old girl had a habit of striking her pet sheep with a switch. She may have tried this on Man, which might have earned Man's dislike, for she received hoof bruises from him on her cheek and back. A few days later, while we were burning brush, the two mutually jealous and antagonistic little creatures—girl and deer—approached each other again. Up went Man's front hoofs, and he danced forward, like a boxer sparring. Then, as she backed away, he dropped on all four feet again.

Except with the one child, who had given him a good reason for his distrust of her, Man never exhibited the dangerous characteristics that male deer are supposed to have. He never turned on us, even when the velvet was gone from his horns and he needed places to whet the new, itchy horn material. He often got one of my legs between his spikes, but always in a mild and courteous manner.

A gentle, intelligent creature, even more sensitive than humans, he promised ever to be so; but we were not able to enjoy his companionship beyond his sixteenth month. The opening of hunting season, the fear of the small girl's mother, and Man's love of human companionship—all decided us in favor of taking him to Woodland Park Zoo in Seattle. There he now has constant human companionship, if not the exotic range of food and perfect freedom of movement that he enjoyed at our home. Man had adjusted to a world not his, and in his maturity he needed the protection from it that only captivity could give him. Perhaps it was his human friends that had profited from his companionship, for his coming of age had been a wonderful, instructive experience for all of those who had known him.

The Mystery of the Big Hop

WILLIAM BYRON MOWERY

FOR SEVERAL YEARS AFTER I BEGAN DOING WHAT A friend humorously referred to as "collecting rabbit tracks," I was puzzled no end by certain huge cottontail leaps that I occasionally saw in the snow. It was comparable to coming across the trail of a man who had been walking along at an ordinary stride, but every now and then had taken three or four gargantuan ones of twenty-five or thirty feet each.

Though I didn't see the record of these tremendous rabbit jumps very often, I did run onto them enough to show that they were a part of a rabbit's routine. Just as definitely, they were none of the half-dozen kinds of rabbit hops and leaps I was familiar with but something very special.

In just hopping around to feed or play, a rabbit covers only from one to three feet per hop. In its first burst of speed when flushed from its form, it averages four or five feet per jump. In full, straightaway flight, to escape a fox or coyote, it will do six to eight feet per leap, with an absolute top (in my records, at least) of nine feet. But these super-duper leaps ranged from twelve to fifteen feet! Furthermore, they seemed entirely without rhyme or reason. In the snow I'd see where a cottontail had been hopping along ordinarily, then suddenly had taken three or four of these huge jumps, then back to ordinary ones again.

In my field notes, chiefly about rabbits' feeding habits and the home range of individuals, I had the explanation of the big hop all the time, in the form of scattered clues; but somehow I hadn't put those clues together. My point is that reading snow trails correctly and understanding them fully can be a very recondite business.

To the knowing eye an animal's snow trail can tell quite a story, and often it yields information obtainable no other way. For instance, the habits of the rare pekan or fisher are known very largely from its record in the snow. To be sure, some trails, like the deer's or the skunk's, are not too informative and may be monotonous; but others are so engrossing that you'll follow them across two counties. Of our common animals the weasel and fox are, to me, the most interesting to snow-trail and study. But the cottontail is high on the list, and some surprising new knowledge about this odd, likable little creature has come from its snow record.

By this record you'll discover that the home range of a rabbit is astonishingly small. Give it a den-shelter against vile weather and a dense covert or two against the sudden swoop of enemies, and it will live its whole life contentedly within an acre or so, especially if its range touches that of another rabbit, with which it can play. You'll discover that it's not a creature of the deep night, as commonly supposed, but of the evening and dawn twilights. True, when the moon rides high it does cavort all night, mostly going through its queer, intricate, little-known play maneuvers with other rabbits; but during pitch-dark times it runs little if any. You'll also learn that it's a very abstemious eater and can get along fine on a dibble of coarse, unpalatable food at which most other nibblers and browsers would turn up their noses. While it prefers those plants that stay green all winter, it readily eats bark, dry grass, twig ends, pine needles, and suchlike, and a frozen apple seems a feast for it.

Most of the complaints about rabbit depredation in orchards and gardens are ill-founded. For county agents and others I have many times investigated these complaints, and four times out of five the damage is referable to the groundhog or to meadow mice (*Microtus*). As stated, a rabbit eats very sparingly—a couple of ounces in the evening and a couple in the morning twilight. Pound for pound, a groundhog eats approximately fifteen times as much as a rabbit.

Contrary to popular belief, especially among hunters, a rabbit does not run its fastest uphill, but on the level. However, it does seem to run fastest uphill because there it outdistances a dog or fox more easily than on the flat.

As for its enemies of the winter night the list is so formidable that a person wonders how the cottontail ever manages to survive at all.

The weasel, cat, owl, fox, coyote, lynx, wolf and still others hunt it continually and with great skill; yet the rabbit not only holds its own against them all, but spends most of its time in play! The snow record explains its success. After a bit of study, you'll begin to recognize the rigid safety patterns of a rabbit's movements when it feeds or plays. An invisible tether of instinct keeps it from getting more than three or four jumps away from a hole or covert. This is just one example, and a rather simple one, of these complex safety patterns.

Occasionally, it's true, you do see where a rabbit trail ends with tragic abruptness in a few flecks of blood and the telltale sweep of big pinions on the snow, or in a few draggles of fur where an ambushed fox scooped up a cottontail, gave it a quick brainbite, and lugged it off. But for every one of these sad little tableaux you will see many dozens of encounters where the rabbit's safety habits kept it from harm.

You hear it said all the time that the rabbit is a timid, furtive animal. Now I wonder about that. You'll see one of these places in the snow where a fox or owl missed a rabbit by inches, and a few hops farther on that rabbit starts nibbling calmly on a crabapple twig. That doesn't seem to me any sign of a timid, cowardly nature. The rabbit just isn't a fighting animal. All its instincts are geared to fleeing and escaping, and death hovers over it so constantly that it takes danger in an apparently nonchalant manner.

In the midst of all these familiar stories, there was that unexplained hop. I knew it was no sort of feeding, flight, or scare jump. Nor was it a "spy hop"—where an animal leaps up high to see over vegetation—because the huge leaps nearly always occured in little open areas where there wasn't any vegetation. And from my observations of rabbit play, I was fairly sure it had no connection with that.

Then, one brilliant winter night, I saw a cottontail—in fact, two of them—actually making this tremendous leap and under circumstances that explained it instantly.

During the fall of this particular year three wild rabbits, living in a brushy little grove at the edge of my yard, had been coming out at twilight and cavorting around on a level terrace outside my study window. With a few tiles and a box I built them a fine, dry shelter-den just inside the grove, and they took to it thankfully when winter came on. Tom, Dick, and Harry, I called them; but along toward the middle of February I was compelled by good and sufficient reason to change this to Tom, Dick, Mary.

On the night in question a large cottontail stranger appeared on the terrace. I found out later, by tracking him, that his home range was a little clump of pines four hundred yards away—a far distance indeed for a rabbit to journey.

For a while after the stranger appeared, Tom and Dick confined themselves to stamping their feet at him, as buck rabbits (and some people) do. No doubt they were telling him that they'd butt his brains out if he didn't go back where he belonged. But the stranger paid no attention to them. His interest was centered on Mary, nibbling at a cabbage head I'd staked up in the middle of the terrace.

Then, as I watched, I saw Tom take a quick little run, somewhat like the approach run of a broadjumper, and go sailing through the air on one of those tremendous leaps. And another, this one arching high up over Mary and the cabbage head.

Immediately the stranger cottontail set out to show what *he* could do along that line. He took the momentum run and gave *three* leaps, even more tremendous than Tom's. Those three leaps carried him nearly all the way across that fifty-foot terrace. Twice more this strange performance was repeated, the two buck rabbits hopping around and across the terrace like two outlandish Mexican jumping beans.

Well, there it was, at long last, and no doubt about it. A "show-off" hop. A part of the rabbit mating ritual. A display of male prowess, in rabbit terms. Evidently in the eyes of a doe cottontail the ability to hop big is a very impressive point.

When I went to my notes and examined them, I saw that all my records of the puzzling, oversized leaps referred to February or March (the mating season coincident with snow), and that these leaps occurred only when one or more other rabbits were around to watch the jumper.

Clearly the cottontail stranger out-hopped Tom—and presumably Dick, too—and by all the rules of the game he should have taken over, the winner, while Tom and Dick retreated to the far corner of the grove and gnashed their teeth. But it didn't work out that way, and don't ask me why. A good many of those pat rules and sayings about the outdoors and its creatures don't hold water too well. Anyhow, as I discovered the next morning by the snow-trail story, the cottontail stranger left soon after the exhibition of big-hopping and returned to his home pine thicket. Once again now, it was Tom, Dick, and Mary, playing and consorting around on the moonlit terrace.

The Redoubtable Kingbird

CHARLTON OGBURN, JR.

THE KING OF THE KINGS! YOU WOULD think the name *Tyrannus tyrannus,* if bestowed upon a bird at all, would be reserved for the most formidable of the predators, perhaps one of the giant eagles of bone-crushing talons. The bearer of this awesome title is in fact a bird smaller than a robin; undistinguished in appearance; unpossessed of any physical weapons to substantiate a claim to sovereignty; unmusical of voice; and, doubtless for these reasons, largely unsung in literature. This is an impressive series of negatives, but there is more to come. The kingbird is unaware of his insignificance. That is why he is the kingbird.

I was eleven years old and just discovering the incomparable world of natural history when I first read about the kingbird. Reading about the kingbird meant, of course, reading about his attacks upon birds five or ten times his size. Phrases like 'four ounces of feathered fury" and "uttering his characteristic battle cry" come back to me from those days. I remember seizing upon any depiction I could find of the kingbird. It was shown as sooty-colored above, nearly black on the head and tail, and generally white below. A color plate I had portrayed the male with a flame-colored strip along the top of his head. It appeared that while this crown was normally concealed, its wearer had the engaging habit when aroused of exposing it by raising his crest, as a diminutive monarch of an obscure principality might throw off an incognito at the climax of combat in the expectation that it would unnerve the most formidable antagonist.

These things could not fail to appeal to a young boy. We forget as we grow older the menacing and overbearing aspect the world has for us in our earlier years, how it confronts us with an enemy more mysterious, more authoritative, and with more arms to grasp and confine us than a Hindu god. The spectacle of a predetermined victim who turns the tables to triumph over heavy odds is one that captures our imagination at a very young age. The kingbird captured mine from the very start.

I read that a walk in the summer down a country road in almost any part of the eastern United States where there are trees and open spaces together was likely to take you across the domain of a pair of these birds, but this seemed too good to be true. It seemed even more so when, on my first trip out from town the next May, I actually saw a kingbird. It was perched on a blackberry cane, and as I came within ten or fifteen paces it launched out with its square-cut, white-tipped tail spread fanwise to veer away with curiously shallow and rapid wingbeats, just as I have seen countless kingbirds do since then. The wonder was not only that I had seen a kingbird but that it had looked just as it should. When as a boy learning about birds you see a new species and find it corresponding meticulously with the plates in the books, the thrill is one that lingers. It is like witnessing a contemporary miracle of creation: "Let there be kingbirds . . . and there *are* kingbirds!"

A few weeks later I moved out to the country for the summer. I could not have been there more than a day or so when, attracted by a sound like the excited jingling of coins in a purse, I looked up and for the first time beheld a kingbird in pursuit of a crow. The crow was beating pell-mell down wind with the smaller bird assaulting it in a flurry of wings and a frenzy of passion. The crow would twist and dodge in an effort to elude the attack or try to ward it off by turning sharply upward and throwing back its head to snap at its assailant, whose wild, staccato cries rent the summer hush.

Neither maneuver appeared to avail it very much. The kingbird charged down from above and behind in short power dives, striking with its beak and dancing aloft again to repeat the attack in an outpouring of sizzling indignation. Its voice, which might be likened to the shrill crackling of a sparking generator or to Morse code played on a high-pitched steam jet, had a sound of pent-up, stammering exuberance. While appearing ill-equipped to inflict any punishment, the kingbird was evidently succeeding in doing a good deal. Once its victim, emitting a strangled caw, turned almost over on its back to get at its attacker, and a few black feathers hung in the wake of the chase like miniature flak.

The crow gained a respite by pitching into the crown of a tree. The prince of virtue—as my kingbird plainly considered himself to be—balanced on the tip of an outer branch (kingbirds fight only in the air), a chesty little figure, rather large-headed, short-necked, and broad-shoulder. His wings quivered with anticipation, and he chattered of his prowess in putting the egg-stealing marauder to rout. His short crest, I could see through my binoculars, was raised; and it was then, I thought, that if I had been close enough and in the right position I could have seen the crown of scarlet feathers.

In time the crow decided to brave it, and the pursuit instantly resumed. As it extended high over the field, I saw the kingbird fall behind, like a winded terrier in the wake of an accelerating truck. I thought perhaps he had had his fill; but in a moment he appeared to recollect himself and, with a renewed shrill chattering that seemed to have more jubilation in it than venom, catapulted to the attack, closing the gap with such dispatch that the crow appeared to be fanning the air without moving. With wild abandon the kingbird, apparently inexhaustible, again bore down upon the quarry. The chase ended finally when it carried to the border of a patch of woods, into which the crow, closing its wings, dropped like a stone.

I was transported. Something important to me, something I was too young to try to find words for, had been vindicated.

The farm on which I used to spend my summers, beginning with my twelfth, was forty-some miles north of New York City. Most of Westchester County has become suburban since then, but the Norway spruce that stood between our front porch and the nearest chicken house still stands and there are still kingbirds nesting in it. Conceivably these are descendants of the pair I used to watch, which every year saddled their nest near the end of a limb in plain view; kingbirds, which never deign to take cover from danger themselves, seldom trouble to conceal their nests.

More often than not, the kingbirds in the spruce were the first birds to be heard in the morning, just when the dark began to thin; and they were the last to be silenced at night, after the deepening dusk had brought the male back from his evening cavortings over the lake, his contrasting pattern of silver and black almost indistinguishable in the halflight. Between those two hours they were generally the most alive objects within view.

The topmost twig of the spruce was the male's favorite lookout station. Balancing there, seventy feet up, watchful for invaders of his realm, he resembled a tiny, vizored knight. Sometimes he would go hawking after insects, and at dull times he would drop to the level of the fields to skim the tops of the timothy with that distinctively restrained flight kingbirds affect when coursing over their domains, "flying on his wing-tips" as it has been described. He reminded one then of a frisking, mettlesome steed under a firm curb. He was always the incarnation of alertness and explosive vitality. At rest he would break repeatedly into his ringing cry, a random challenge. He was like a safety valve on the forces of nature, constitutionally at the simmering point.

He would take no notice of a chipping sparrow or yellow warbler that alighted in his spruce, but another time when a robin crossed the lawn he would swoop and drive it into the shrubbery or smack onto the grass, apparently in a passing fit of irrepressibility. One July day a flock of starlings, thirty or forty of them, wheeled over the farm and came in for a landing, heading for the spruce. The kingbird met the flock just as it cleared the barn. It was as if there had been an explosion in its ranks. For a few seconds there seemed to be five kingbirds in the air at once, and the starlings were reeling in every direction. At the end, the spruce stood inviolate, with the interlopers dispersed among the maples on the other side of the house.

No large bird that came by ever escaped unscathed. Not even the harmless herons—the night herons and the lumbering great blues—were spared. The female would join in the initial pursuit and the male would harry the hapless creature across the lake, even alighting on its back to deliver more telling blows and clinging to it like a cowhand on a bucking steer.

The northern end of the ridge across the lake from the farm was covered by heavy woods. It formed the preserve of a pair of red-shouldered hawks, members of the genus *Buteo,* which comprises the massively built hawks you generally see circling high overhead, buoyed up by a rising column of warm air. If one of these came south along the ridge, I fancied I could detect in the kingbird's cry the kind of exultance that is said to ring in the lookout's voice from the mast-head of a whaler when, after a succession of blackfish and hump-backs, a forty-barrel sperm bull breaches. It was for this—you could hear it in his voice—that kingbirds were put into the world.

The *Buteos* are heavy but powerful flyers, rigged for the open sky and capable of soaring out of sight without appreciable effort. To overtake the red-shouldered hawk in the first place would require a major effort on the kingbird's part, a sustained sprint of several hundred yards. You could almost see his head lowered as he charged. The angle of climb would grow as the kingbird gained on the hawk; the first essential was to get above it. With this achieved, the battle would be on, the kingbird lunging at the hawk's head and shoulders, the hawk nosing off downwind to pick up speed, bucking and side-slipping under the blows of his assailant. The fight would become a straightaway race, the kingbird on the red-shoulder's tail, following every twist and turn like the tail on a falling kite. Regaining his stance as the hawk would wheel upwind again—for the hawk had the object of outclimbing the attacker—the kingbird would strike again and again, taking care at close quarters to be always on top and sputtering in ear-splitting sibilants. The course would be an ascending one, the red-shoulder swinging out in great arcs, describing a steep spiral as it strived for altitude. Sometimes the pursuer would fall so far behind that you thought this time surely he was spent. To come even again with the towering *Buteo,* the kingbird would fly almost straight up—a feat no soaring bird can accomplish.

If the kingbird were fully aroused, the chase would lead to a lofty altitude, the metallic cries of the attacker growing fainter, if little softer, until, from below, the kingbird would look no larger than a gnat. In the end, the hawk would be seen to steady itself, and tilting slightly, against the wind, fall away across the sky in a level glide. A moment later the victor would materialize dropping earthward, resembling a tiny skier swooping breathlessly down a descending series of invisible hills. The last dive would bring him up at the summit of the spruce where, still filled with the exhilaration of combat high above the earth, he would break the silence of the descent with a paean of self-praise.

What was it about the kingbird? What made him act as he did? I asked myself this question as a boy and I have asked it often since then. With age I have come to see that it is not his success in combat, on which I used to set such store, that matters. It is not his speed in a sprint, which, when I saw him overtake the graceful, plunging swallows and even the scimitar-winged, torpedolike swifts above the farmyard, I was wont to assure myself was unsurpassed. The important thing is that he makes the effort. In all his enterprises, the kingbird appears to be unreckoning of the odds against him. The last factor that enters into his appraisal of the world, of which he traverses as much as three thousand miles twice a year, is the lowly character of the place allotted to him in it. He has no equipment for the gladiator's role—and the lack of it deters him not at all.

Some other birds of the kingbird's size will attack crows and hawks, but none—not even the mockingbird and red-winged blackbird, which are probably next to him in pugnacity—approach him in dedication and zeal. And no others, at least in my experience, will rise to meet a sharp-shinned hawk or a Cooper's hawk. This, as no bird-watcher needs to be told, is a dangerous game. The lean, low-flying *Accipiters,* unlike the *Buteos,* are pre-eminently bird-killers, capable of plummeting through a tree with the speed of a meteor and so fanatic in pursuit of the quarry that they have been known to follow it on foot through the underbrush. They look their part, too, with their blood-red eyes. The appearance of an *Accipiter* coming in purposefully over the treetops is a signal for every other bird to freeze into immobility on its perch. In fact, you can usually foretell the approach of one of these hawks by the sudden silence, as if all the birds around you had disappeared. To see a kingbird, in these circumstances, appraise the situation with cocked head from his lookout station, then crouch and dart forth to intercept the oncoming corsair, dancing above him like a mongoose and chivvying him until he quits the neighborhood, is as heartening a spectacle as any I know in the world of animals.

What the kingbird has is spirit. There is an unmistakable gaiety in his combativeness and in his violence when executing the intricate paces of a close-in battle in a paroxysm of flailing wings and shrieks. Life is an adventure with him. He is exhilarating in everything he does. That is why, increasingly with the passage of years, I look forward to his advent in the spring. The first indication that the kingbirds are back is likely to be quite in kingbird character: a sudden *pfft-pfft!* just above your head as two of them streak by in hot pursuit of each other. A couple of seconds later they come into view again a hundred yards away, set in a furious course through the tops of the trees. Either because the claiming of a mate and the staking out of territory are the most important tasks in a kingbird's life or because it is more fun to take on someone who can match you at your best, a kingbird is never more exuberant than in contests with his own kind.

To appreciate him fully, you must witness his evening flight. I have seen it numberless times, but the performance I shall always remember best is one I watched in Mississippi. A kingbird rose from the top of a sweet gum in one of the bottomlands fleeced with magnolia and honeysuckle that traverse the pine woods of that moody country. A thunderstorm was coming up, and the stillness preceding the wind had a trenchant heaviness. The first ascent carried him above the river bottom, where the clear notes of a Carolina wren carried from far down stream. Leaving a flock of swallows beneath him, he broke his steep ascent with a flurry of gyrations impossible to unravel with the eye—twists, turns, darts, all executed at once amid a tremolo of metallic cries. This was the kingbird's dance, analagous to the song-flight of the skylark. It carried him above the mechanically darting swifts and the loping, coursing nighthawk, against the dark background of the thunderhead. The sunlight that had already left the valley caught the black and white of his plumage and picked him out of the sky while he performed his outbursts of gymnastics as if shaken to pieces by the force of his emotion.

His performance, I thought, was comparable to the cadenza in a concerto, when the orchestra falls silent and the violin, interspersing its crescendoes with passages of intricate virtuosity, carries alone the theme of the composition. Still higher the kingbird flew, until he leveled off, finally, to continue the evolutions of his dance at the ceiling of the evening in obedience, as it were, to an obligation laid especially upon him, the king of the kings, to express to the world the excitement of living and the ecstasy of freedom.

Alta, My Friend the Eagle

V. W. TURBIVILLE

NOT SO MANY YEARS MORE AND THE GOLDEN EAGLE, like the wild pigeon and several other forms of wildlife, may be something to read or hear about, and not to see.

Of course, future generations may not care to even hear about such things; but I think that the passing of this bird, which often is falsely accused, will be one of the great tragedies to befall our bird-life.

In some localities of the West, aviators are hired to fly and kill eagles, and are ready to take off as soon as some sheepherder has reported seeing one of the great birds. Of course, even an eagle has no chance against an airplane and a machine gun or shotgun.

Some years ago I was living on a rather isolated Texas ranch, and there were a few golden eagles in the locality. Sometimes I would see one of the big birds in the sky, sailing in an ever-widening circle, occasionally letting out that freedom-sounding scream that is such a pleasure to hear.

On one hot day in July, I spent the better part of an hour watching two of these birds as they sailed high in the heavens. As I watched, a conflicting element appeared in the sky; and, as soon as I saw the gaudy silver, green, and yellow markings on the plane, I knew that my beautiful birds were doomed.

Fearless creatures that they are, the eagles paid not the slightest attention to the oncoming plane. On the first blast of the gun, one of the eagles came tumbling to the ground. The pilot of the plane, not checking his speed, sped for the remaining eagle. It, too, came tumbling down.

The plane then circled, going back in the direction from whence it had come. Not interested in the plane, I watched the last victim of the gun as it tumbled end over end in its fall. As it neared the earth, I could see that one of its wings was broken, but that the other wing was spread full length, and that the eagle was making some effort to use it. When possibly a thousand feet from the earth, it almost righted itself and, with much flapping of the one good wing, disappeared beyond a hill about a mile away. Mounting my horse, I went to look for it, but I did not find it.

Two days later, as I was coming off the range, I found the wounded eagle near one of my watering troughs, flapping her one good wing for locomotion and dragging the other one in the dirt. Riding around so as not to disturb the bird's slow and painful progress to the water, I went to the barn, unsaddled and fed my horse, and then returned to see how the poor eagle was making out. She had reached the trough and was standing near it with her mouth open, her maimed wing dragging limply on the ground. The trough was built for cattle and was much too high for the bird to reach.

Securing a pan, I dipped some water from the trough and offered it to the eagle. She made no effort to get away, but stood passively, watching my every move with feverish, bloodshot eyes. She looked first at me and then at the water. Then, with much flapping of her good wing, she went to the water and drank heartily, afterward hopping to the shade of a nearby tree. There I left her.

Early the next morning, I went to see whether she had died or had gone away during the night, but I found her as I had left her. I watered her once more and then realized she must be hungry. I had some diced beef on hand and I took a goodly portion of it and put it in a box within her reach. With no ado whatever, she gobbled it down.

For several weeks, the eagle kept her place beside the tree, and each day I fed and watered her. Like most crippled wild things, she came to depend upon man for succor and relief, and it seemed that she accepted my attention as a matter of course.

From my experiences with this bird, I suppose that eagles are strictly meat-eaters, for at no time could I get her to take anything but flesh, which consisted mainly of rabbits and other small animals that I could secure. She herself did her best to catch the birds and other small creatures that approached the watering place; but, being hampered by her dragging wing, she had little success. I doubt whether she caught as much as a single lizard, though I saw her try many times.

As the weeks went by, one of the eagle's wings healed, but the badly maimed wing still held on. I knew that I should remove it, but how?

I thought about this problem for some time and then realized that the first step was to become better acquainted with "Alta," as I had come to call her, *alta* being the Mexican word for "high." I knew that it was no simple thing to get familiar with a wild eagle. Nevertheless, I began feeding her small bits of food by hand, wearing gloves for protection against her sharp beak. A few days of this and I was able to stroke and ruffle the feathers along her neck and back.

It was some time before she would allow me to touch her when there was no food in sight. But weeks of patient treatment finally brought results. A day came when she didn't threaten me with that saberlike beak that can cut through the skin of the toughest animal.

Before long, Alta seemed to expect me to ruffle her feathers and to stretch her good wing to its full width. I never dared to touch the other wing. Although it appeared healed, I was sure that it was still sore. The dried flesh and skin that held it to her body were almost as large as a man's wrist. Without examining it, I couldn't tell whether there was life in it or not, but one thing I knew for certain —the wing must come off. Winter was approaching, and three-and-a-half feet of wing dragging along the ground would be too much of a handicap for Alta.

When the balmy days and crisp nights of September had arrived, Alta had been with me for two months. With the aid of her good wing, she could make eight to ten hops and so could range some little distance from the watering trough. She had learned many things and responded readily to her name. I would call "Alta!

Alta!"; and, whether she were far or near, she came as fast as she could.

By now, too, I could take all kinds of liberties with her, such as pulling her beak open, folding my hands around her head, and spreading her good wing. All this apparently pleased her, and she seemed more like a friendly dog or cat than a wild eagle. But just let me touch that broken wing, and all friendship ceased!

Finally, I decided that if I couldn't prepare Alta for the operation by friendship, I would have to resort to other tactics. Getting a large cedar post, I placed it near the watering trough. Then I went for my hand-axe and some scraps of beef. With these, I started feeding Alta, maneuvering her alongside the post so that she dragged her bad wing along its top. When the right time came, I brought down the axe, and off came the wing.

Alta almost choked on the meat she was swallowing. She jumped to one side, threatening me with her talons and snapping her beak. After it was all over, however, she remained my friend.

Relieved of the useless wing, Alta became more active, hunting far and wide. She was learning to use the one wing to some extent, not to fly with, but to make long, half-circular hops that propelled her across the country with considerable speed. For days she wouldn't appear for food. On occasion, I would see where she had picked the bones of a rabbit or a snake. She continued to make daily trips to my watering trough and always roosted under the same nearby tree.

A mile or so from my ranch house was a sizable butte, the top covered with boulders. One day, riding in the vicinity of this butte, I heard the scream of an eagle. I looked toward the heavens, hoping to see more of the great birds, as I had seen them that day when Alta had been blasted down, but I saw nothing. Then, again, the stillness was shattered by the sound that no other bird or beast can duplicate—a sound at once magnetic, powerful, commanding, and prideful. I looked in the direction of the sound and saw Alta, perched on the topmost pinnacle of the butte.

After that, Alta continued coming to my well for her daily drink and accepted an occasional handout, but she abandoned her old roosting place under the tree, moving instead to the top of the butte. Here, for hours on end, she would stand looking across the Kansas and Nebraska hills toward the Rockies, calling for the mate that would never come. Many times I climbed to the top of the pinnacle to stand with her. She would passively allow me to comb my fingers through the beautiful feathers on her neck and back and let me stretch her wing to its full length.

When the warm days of April came, Alta started building a nest on the top of her butte. It was not much of a nest as far as eagles' nests go, but she did her best. Sticks as long as a man's arm she carried to the ledge. With her sailing skip and hop she came to my corral, pulling bark from the cedar posts, which she used for lining the nest. Within a week, she had finished her nest, and a few days later she laid her first egg. In all, she laid three eggs. They were infertile, of course, but Alta was following the dictates of nature to reproduce her kind.

Though I knew that the eggs would never hatch, I hadn't the heart to break up the nest. And so, all through the summer, Alta sat on her eggs, coming to my well occasionally. She began to look bedraggled and poor. Her once beautiful feathers were now dead-looking and rusty, and her eyes had lost much of their former brightness.

Finally, during the last hot days of August, she stopped coming to the well. Wondering what had happened to her, I went to the butte. When I climbed to the top, I found my great American eagle, the heroine of them all—dead. I think that Alta's proud heart just withered away and stopped from the uselessness of it all—the inadequate nest, the three infertile eggs, the lack of a mate, and no pair of great wings to carry her beyond the distance that man can see.

I suppose that the man who flew the gaudy little plane will some day be telling his grandchildren how he helped to blast "vicious" eagles, like Alta, from the sky.

NOTES by John K. Terres, Editor

A Whooping Crane Named Bill

By S. W. Oliver

In July, 1955, Robert P. Allen, Research Associate of the National Audubon Society, flew over the wilderness of Wood Buffalo Park, Alberta, Canada, and saw five whooping cranes and four young ones near their nests. They had been driven there by the agricultural development of the prairie country which had routed them from their last nesting marshes in the United States and southern Canada. The whooping cranes had come to a northern land avoided by both white man and Indians because of its impenetrability. Although he had searched the northern wilderness before, Mr. Allen had never found the nesting grounds of the cranes. On August 6, in the same area, W. A. Fuller, a Canadian biologist, who had discovered the nesting cranes even before Mr. Allen did, saw five young ones and six adults, eleven of them, or about half of all the whooping cranes left at that time in the world.

Mr. Allen's exciting experience climaxed the long fight of the National Audubon Society and of the U. S. Fish and Wildlife Service to save the whooping cranes. He had studied the last of them on their Texas wintering grounds; he had learned about their relationships to each other, and to other animals in their environment; their food supply and its nature; and other facts so desperately needed if he were to unearth every possible threat to their lives. In 1952, the National Audubon Society published its Research Report No. 3, "The Whooping Crane," by Robert P. Allen. It contained all that was known about the whooping cranes up to that time.

But the present nesting grounds had never been found, and no one, not even Mr. Allen, knew what threatened the cranes there. To find the breeding grounds meant encroaching upon their last privacy, but he believed that what he might discover there would save whooping crane lives.

In the summer of 1955, Mr. Allen studied the foods of the cranes in the Canadian waters and lands about their nests. Science needed these and other facts, and Mr. Allen came back with the encouraging news that for the time being, in that remote land, the cranes were safe from the guns of man. Nothing apparently threatened the cranes on their breeding grounds that they could not cope with themselves. The last resident area of the cranes that held a potential threat to them had been analyzed. Protected on their wintering grounds in Texas, and safe on the northern breeding grounds because of their isolation, Mr. Allen became reasonably certain where the greatest threat to the cranes must lie. He knew, at last, why the whooping cranes had come to Texas in the fall of 1954, *without a single young one, for the first time in many years.*

The young cranes had probably been shot somewhere along their migration route.

Weasels Are Wonderful

by Helen Hoover

The short-tailed weasel, or ermine, *Mustela erminea,* the major subject of this article, lives in Alaska, throughout Canada, and southward to New England, New York, and Pennsylvania. It ranges westward to northern California. In summer it is dark brown with white underparts and white feet; in winter it is all white, excepting the black tip at the end of its tail.

The long-tailed weasel, *Mustela frenata,* ranges from southern Canada southward over the entire United States (with the exception of southeastern California and southwestern Arizona). Its range also includes Mexico and Central America. It is the most widely distributed and commonest of all weasels. Throughout the year, over the southern part of its range, it is brown with yellowish-white underparts with a black tip to its tail; but in the North, in fall, it changes to a coat of winter-white. In winter only the tip of its tail is black. The change of color, from summer-brown to winter-white, is accomplished by a molt in the fall of the year. In spring, the weasel molts again and changes its white coat for the brown-and-white coat of summer.

The least weasel, *Mustela rixosa,* is the smallest of all living carnivores and is rare throughout its range. It lives from Alaska southeastward through the provinces of Canada and well down into the Prairie States and over the northeastern United States, generally;

southward, in the mountains, to Tennessee. In summer, the least weasel is brown above with whitish underparts. In winter it is white all over and does not have a prominent black tip at the end of its short tail.

CALIBAN

by Henry S. F. Cooper

The word "Caliban" in literary usage means "rude, uncouth, unknown." The allusion is to Shakespeare's Caliban in *The Tempest,* the deformed, half-human son of a devil and a witch, a slave to Prospero.

Cooperstown, the locale of this story, is a village about seventy miles west of Albany, probably best known for its Hall of Fame for baseball players and its National Baseball Museum. Cooperstown was the home of James Fenimore Cooper, called "the first great novel writer in American literature." The scenes for some of his famed *Leatherstocking Tales* were the densely forested hills about Cooperstown in the early nineteenth century. James Fenimore Cooper was the great grandfather of Dr. Henry S. F. Cooper, a New York City physician, and the author of this article.

GEOFFREY

by Penelope Weigel

The phenomenon of two-colored animals, as exhibited by the screech owl, is called dichromatism. It does not indicate a different age, sex, or stage in the bird's plumage. The screech owls of the eastern United States seem to be more of the red phase than of the gray; in the western United States they are said always to be gray.

THE DESERT TORTOISE

by Lillian E. Miles

The desert tortoise, *Gopherus agassizii,* lives in the deserts of southeastern California, the southern part of Nevada (Clark and Nye Counties), southwestern Utah, western and southern Arizona, and

Sonora, Mexico. In California it is found in northeastern Los Angeles, eastern Kern, and southeastern Inyo Counties, over most of San Bernardino and much of Riverside and Imperial Counties. Males are a little larger than females, one series averaging about eleven inches (length of carapace or "back" shell) compared with a length of about nine and one half inches for females. The slow, plodding desert tortoise is related to the Berlandier's tortoise of southern Texas and Mexico and the gopher tortoise of the southeastern United States.

Tortoises have well-developed middle and inner ears but are not believed able to hear as human beings and other animals can. No one has yet proved that turtles respond to sound waves transmitted through the air, although some careful experimenting with them has been done. They respond to the slightest ground vibrations, and they feel the lightest tap on their shells. Their eyesight is keen and they can distinguish about the same range of colors that a man can.

Desert tortoises, like all reptiles, are quite sensitive to heat and cold. They are active in the early morning and late afternoon, between the cold of the desert night and extreme heat of the day, also during cool periods after thunderstorms. During the hottest periods of the day, they rest in the shade of shrubs, rocks, or in their burrows. A desert tortoise kept in strong sunlight too long would probably die.

Beneath the desert tortoise's head, projecting forward from the lower shell, is the curious two-pointed horn with which he rams his opponents in his efforts to overturn them. The combatants meet head-on with their heads drawn partly into the shell.

Mating is usually in early spring but is thought to continue for several months. Two to six eggs are laid by the female any time between June and October, so that the record of nine eggs for these captive desert tortoises is more than the usual number.

Jumping Phantoms of the Desert

by Alfred M. Cooper

The species referred to in this article is *Dipodomys deserti,* the desert kangaroo rat. This pale, yellowish, four-toed species inhabits areas of soft sand, usually dunes, in the desert areas of eastern California, southern Nevada, and southwestern Arizona. From the tip of its nose to where its tail joins its body, it is five to six-and-one-half inches long; its tail is seven to eight inches long, with a white tip. It is, with *Dipodomys merriami,* the Merriam kangaroo rat, the most common and widespread species of its kind in the southern California deserts. Kangaroo rats live chiefly on plant stems, seeds, insects, and fleshy fungi. They have cheek pouches in which they carry off large numbers of seeds or other dry foods, which they store in their underground burrows.

Our "Minnesota" Barred Owls

by Rachel D. Tryon

The northern barred owl, *Strix varia varia,* the subject of this article, nests from Canada and Newfoundland south to Arkansas, Tennessee, Kentucky, northern Georgia, and parts of South Carolina; westward to eastern Wyoming, central Montana, and eastern Colorado. The southern form, the Florida barred owl, *Strix varia georgica,* lives in the southeastern United States from eastern Texas and Arkansas to northern Alabama and southward. It is especially common in Florida. Another subspecies, the Texas barred owl, *Strix varia helveola,* is a much paler form that lives in southcentral Texas, from the eastern border of the Edward's Plateau (Bexar County) to the coast.

The Roadrunner

by Frank F. Gander

Geococcyx californianus, the roadrunner, chaparral cock, ground cuckoo, or lizard bird, is a member of the cuckoo family, or Cuculidae. According to the A.O.U. check-list of North American Birds (Fourth Edition), it ranges from California to southern Utah, Colorado, Kansas, middle Texas and the lower Gulf coast south through Lower California and into Mexico.

Pelorus Jack—A Dolphin Diplomat

by Cyrus Cress

The story of Pelorus Jack is given full credence by Dr. A. Remington Kellogg, Director, United States National Museum, Washington, D.C.; and by Dr. George G. Goodwin, American Museum of Natural History, New York City, to whom the story is well-known.

Dr. Kellogg, in an article, "Whales, Giants of the Sea," *The National Geographic Magazine,* January, 1940, says that "Pelorus Jack," the famous Risso's dolphin of Pelorus Sound in New Zealand, "accompanied vessels for about thirty-two years and was last seen in 1912. . . . It [the Risso's dolphin] differs from all other dolphins in that the few teeth it possesses are restricted to the front end of the lower jaw."

The maximum length of adult Risso's dolphins is twelve or thirteen feet. When on or near the surface of the water the recurved dorsal fin identifies it. It is a "beakless" dolphin; the front of its head rises almost perpendicularly from the tip of the upper jaw.

The Risso's dolphin lives over a wide area—in the North Atlantic Ocean; in the Mediterranean; and, in the southern hemisphere, off the coast of New Zealand and at the Cape of Good Hope. It may range about alone or in small schools of less than a dozen. Cuttlefishes, as far as is known, are its only food.

The dolphins often photographed leaping out of water for food at Marineland, St. Augustine, Florida, are bottlenose dolphins. They range the Atlantic Ocean, off the coast, from Maine to Florida.

Passengers on ocean liners often see schools of the common dolphin, *Delphinus delphis,* sporting in the sea.

Dolphins and porpoises, though smaller than whales, belong to the same class of animals—the cetaceans. Among the smaller ones, those with beaks are called dophins; those without beaks are called porpoises.

Common porpoises, *Phocaena phocaena,* live in the North Atlantic Ocean and range south to Cape May, New Jersey. They are rarely seen far offshore, and usually travel in schools, from a few to fifty, or even one hundred. They are four to six feet long and have a blunt, rounded snout, without the distinct beak of the dolphins. A related species, *Phocaena vomerina,* ranges along the Pacific coast from the Pribilof Islands south to Mexico.

Dall's porpoise, a black-and-white one, is the species most frequently seen by passengers on ships traveling the Inside Passage from Seattle, Washington, to Juneau, Alaska. In summer this species may travel as far south as Santa Barbara Channel off the coast of Southern California.

Common Porpoise

Bottlenose Dolphin

Common Dolphin

I Lived With a Black-Tailed Jack Rabbit

by Henry Paul Jackson

Many people confuse hares with rabbits, not realizing that they are different animals. The name "rabbit" should be applied only to the cottontails, genus *Sylvilagus*. Hares, *Lepus,* which include, in this country, the varying hares, arctic hares, and jack rabbits, have longer ears and longer hind legs than rabbits, and their digestive tracts are different in structure. When hares are born, their eyes are open and their bodies are well-covered with fur; rabbits are born naked, or without fur, and have their eyes closed for a week or more after they are born.

The black-tailed jack rabbits are generally recognized as of three species in this country: *Lepus californicus,* the subject of this article; *Lepus alleni,* and *Lepus gaillardi.* These three have white tails, of which the upper surface is more or less black; they live in the Far West and Southwest, from Oregon east to Central Nebraska and Western Missouri, and southward through Texas, Arizona, New Mexico, California, and into Mexico.

Jeff

by Alexander Sprunt, Jr.

According to the A.O.U. *Check-List of North American Birds* (1957 Fifth Edition), the eastern sooty tern, *Sterna fuscata fuscata,* nests on the Dry Tortugas, Florida, the Gulf Coast of Texas, and Louisiana; the Bahamas Islands to Honduras; Cuba, Jamaica, Mona Island, Virgin Islands, the Grenadines, Margarita Island, Fernando de Noronha, Rocas Reef, Ascension Island, South Trinidad, Martin Vas, and St. Helena. In winter it ranges widely over the open seas, and may appear casually, usually after hurricanes, near Bermuda and off the coasts of the United States and north to Nova Scotia.

Fence Lizards in My Garden

by Frank F. Gander

The fence lizards described by the author in this article are probably the western fence lizard, *Sceloporus occidentalis biseriatus.* It ranges through southern, central, and western California, north to southern Oregon and southern Idaho, throughout Nevada, and in extreme western Utah. It is considered the most abundant and conspicuous reptile, in its preferred habitats, in southern California.

Fence lizards, or swifts, of the family Iguanidae, genus *Sceloporus,* live in many parts of the United States. One group, *Sceloporus undulatus* and its subspecies, includes the northern and southern fence lizards and the prairie and plateau lizards. These little reptiles are usually from two or three inches or more long, from the tip of the nose to the end of the body. This does not include the long tail, which may be as long, or twice as long, as the body length in some species. The western fence lizard, *Sceloporus occidentalis biseriatus,* is a different species from the eastern fence lizards; but superfically it resembles the eastern forms, and its habits are much the same. Its body is about three inches to three and one-half inches long; the tail may be three or four inches long.

The Handsome Little Ringtail

by Norman G. Woolsey

The ringtail, *Bassariscus astutus,* is one of the most winsome of all wild mammals. Although it lives over a wide area of the western United States and south to Costa Rica, few people have ever seen one. It is usually quite shy, lives in and about dark caves, and does most of its hunting at night.

Mexicans call the ringtail the Aztec name of *cacomixtle;* in Baja California it is called *babisuri.* It is often called civet cat, in the Southwest; but it is a very different animal from the civet of the Old World, which, phylogenetically, is close to the felines, or true cats. Scientists place the ringtail in a family by itself—Bassariscidae—between the raccoons and coatis (Procyonidae), and the marten, weasels, etc. (Mustelidae). This agile creature is as much at home in trees as it is on the ground. Other local names for it are mountain cat, miner's cat, and cat squirrel. The common name of "cat squirrel" is an even greater misnaming of this animal than "cat." The ringtail is not at all related to the squirrel family. There is already a common name of "cat squirrel" that has been given locally to the southern gray squirrel. Ringtail seems to be far and away the best common name for this beautiful little animal. In the United States, it lives from Oregon southward into California, and eastward into Nevada, Utah, western Colorado, Arizona, New Mexico, and Texas.

The Black "Cat" of the Forest

by Robert G. Snyder

The fisher, *Martes pennanti,* has become alarmingly scarce in the United States during the past twenty-five years. Fishers once lived in the Appalachian Mountains of the eastern United States as far south as North Carolina. Their most southern outpost in the east is now the Adirondack Mountains. Fishers range across Canada to the coast of British Columbia and south, in the mountains, to Wyoming and east-central California. There is only one species.

The fisher is slender, about the size of a gray fox, and is from thirty-six to forty inches long. It is about ten inches high at the shoulder. Males may weigh up to eighteen pounds, although rarely more than twelve pounds; females are considerably smaller—about one half the weight of males.

The Ptarmigan of Glacier National Park

by J. Gordon Edwards

Dr. Edwards is an associate professor of entomology at San Jose State College, San Jose, California. Beginning in 1947, he has spent his summers employed as a ranger-naturalist in western national parks. He collects beetles, studies the ecology of animals and plants, and is a photographer and mountain climber.

Aloysius the Independent

by William D. Berry

The yellow-haired porcupine of the West, *Erethizon dorsatum epixanthum,* once considered a separate species, is now classed by mammalogists as a subspecies of the dark brown porcupine of the eastern United States.

Porcupines, according to a recent study, are often killed and eaten by lynxes, foxes, and fishers. Fishers, which can climb trees in pursuit of their prey, are said to be "habitual porcupine killers." Wolverines in California are known to eat porcupines; and, in "wolf country," wolves eat them. Foresters interested in the control of porcupines where porcupines become so populous as to cause economic losses to forest trees might well urge the protection of predatory species.

My Favorite Bird

by Frank F. Gander

According to the A.O.U. *Check-List of North American Birds,* (1931, Fourth Edition), *Spizella breweri breweri,* the Brewer's sparrow, "breeds mainly in the Transition Zone from southeastern British Columbia, southern Alberta, east-central Montana, and northwestern Nebraska south to southern California, southern Arizona, and central western Texas. Winters from southern California and central Texas south through Lower California and Mexico to Jalisco. Accidental in Massachusetts."